A Guide to Writing Sociology Papers

A Guide to Writing Sociology Papers

SIXTH EDITION

The Sociology Writing Group

COORDINATOR AND EDITOR

Roseann Giarrusso

AUTHORS

Roseann Giarrusso

Judith Richlin-Klonsky

William G. Roy

Ellen Strenski

WORTH PUBLISHERS

A Guide to Writing Sociology Papers, sixth edition

Publisher:	Catherine Woods
Acquisitions Editors:	Sarah Berger
	Erik Gilg
Marketing Manager:	Amy Shefferd
Art Director:	Barbara Reingold
Senior Designer, Cover Designer:	Kevin Kall
Associate Managing Editor:	Tracey Kuehn
Project Editor:	Dana Kasowitz
	Dan Fitzgerald, Graphic World Inc.
Production Manager:	Barbara Anne Seixas
Composition:	Graphic World Inc.
Printing and Binding:	RR Donnelley

Library of Congress Control Number: 2007930375

ISBN-13: 978-0-7167-7626-0
ISBN-10: 0-7167-7626-X

First printing

Worth Publishers
41 Madison Avenue
New York, NY 10010
www.worthpublishers.com

CONTENTS

TO THE INSTRUCTOR

A Guide to Writing Sociology Papers has been extremely well received by instructors in a wide range of sociology courses since the publication of the first edition. Both instructors and countless students have benefited from its clear, straightforward, and engaging style.

The quality of student writing is a constant concern to college teachers. Like their colleagues in other disciplines, many sociology instructors, preoccupied by the demands of their profession and dreading the likelihood of poorly written or perhaps plagiarized papers, despair of assigning writing and rely instead on tests. But to do so deprives students of the active, personal engagement with sociological concepts and data that only writing about them can provide. This book is an attempt to do something about this problem.

Flexible Design

A Guide to Writing Sociology Papers grew out of our collective experiences as sociology and English faculty members, teaching assistants, counselors, and tutors at UCLA. The book is designed to relieve you of some of the burden of writing instruction and to provide your students—from beginning to advanced—with practical advice. Its format is flexible enough to accommodate specific modifications, yet "spelled out" enough to guide those who need to pay special attention to all steps in the writing process, from initial conceptualization to final presentation.

Writing as Exercising the Sociological Imagination

The underlying premise of the book is that thinking and writing are integrally related and, therefore, that writing a sociology paper involves exercising the "sociological imagination." Throughout the book, our advice and examples are informed by this practical pedagogical observation. When instructors comment to students that their papers "are too psychological" or "really don't address a sociological issue," for example, students tend to be confused and rarely learn how to correct the problem in later papers. Similarly, comments that a paper "has no structure," "follows no clear logic," or "lacks sufficient evidence" often baffle students. Our goal here is to provide both you and your students with illustrations and a common language for discussing and improving papers in these areas.

Accessibility to Students

The book can be used in a variety of ways in both lower- and upper-division sociology courses. For example, you can assign it as a reference tool for students to consult on their own. Or you can refer in class or in discussion sections to specific parts when you mention papers, explaining how students can apply our advice to your assignment and how our sample student papers do or do not represent what you expect. Or, in your comments on drafts or in individual conferences with students, you can refer students to specific pages in the text.

In addition, the book can be used in a range of writing classes from remedial to advanced. It is especially appropriate for adjunct writing courses paired with sociology courses. However, since much of the advice we present can be generalized to other disciplines, the book is also suitable as a basic text in advanced writing courses that emphasize the social sciences. Much of the book—Chapters 2, 3, 4, 5, and Part 3—applies equally to courses in the humanities.

Student-Friendly Writing Style

While we focus on the priorities most commonly identified by instructors, our own writing style is intentionally "student-friendly." Students report that learning about writing is sometimes boring or intimidating. Thus, our tone is deliberately easygoing, avoiding prohibitions where possible, including contractions where they soften the prose, and offering guidelines rather than commandments. We also include many concrete examples, some taken from student papers, to make the guidelines less abstract.

A Note about the Sixth Edition

The order of the chapters has changed to be more consistent with the flow of the writing process. The beginning chapters now include only information students need to know early on, such as how to outline and revise, while things they need to know later in the writing process, such as editing and formatting, have been moved to the end of the book.

The order of the chapters based on different data sources also has changed to better show how later chapters build on earlier ones. That is, unless the students are given a text or journal article to review, they must begin the writing process by searching for sources in the library or on the Internet (Chapter 4). After students have found a text or journal article to review, they need know how to analyze and evaluate their source(s) (Chapter 5). Students then can synthesize material from several textual analyses and/or article critiques to form the basis of a literature review section of a quantitative research paper (Chapter 6).

The new order of the chapters also reflects the similarity of papers based on three data sources (Library/Internet, Textual Analysis/Article Critique, and Quantitative Research): all develop a thesis or hypothesis—an anticipated answer—in response to a sociological question. Conversely, papers based on ethnographic data do not begin with either a thesis or a hypothesis; rather, they approach the study of social phenomenon unfettered by preconceived notions about the answer to their question.

Chapter 4 (formerly Chapter 6) has been extensively revised to reflect the fact that students can now search their library catalog and specialized databases such as *CSA Sociological Abstracts* electronically, either at school or at home (if using a proxy server). The chapter points out that search engines such as *Google Scholar* and *Google Book Search* also can provide access to scholarly journal articles and books. Previously the chapter treated paper research as the default, while informing the reader of electronic resources; now the chapter treats electronic research as the default, persuading the reader that there is still virtue in paper. The chapter now includes a sample student paper based on library/Internet data, with comments about the strengths and weaknesses of the writing.

Chapter 5 has been revised to show that the same valuable techniques used to write a textual analysis paper also can be used to write an article critique. Both Chapter 6 (formerly Chapter 8) and Chapter 7 have been updated and include new sample student papers.

Acknowledgments

Special thanks go to the students who granted us permission to use all or part of their work as examples: Lysa Agundez, Tanaya Burnham, Mayank Chawla, Christina De Roulhac, Gloria Fong, Dana E. Knickerbocker, and Shannon Prior.

Profound thanks are also due to Constance Coiner, Arlene Dallalfar, Lisa Frohmann, and Nancy A. Matthews, contributors to previous editions of *A Guide to Writing Sociology Papers*. This book continues the commitment to teaching of our friend and colleague Constance Coiner (1948–1996), who contributed in a major way to the first edition of this book.

We would like to acknowledge our gratitude to the following professors who assisted in the revision of this book by responding to our questions about the previous edition: Lynda J. Ames, SUNY–Plattsburgh; Barbara Karcher, Kennesaw State University; James A. Kitts, University of Washington; Andrew J. Knight, Arkansas State University; Ann Marenco, California State University, Northridge; Ben Nefzger, Augustana College; Linda L. Yellin, California State University, Northridge; and Lisa K. Zottarelli, Idaho State University. We are also grateful to librarian Romelia Salinas of California State University, Los Angeles, for advice on Chapter 4.

Finally, we are grateful to Linda Hall of USC, and Associate Editor Sarah Berger, Acquisitions Editor Erik Gilg, and the editorial and production staffs at Worth Publishers for all their help in preparing the sixth edition.

ABOUT THE AUTHORS

The members of the Sociology Writing Group came together in 1984 to prepare a guide for instructors and students in sociology and writing courses at UCLA. *A Guide to Writing Sociology Papers* grew out of this collaborative effort. Judith Richlin-Klonsky and Ellen Strenski coordinated the group's work and edited the first five editions of the book; Roseann Giarrusso took over this role for the sixth edition of the book.

Roseann Giarrusso is Assistant Professor of Sociology at California State University, Los Angeles, where she teaches courses in writing for sociology, social gerontology, and social psychology. She is also a consultant at the Andrus Gerontology Center at the University of Southern California, where she conducts longitudinal research on intergenerational family relationships. She has over 40 publications, most of which apply a social psychological perspective to the study of family relationships and aging. Roseann Giarrusso's contributions to the book include Chapter 6 and major portions of Chapters 2, 3, and 4.

Judith Richlin-Klonsky has taught sociology for more than 25 years at institutions such as UCLA, UCLA Extension, UCSD, and Santa Rosa Junior College. Among the classes she has taught are the sociology of everyday life, aging and society, introductory sociology, sociology of mental illness, group processes, and race and ethnicity. As director of the UCLA Student Affairs Information and Research Office, she conducted research about the experiences and needs of undergraduate students. Judith Richlin-Klonsky holds a master's degree in family therapy and received her Ph.D. in sociology from UCLA, where she was trained in qualitative research methods and an interpretive theoretical framework. Her contribution to the book includes Chapter 7, as well as major portions of Chapters 1 and 5.

William G. Roy is Professor of Sociology at UCLA, winner of the 1989 Luckman Award for Distinguished Teaching, and author of *Socializing Capital: The Rise of the Large Industrial Corporation in America* (Princeton University Press, 1997) and *Making Societies: The Historical Construction of Our World* (Pine Forge Press, 2001). He specializes in the sociology of music and comparative-historical sociology, particularly long-term political and economic transformations. William G. Roy contributed major portions to Chapters 1, 2, 3, and 4.

Ellen Strenski is Composition Director in the English Department at the University of California at Irvine. In addition to co-authoring *The Research Paper Workbook* (New York: Longman, 3rd ed., 1991) and *Making Connections across the Curriculum: Readings for Analysis* (Boston: Bedford, 1986), she has published articles in many pedagogical journals on the subject of writing in diverse disciplines. Most recently, she has exercised her sociological imagination in several articles and chapters that analyze issues in writing program administration. Ellen Strenski contributed to Chapters 2, 3, 4, 5, and Part 3.

TO THE STUDENT

If you're uneasy about the prospect of writing a sociology paper, you're not alone. Many students feel as you do; that's why we wrote this book. We can't promise that your assignment will be easy, but it *can* be done, and done well. This book can help you feel in control of the writing process from beginning to end, and it can help you produce your best work.

We've written the guide we wish we'd had as undergraduates. We experienced many problems in writing our own papers and we want to spare you some of the trouble we endured. And we have learned that procrastination—our own and that of others—is not always the result of laziness but often a sign of uncertainty about just how to begin and complete a given writing task.

What Your Instructor Expects

Our students often tell us that they don't know what they're expected to do in a paper or that they don't know what the instructor wants. So we've tried to demystify the whole process. For example, we explain in Chapter 1 what makes a sociology paper different from papers in other disciplines and what sociology instructors want in terms of a paper's logic and structure. We suggest ways to get started and to stay on track, ways to deal with and present your data, ways to troubleshoot your writing, and ways to make your prose look and sound professional. All along the way our book gives practical illustrations, including sample student papers that you can compare with your own. These sample papers are very good but they are not perfect. We comment on their fine features and suggest alternatives where problems remain.

We recommend that everyone read all of the chapters in Part 1, "Essentials," and Part 3, "Finishing Up." The chapters in Part 2, "Writing from Various Data Sources," can be used selectively. Use the table of contents and the index to look up what you need.

Getting Started

Part 1 includes chapters on the essential aspects of writing. Chapter 1 focuses on the conceptual starting points that are fundamental for writing a good sociology paper. Chapters 2 and 3, respectively, present basic guidelines on writing and revision, and keeping track of notes and references to avoid plagiarism. Follow these guidelines from the beginning of your project.

Doing Your Research and Writing It Up

Part 2 includes chapters on the four typical kinds of sociology papers that are, in turn, based on four different data sources: library and Internet (Chapter 4), textual analysis or article critique (Chapter 5), quantitative research (Chapter 6), and ethnographic field research (Chapter 7). All four chapters contain student papers as illustrations.

Part 3, "Finishing Up," includes guidelines on editing and formatting your paper, a checklist for your final draft, and suggestions for expanding your sociological imagination.

How to Use This Book

Don't try to read the whole book at one go. The four chapters in Part 2 are meant to guide you through steps in a process. Use these chapters as you would instructions for assembling anything—first scan the chapter to get a sense of what you're in for and then consult it carefully as you move along step by step. Sometimes a writing assignment can loom as an enormous, mysterious undertaking because students don't know how to break it down into smaller, more manageable tasks. This guide does that for you. There may be portions of the guide that you'll have to reread before they make sense to you and other portions that you'll refer to again and again for present and future writing assignments.

The primary purpose of this book is to help you prepare good sociology papers, and, except for Chapter 6 on quantitative research, which is more technical than the other chapters, you'll be able to use this book from day one of any sociology course. But you'll also find that much of this book applies as well to other social sciences and that many parts will even help you write papers in the humanities. *A Guide to Writing Sociology Papers* will help you from the start to the finish of your college career.

Other Suggestions

Your own campus may offer other resources to help you further.

+ Find out if your campus library offers tutorials on how to search their online catalog and any specialized electronic databases such as *CSA Sociological Abstracts* to which they subscribe. Also find out if the library offers a proxy server that allows you remote access to these and other resources. A short time invested at the beginning of the quarter or semester when schedules tend to be less demanding may save you many hours later.
+ Find out if your English department offers composition courses in which you can practice and develop writing skills. Investigate writing courses even if you have fulfilled the requirement for basic English composition. (Don't let English majors corner the market on intermediate or advanced courses.) At some colleges, special writing courses are attached to sociology and other courses, a combination that benefits you doubly. If you are concerned that your present writing skills might earn a less-than-satisfactory grade in a composition class, check out the possibility of taking the course as an elective on a pass/no-pass basis.
+ Find out if your campus has a tutoring center where peer or professional tutors can review your work with you and help you strengthen your writing skills.

A Note on Our Writing Style

Before going on, we would like you to note two features of our writing style: our occasional use of contractions (for example, "we've" instead of "we have") and our avoidance of sexist language.

First, we have tried to make this book as down-to-earth and practical as possible. We imagine ourselves talking to you as we talk to our own students—trying to be direct, friendly, and helpful. Our prose is therefore rather informal and includes contractions. Academic papers, on the other hand, have a different purpose and are usually more formal. Some instructors might object to your using contractions in a formal sociology paper.

Second, we have deliberately used inclusive language when we refer to people in general. Historically, masculine nouns and pronouns have been used to refer to women and men both—for example, *"Man* is a social animal." As a result of the women's movement, this usage has become unacceptable. Chapter 2 explains ways of avoiding sexist language.

Finally, we wish we could show you some of the drafts of this book. Writing anything worthwhile—a paper or a book—is always a frustrating, creative, and rewarding process. Our own experience has been typical. Final written work usually looks so straightforward that it's easy to forget all the drafts and revisions. So don't be discouraged if you don't like what you first write. That's normal. The paper will improve, and you will like it better with each succeeding draft. *A Guide to Writing Sociology Papers* will show you how this happens as it guides you through the writing process.

A Guide to Writing Sociology Papers

Essentials

Perhaps the most disabling myth about intellectual activity is that writing is an art that is prompted by inspiration. Some writing can be classified as an art, no doubt, but the art of writing is a trade in the same sense that plumbing and automotive repair are trades. Just as plumbers and mechanics would rarely accomplish anything if they waited for inspiration to impel them to action, so writers would rarely write if they relied on inspiration.

RODNEY STARK
Sociology

Writing is a craft as well as an art. As with any other craft, becoming a good writer requires understanding the principles of how papers work. A first-rate plumber must know some principles of hydraulics, and an outstanding auto mechanic, the principles of combustion. Writing a good sociology paper requires understanding principles of both sociology and writing.

Part 1 presents these fundamentals of craftsmanship. Chapter 1, "Getting Started," explains some topics that might be considered as much inspiration as perspiration, such as how to use a "sociological imagination" in writing. More specifically, this chapter covers some of the qualities that instructors look for in papers but that students sometimes have difficulty grasping. An instructor will frequently criticize student papers as being "not sufficiently sociological," "not addressing a real question," or "having problems of logic and structure." But often students are not sure what the instructor means, and instructors often find themselves at a loss for how exactly to interpret their own comments. So we have explained what sociologists mean when they require papers to "take a sociological perspective," to "be logical and well structured," and to "answer a well-formed question."

Chapter 2, "The Writing Process," recommends techniques for harnessing the power of the writing process itself to trigger insights and to continually clarify your ideas. Chapter 3, "Working with Sources," explains when and how to introduce and cite borrowed information.

Getting Started

Additionally, and especially in the social sciences, much unclear writing is based on unclear or incomplete thought. It is possible with safety to be technically obscure about something you haven't thought out. It is impossible to be wholly clear on something you do not understand.

JOHN KENNETH GALBRAITH
Writing, Typing, and Economics

Writing a good sociology paper starts with asking a good sociological question. Picking a topic is just the beginning of planning your paper. You need to frame your paper's topic in the form of a *question*. Asking a good question will make the other tasks of writing your paper much easier and will help you hand in a good finished product.

Everything else follows from the question your paper asks. Think of taking a photograph. The deepest artistic sensitivity or the most sophisticated technical skills cannot create a beautiful picture unless you point the camera in the right direction. But carefully aiming the camera in the right direction can combine with simple competence and a personal point of view to produce a fine and, if you are lucky, breathtaking photograph. Likewise, when you create a sociology paper, you can produce interesting, high-quality results without being the smartest or most eloquent student in the world: the key is to take the time to "point" your work in an effective direction by asking a well-formulated question.

Sometimes instructors assign papers by requiring students to respond to a particular question. When that happens make sure you thoroughly understand the question and keep it in mind as you work on the paper. Not answering the instructor's question is one of the most frequent pitfalls of student writing. Even if you have a thoroughly researched, insightfully reasoned, and eloquently written paper, if it does not answer the assigned question, most instructors will find it unsatisfactory. Read the question carefully when you begin your work, reread it as you are doing any reading or research that may be required, reread it when you sit down to write, and reread it as you begin your final draft. People's minds, especially intelligent

3

people's minds, have a tendency to drift to interesting and related, but not always pertinent, topics.

Even when the assignment is not presented as a question, you must formulate one to address in your paper. Three features distinguish a question that will serve as a strong foundation for a sociology paper. First, a helpful question reflects an understanding of sociology's distinctive perspective on human life. Second, it is carefully posed and framed. Third, it is asked in such a way that it lends itself to a logical and well-structured answer (in contrast to a question that suggests an endless list, such as "What are all the roles adopted by leaders?" or one that is too open-ended, such as "Why are people irrational?"). The following sections will help you to meet these three criteria for asking good questions.

WHAT IS SOCIOLOGY?

Failing to understand what sociology is and what sociologists do is a main reason that students experience difficulty in writing successful sociology papers. Since asking a good sociological question depends on understanding what sociology is, this section defines sociology and discusses how it is different from other fields.

Sociology is the study of human social behavior. Sociologists investigate how individuals are shaped by their social groups, from families to nations, and how groups are created and maintained by the individuals who compose them. Sociology's basic insight is that who a person is, what she or he thinks and does, is affected by the groups of which that person is a member. To begin thinking sociologically, look around and consider how the world may be experienced differently depending on whether a person is male or female, rich or poor, of one race/ethnicity or another.

Another part of sociology's insight is that interaction takes place in ways that are patterned, even though the people involved may be separated by many years or many miles or may appear to have differences. For example, societies at different historical times or in different geographical locations all find ways to enforce rules, to teach children valued beliefs, and to organize the production of goods necessary to their members' welfare. Sociologists try to understand the consistencies in these processes—the ways in which their similarities and differences follow a predictable pattern.

Finally, sociologists attempt to explain *in*consistency as well. How do new social patterns emerge? For instance, what accounts for changes in dating patterns, parent–child relations, or types of college degrees earned?

SOCIOLOGY AND OTHER PERSPECTIVES ON HUMAN BEHAVIOR

Sometimes new students (and more experienced ones!) are confused about how sociology is distinguished from other disciplines that study people, such as psychology, political science, history, philosophy, anthropology, and economics. In fact, these fields are not totally distinct. Right now, however, we want to focus on what is distinctive about sociology because, in order to write successfully in any discipline, you need to have some idea of its boundaries. Our brief sketch necessarily simplifies the definitions of sociology and its "neighbors" and exaggerates their dissimilarities. The differences we discuss here are intended primarily to sensitize you to sociology's distinctive features; they are not rigidly observed by theorists or researchers. In fact, many scholars describe themselves explicitly in terms that cross these boundaries (such as social historians, political economists, and social psychologists), often incorporating a sociological perspective into other disciplines. More and more scholars are adopting an interdisciplinary approach to study sociological issues, such as race, gender, class, crime, family, and the like.

The following summary compares and contrasts sociology with psychology, political science, history, philosophy, anthropology, and economics. We have illustrated their differences by showing how researchers in each field might approach one aspect of human life—deviant behavior.

Sociology and Psychology

Similarities: Both are concerned with attitudes, beliefs, behavior, emotions, and interpersonal relationships.

Differences: Psychology is more likely to focus on the individual level of human behavior, especially the role of biological factors. When sociology considers the individual, it is within the context of social groups.

Studying deviance: Psychologists investigate psychological dispositions that make some people more likely to commit crimes. A sociologist might try to discover whether activities of one socioeconomic class are more likely to be labeled "criminal" than activities of other classes.

Sociology and Political Science

Similarities: Both study government.

Differences: Political scientists analyze different forms of government and their underlying philosophies and study the political process. A sociologist is more likely to examine the relationship of political structure to behavior and other aspects of society, such as the economy, religious institutions, and the attitudes of various social groups.

Studying deviance: A political scientist might analyze why groups make choices to support one kind of criminal law over another. A sociologist might examine how such laws change as the members of society adopt different ideological beliefs or how they serve the interests of some classes more than others.

Sociology and History

Similarities: Both look at human life over time.

Differences: Historians are more likely to focus on the influence of individuals and on the causes of specific events. Sociologists concentrate on the causes and effects of changes in large-scale patterns of social life, especially institutions such as politics, economy, religion, education, and so on.

Studying deviance: A historian might interpret the motivations and actions of influential deviant individuals and attempt to explain their influence. A sociologist is more likely to trace changes in society's ways of defining and controlling deviant behavior.

Sociology and Philosophy

Similarities: Both are interested in beliefs about the nature of life.

Differences: Philosophy is a system of abstract reasoning that follows specific rules of logic. Sociology is empirical: it seeks to discover information about the real world by gathering data about what people actually do.

Studying deviance: Philosophers might ask "What is good?" and "What is evil?" or analyze the appropriate uses of the term "deviance." Sociologists stick to what actually goes on in the social world, asking, for instance, "What do members of this particular society or subculture believe is 'right' and 'wrong'?"

Sociology and Anthropology

Similarities: Both are concerned with social life, including culture, beliefs, decision making, relationships, and so on.

Differences: Anthropology is more likely to study societies other than our own, and to compare aspects of society cross-culturally.

Studying deviance: Anthropologists might travel to an isolated, nonindustrialized society to study how it defines and treats deviant behavior. Sociologists would study the same processes by focusing on complex, industrial societies.

Sociology and Economics

Similarities: Both are concerned with how society produces and distributes goods and services.

Differences: An economist concentrates on the economy in its own right, treating it as the aggregation of individual choices. Sociologists are more likely to consider how the economy affects and is affected by other social processes that shape individual choices.

Studying deviance: An economist might study the contributions and costs of deviance to the gross national product. A sociologist might study how the control of the economy by upper social classes provokes deviant behavior, such as burglary and theft, by those without access to a fair share of goods and services.

THE SOCIOLOGICAL IMAGINATION

One way to describe what is distinctive about a sociological point of view is the "sociological imagination," a phrase coined by C. Wright Mills ([1959]

2000). Using the sociological imagination means recognizing the connection between individual, private experience, and the wider society. Mills calls the personal level an individual's "biography"; he uses the term "history" to refer to patterns and relationships on the larger scale of society.

As a student, for example, you have followed your own life path to college. Being a college student is part of your personal life story. Your family has its own beliefs about what a college education means. You have your own academic and career goals. You have individual feelings and attitudes about the subjects covered in your classes and your own mixture of college and work schedules. All these things make up your personal, *biographical* experience of your life as a college student.

Applying sociological imagination to your college life expands your perspective. It is like a wide-angle lens that allows you to see yourself in a larger, more complex (and, in many ways, more interesting) picture. Using sociological imagination, you can begin to see where your experience as a college student fits into the social world in which you live, the *history* of which your biography is a part. Perhaps you are part of a trend among your peer group to major in computer science or communication studies. It could be that you are part of an ethnic group whose members are underrepresented in higher education. Perhaps your academic goals have been affected by social values (say, an increasing emphasis on the need for a college degree), or maybe your career choice, combined with many others', will affect the way society's workforce is balanced between producing goods and providing services.

To use sociological imagination, then, is to identify the intersection of biography and history, the ways in which people are affected by social forces and social groups are affected by their members. As Mills ([1959] 2000) himself puts it:

> Every individual lives, from one generation to the next, in some society; . . . he [or she] lives out a biography, and . . . he lives it out with some historical sequence. By the fact of his living he contributes, however minutely, to the shaping of his society and its history; even as he is made by society and by its historical push and shove. (P. 6)

Mills's deceptively simple insight—that people both affect their own destiny *and* are swept by currents of history—challenges and eludes sociologists from first-year college students just beginning to study the field to seasoned scholars. The key to using sociological imagination is to not lose sight of either side of this relationship.

SOCIOLOGY'S FOCUS AND METHODS

One of the major differences between high school and college is that in high school, "learning" usually means learning facts. Those high school students who demonstrate that they have learned the most facts generally earn the highest grades. In college, however, there is greater emphasis on analytical reasoning and thinking. Students are expected to understand entire systems of knowledge. Moreover, college students often find that there is more than one correct way to approach a topic; that is, that there is more than one *perspective* on an issue. A perspective is a way of looking at a topic. For example, think about the various ways of looking at a house. If you view it from the front, you see a door and windows with a roof overhead. If you look at the house from the side, you might see no doors, only windows. If you take your perspective from above, you see neither doors nor windows, only the roof. Although all three perspectives involve the same house, your observations from each perspective result in very different descriptions of that house.

Intellectual perspectives can differ as well. Earlier we saw how a number of disciplines take different perspectives on deviance. They all look at the same behavior, but each discipline paints a different description and develops a different explanation of it. Even *within* sociology there are several perspectives. Beginning students may find this confusing. For example, by adopting a *conflict perspective,* we can look at society in light of the ever-present conflict that goes on within it; by contrast, taking on a *consensus perspective* points us toward examining society in terms of the enduring ties that produce stable patterns of relationships among people. Likewise, whereas *microsociological perspectives* consider social life in terms of everyday interaction among small groups of people, *macrosociological perspectives* see things from the point of view of long-term change and societies as a whole.

To some extent these perspectives disagree about what we might generally consider the "facts" of society—about whether it is stable or conflicted, about whether it is defined by what occurs on a large scale or in direct interpersonal relations. More often than not, however, different perspectives are simply asking different questions. It's like looking at the house from different perspectives. A microsociologist might examine the process of becoming deviant from the deviant's point of view, whereas the macrosociologist might ask how definitions of deviance have changed over time. A sociologist operating from a conflict perspective might examine how deviance is produced as a result of the opposing needs of different social groups, whereas a colleague with a consensus perspective might ask how deviance serves to reinforce the established rules of society. All of these perspectives share the features of sociology discussed earlier. All ask different questions—but within a sociological framework.

Some students struggle with the cognitive ambiguity that can arise when different perspectives with very different implications are all considered acceptable. This is one of the great intellectual feats of a college education: to be able to juggle more than one perspective in one's mind at the same time. As a novice sociologist, your task is to understand these different perspectives and to learn how to support whichever approach *you* take with empirical evidence.

Sociology not only encompasses a range of perspectives, but also allows sociologists to apply these approaches to questions about an innumerable array of topics. Like other disciplines, sociology has several major subdisciplines—variations on a theme, as it were. Sociology may examine events that are as momentary as the eye contact between strangers on a bus or as long-term as the industrialization of society. It may deal with social life in terms of its structure, attempting to uncover stable, underlying patterns, or it may look at the fleeting interactional processes through which individuals relate socially.

In sociology classes, then, you might study anything from the sociology of sports to the sociology of religion. You might learn about how those engaged in different occupations perceive their work lives, how a thief accomplishes her or his crime, or how children learn table manners. You might study birthrates, medical decision making, or the sex lives of teenagers in the 1930s versus the 21st century. And, for each of these subjects, sociologists may disagree about the kinds of questions to ask and the methods to use in order to answer them.

It should come as no surprise, then, that just as there is no one "right" way to think sociologically, there is no single "right" way to do sociological research. Sociology's methods vary considerably. Most sociology texts and many instructors describe sociology as a "science." By this they mean that sociologists systematically collect information about the social world and then methodically analyze this evidence or "data." The data may come from any of a number of sources—from controlled laboratory experiments, from written accounts of social life, or from observing, interviewing, or surveying people involved in the phenomenon being investigated. (Part 2 of this book presents tips on how you can use four types of data sources commonly found in undergraduate sociology papers.)

Many sociologists literally *do* use the scientific method, in much the same way that a botanist or chemist would: they set out to support or reject a prediction, or "hypothesis," about the relationship among several facts of the social world. To do that, they collect quantifiable data—information that can be transformed into numbers and analyzed statistically. (One example of this method is the survey research described in Chapter 6.) Those who adopt this "positivist" approach to sociology believe that we can observe and quantify the relationship between selected social variables (such as age, race, or gender) and particular social experiences (such as deviant behavior). After collecting and analyzing data on prisoners, for instance, the researcher might generalize about whether a 20-year-old or a 45-year-old is more likely to end up in prison. The generalizations produced by these kinds of methods often form the basis of decisions regarding public policy, social programs, and the like.

However, not all sociologists see sociology as a science in the narrow sense. Some sociologists believe that the complexity and subtlety of human experience make understanding social relations a very different endeavor than, say, measuring the effects of gravity on a falling object, as a physicist would do. Instead of quantifying social forces, these "interpretive" or "constructivist" researchers concentrate on probing how aspects of everyday life are constructed—given meaning—through social interactions. In studying deviance, for example, they might ask how an individual who breaks the law comes to see him- or herself as a criminal (or if he or she does at all). Or they might explore how social interactions produce different ideas about deviance in different subcultures. To accomplish their goals, these sociologists use qualitative methods, conducting research that is quite different from that done in the biological or physical sciences. Examples of these methods include the participant-observation method and open-ended interviewing (discussed in Chapter 7). Rather than trying to generalize, interpretive sociologists want to specify in as much detail as possible just *how* the social world is constructed. Despite their different approaches, however, all sociologists base their conclusions on a combination of insight and carefully collected and analyzed evidence.

Although some sociology departments specialize in one perspective, topic, or method, most departments include faculty members who represent a range of sociological concerns and styles. Course curricula, including writing assignments, reflect this variety, and students typically have the opportunity to become familiar with several ways of asking and answering sociological questions. When you are trying to understand what an assignment requires of you, it will help to keep in mind the focus of the course as a whole and the particular approach your instructor is presenting.

Sociology, then, is a diverse field. But across all sociological methods and topics, *a sociological perspective involves seeing individuals interacting as members of social groups.* As you prepare to formulate the question that will underlie your sociology paper, remember that *adopting the sociological perspective is always the first step* in writing a successful paper.

FRAMING A QUESTION

Writing a good sociology paper requires using your sociological imagination to frame an interesting question that then guides your research effort. Asking a sociologically imaginative question is one of the tasks students find most challenging and most difficult to pin down. There is no magic recipe, but here are some tips that might help. Your instructor may feel that some aspects of what we say are more important than others, so remember that these are just suggestions.

Remember the "history" part of the sociological imagination. Avoid overly individualistic or psychological questions, questions that concern only what happens inside a person's head. For example, asking whether criminals are motivated more by aggression than by greed is more interesting psychologically than sociologically. (We are in no way implying that psychological questions are inferior to sociological questions, but our purpose here is to emphasize the sociological aspects of human life.) A sociologically imaginative question might ask what aspects of social life—such as race, class, or gender—influence people to act out their aggression or greed in socially acceptable or unacceptable ways.

Remember the "biography" part of the sociological imagination. Avoid overly economic questions that drop people out of the picture. (Again, economic questions are often interesting and important, but we want to emphasize the sociological aspects.) For example, asking how much income is lost to crime each year is less sociologically imaginative than asking what types of crime typically victimize wealthy people as compared to poor people.

Ask a question concerning *differences* between individuals, groups, roles, relationships, societies, or time periods. Only rarely do sociologists make claims about all people or all societies. They are typically more interested in how and why people or societies differ from each other; that is, they more frequently ask questions about variation than about uniformity. For example, they would probably not ask whether people are by nature aggressive but rather why some people are more aggressive than others. Are highly aggressive people socialized differently, part of a different subculture, vulnerable to different social pressures, or aspiring to different goals than less aggressive people?

The remaining five suggestions apply to questions for any discipline, not just sociology.

Ask a question that requires more than a simple "yes" or "no" answer. A "yes–no" question is a dead end. The case is already closed and there is nothing to investigate or argue. For example, the question "Does socioeconomic status affect marital stability?" can be answered "yes," and there is no more to say. So, too, with this question: "Can children born with severe language/communication deficits caused by aphasia be socialized to participate in society on a par with nonaphasic persons?" One way to improve such questions is to put the phrase "To what extent . . ." in front of them; for example, "To what extent does socioeconomic status affect marital stability?" Another remedy is to rephrase the question; for example, "What are the most effective ways for primary schools to enhance the normal socialization of children born with severe language/communication deficits caused by aphasia?"

Ask a question that has more than one plausible answer. The paper's task is to demonstrate why your answer is more valid than other plausible answers. "Do social conditions affect the crime rate?" is not a genuine question because "no" is not a plausible answer. "Are crime rates more sensitive to economic inequality or differences in family structure?" is a better question because you will find sociologists arguing for both answers. Belaboring the obvious wastes both your time and your reader's. Before starting the research, specify different plausible answers to your question. Can you imagine anyone seriously taking the other side? If not, you need to reformulate the question.

Unless your assignment specifies otherwise, ask a question that draws relationships between two or more concepts. (Some exceptions are a definition paper, a "feeling" or reaction paper, and a story or narrative paper.) Typically, assigned questions concern the relationship between concepts. Instead of asking about the relationship between two concepts, you could ask about the interaction of two institutions. For example, "What are the similarities and differences in how medical and criminal justice systems have supported drug use?" Unless specifically instructed, avoid questions that address only one concept, such as "What is deviance?"

Make sure you have access to the information to answer your question. Although some paper assignments do not require any research outside assigned readings and lectures, many do require you to document your points with evidence. For these papers, you must consider, when you ask your question, whether you can realistically get the necessary documentation. For example, "Has deviance always existed?" is an interesting question with important consequences for sociological theory. But it would be difficult to document adequately whether or not prehistoric societies had deviance. On the other hand, students are sometimes surprised to discover what information does exist and can be tracked down with a little work, so it is best to check with your instructor if you are unsure.

Make sure your question is answerable in the space allowed. This may be the most elusive of our tips and the one students falter on most frequently. Part of the difficulty is that some instructors expect finer detail of documentation or a more fully developed argument than others. Another problem is that students often don't know how much information they will find until they have done their research. Here are two guidelines. First, ask middle-range questions that are neither grand, monumental, deep-truth questions nor minutely exacting, picky-detail questions. Second, check out your question with your instructor before you begin your research.

To sum up this section, then, we want to stress that a good paper should not just be *about* some topic (such as mental health, race, gender, or occupations). For example, rather than a paper about social mobility, you might frame and address the question "Is there more opportunity for upward mobility in America today than there was a hundred years ago?" Notice that this question concerns differences between two fairly specific time periods. And it has more than one plausible answer; reasonable people could disagree about whether there is now more opportunity for mobility or less. Framing an answerable but debatable question is a fundamental, and sometimes the most demanding, part of writing a paper.

TERMS AND STRATEGIES IN ESSAY AND EXAM ASSIGNMENTS

When students are given a paper or essay assignment, they naturally want to know what the instructor wants, but asking "What do you want us to do on this assignment?" usually annoys the instructor. From the instructor's point of view, the instructions already indicate what students are expected to do with the information. Knowing the course content is not enough to do well on a paper assignment; knowing *what to do* with this content and having a strategy for selecting and presenting this information are essential. The way to determine such an appropriate strategy is to scrutinize the wording of the assignment, to clarify for yourself what is expected, and then to use a suitable strategy to produce the paper.

Instructors deliberately design assignments to get you to work with—and think about—course concepts and data in various ways. For example, writing about deviance could involve defining it, illustrating it, analyzing it, comparing it to other behavior, evaluating its effects, summarizing someone's theories about it, and so on. Sometimes instructors will provide you with a well-framed, unambiguous question to start with. At the other extreme, you may be given a very vague assignment ("Discuss deviance") that will require you to create and frame your own question. In the middle of this range are the following common commands that cue you to appropriate questions that can be framed concerning the course information and that tell you what the instructor wants you to do with this information.

Note that sometimes an assignment calls for more than one question because the instructor deliberately combines these commands, thereby requiring you to work with the material in several ways, applying several different strategies. At other times, instructors provide several different versions of essentially the same question but repeat it in different words to help you understand what you are supposed to do. If your assignment seems to call for several questions, first determine whether they are the same single question in different words or whether they involve separate strategies.

Analyze: Break something down into its parts; for example, a theory into its components, a process into its stages, an event into its causes. Analysis involves characterizing the whole, identifying the parts, and showing how the parts relate to each other to make the whole. Corresponding question: "What is the relationship between anomie and frustration in the functionalist theory of deviance?"

Assess/Criticize/Evaluate: Determine the importance or value of something. Assessing requires you to develop clearly stated criteria of judgment and to comment on the elements that meet or fail to meet those criteria. Corresponding question: "How useful is labeling theory for explaining why people join gangs?"

Classify: Sort something into main categories and thereby pigeonhole its parts. Corresponding question: "If someone cheats on an examination to get a better grade, which of Merton's forms of deviance does the behavior belong to?"

Compare/Contrast: Identify the important similarities and differences between two elements in order to reveal something significant about them. Emphasize similarities if the command is to compare and differences if it is to contrast. Corresponding question: "What are the similarities and differences in labeling theory and functionalist theories of deviance?"

Define/Identify: Give the special characteristics by which a concept, thing, or event can be recognized; that is, what it is and what it is not. Defining is more than just describing a word's "essence." You should also place it in its general class and then distinguish it from other members of that class. Corresponding questions: "What is anomie? What behaviors or attitudes indicate that a person or group is anomic?"

Describe: Present the characteristics by which an object, action, person, or concept can be recognized or an event or process can be visualized. Corresponding question: "What is Durkheim's theory of deviance?"

Discuss/Examine: Analyze and/or evaluate a particular topic. You must decide on your own a question concerning the things to be discussed. Instructors usually expect you to go beyond summary. Corresponding question: "What can sociological theories tell us about why gangs exist and why individuals join them?"

Explain/Justify: Make clear the reasons for or the basic principles of something; make it intelligible. Explanation may involve relating the unfamiliar to the more familiar. Corresponding questions: "Why do people break rules that they believe in? What theories do you think give the best explanation of this kind of behavior? What evidence can you present to support this theory?"

Illustrate: Use a concrete example to explain or clarify the essential attributes of a problem or concept. Corresponding question: "Give a concrete example of 'innovative deviance.' How does this example show the defining features of the concept?"

Interpret: Explain what the author of a quotation means (not what you mean). Go beyond just restating what the author said (though that also is important) to say something more about his or her ideas. Corresponding question: "What does Durkheim mean by stating that animals cannot commit suicide?"

List/Enumerate: Give essential points one by one in a logical order. Corresponding question: "What are the forms of deviance in Merton's theory of deviance?"

Outline/Trace/Review/State: Organize a description under main points and subordinate points, omitting minor details and stressing the classification of the elements of the problem or the main points in the development of an event or issue. Corresponding questions: "What have been the major debates over deviance in the past quarter century? How has the resolution of one debate led into the next? Highlight these debates with reference to leading theories and pathbreaking studies."

Prove/Validate: Establish that something is true by citing factual evidence or giving clear, logical reasons for believing it is true. Corresponding question: "Make a case on behalf of or in opposition to labeling theory. What are the strongest justification and best evidence you can present to support your point of view?"

ANSWERING AN ESSAY EXAM QUESTION

Because essay exams test thinking, not ability to memorize details, understanding the directions represented by the terms just listed is especially important. This is particularly true when you are writing under time pressure. What instructors want to see in your exam essay is the big picture—meaningful generalizations. They want you to demonstrate quickly what all the details covered in class add up to. To put it another way, they want you to show that you can see the forest for the trees! Because instructors differ in whether they prefer depth or breadth, you should ask your instructor about how much analysis or how much detail he or she expects. Therefore, answering an instructor's ready-made question requires a special approach.

Begin by reading through the exam sheet(s) **twice** in order to make choices if they are available and to ration your time. Otherwise, especially if you are nervous, you may confuse the number of questions or not understand important directions. Start with the question you feel most confident about answering, even if it's not in the first section of the exam. (Be sure to **label clearly** the number of each question as you answer it.) Other ideas will come to you as you write, and your relatively easy answer will build your confidence for tackling the others.

Underline or circle the key terms like "analyze," "evaluate," "how (in what way)," and "how much (to what extent)." If the instructions simply say "discuss," you're on your own. Are there several theorists, institutions, or concepts, for example? Try a *comparison*. Does the question require demonstrated understanding of key terms? Try *defining* and *illustrating*. Is a process important? Try *analyzing* its different stages. Would grouping help? Try *classification*.

One common essay exam strategy is to begin by cannibalizing the words in the question and using them as a ready-made part of your thesis answer, for example:

> *Question:* "In what ways has the subsequent development of the West confirmed or disconfirmed Marx's theory about class conflict in capitalism?"

> *Answer:* "The subsequent development of the West has disconfirmed Marx's theory about class conflict in capitalism in at least three ways. First, the class structure did not polarize into two unbridgeable classes, but instead gave rise to a very large middle class. Second, life chances for wealth and prestige now depend at least as much on education and occupation as on class background. Third, the revolutions Marx predicted in advanced capitalist societies did not occur, but instead Marxist-inspired revolutions have developed primarily in peasant-based societies."

Such a bald statement might be too obvious for a polished *paper,* but for an exam *essay,* an announcement like this can help you outline your answer and then stick to it.

Focusing on the question is essential. The object of your essay is **not** to demonstrate all the facts you know, but to answer the question as clearly and concisely as possible.

DEVELOPING AN ARGUMENT: LOGIC AND STRUCTURE

In writing, logic refers to the relationship between the paper's assertions and its evidence. Structure concerns how the parts of the paper fit together. If sentences are the "trees" of the paper, then logic and structure are the "forest." According to one faculty survey, structure and logic are among the most important criteria instructors weigh in grading papers.

Logic demands that a good paper go beyond mere assertion ("This statement is true because I say it is"). The answer to your question, which is your thesis, must be supported by evidence and reasoning. One way to accomplish this is to assume that the reader is naive (a Martian, for example) or skeptical. Try to imagine actively what a naive reader might not understand about what you are saying and explain your points to her or him (or it). Try to imagine the kinds of doubts a skeptic might hold and attempt to convince her or him, just like a debater would.

Structure demands that in a good paper each sentence should be well written and make sense; each sentence should also be logically connected to the sentences around it, each paragraph to the paragraphs around it, each section to the sections around it, and all of them to the overall theme of the paper. Whether you write sentence by sentence or begin with a general plan and work down to the level of the sentence, by the time you submit the paper, you should be able to conceptualize the structure of the whole paper in your head (and, if necessary, to explain that structure to the instructor). This means being able to say in one or two sentences what the paper's main thesis is and how you go about arguing that thesis. Imagine your roommate or a friend asking "What's the point of the paper?" and "Why should the reader believe you?" If you can't answer those questions, you still have work to do before turning in the final draft.

The next step after framing your question is constructing a logical defense of your thesis—why your answer is more correct than alternative answers. This defense requires pieces of evidence that support your thesis. The evidence must be logically connected to the thesis so that you can make the statement (either in your head or in the paper) "If the evidence is true, the thesis is true." Many student papers (and some professional papers) falter here, presenting interesting and important evidence in narrative form, or in a controlled study, or sometimes through reasoned reflection, but then drawing a conclusion that is less than warranted by the evidence presented. So be sure to put aside the actual paper and think through the first three items on the checklist presented in Part 3: "What is my thesis? Does my thesis remain evident and central throughout the paper? Have I supported my thesis with adequate evidence?"

Finally, the structure of the paper should reflect the logical connection of the evidence to the thesis. It is the writer's job, not the reader's, to draw the connections between evidence and conclusions and to show how the paper logically proceeds. Thus the paper's introduction, transitions, and conclusions are essential, not just incidental, parts of the paper. The *introduction* should state the question that is being answered and specify the plan for answering it. As the paper unfolds, provide guideposts for the reader telling where the paper has gone and where it is going. These *transitions* indicate how sentences, paragraphs, and sections logically fit together. Transitions can be accomplished by including transitional words and phrases, such as "on the other hand" and "furthermore." (See Chapter 2 for a list of transitions.) Or they can be stated in sentences: "The last section discussed Durkheim's basic presuppositions; this section will show how those presuppositions influenced his theory of religion." A common writing error is the *non sequitur,* a Latin phrase for sentences or paragraphs that have no apparent connection. This often results from a connection that is in the writer's mind but that she or he fails to demonstrate to the reader. A *conclusion* should remind readers where they have been and why you think the thesis has been demonstrated. Try to summarize the paper without repeating specific sentences. This is also the appropriate place to reflect upon the larger implications of your thesis—to answer the question "So what?" But it is not appropriate to present new evidence in the conclusion.

LOGICAL FALLACIES

Logical fallacies are errors in reasoning. Even if facts are accurate, errors in logic can lead writers to inappropriate conclusions, often with the best of intentions. Try not to make any of the following typical errors:

+ **ad hominem** (attacking the person, not the issue), for example, "They believe that they [animals] have 'inherent moral rights.' Some of the people who most vigorously support animal rights are cruel to their own family members."

+ **begging the question** (circular reasoning), for example, "Because they have nowhere to stay, the homeless must live on the streets."

+ **either/or** (also called "false dilemma"), for example, "If school reforms in the last several decades have not created high-quality education for everyone, it is time for school vouchers."

+ **false analogy** (assuming that because people or objects share one characteristic, they share all characteristics), for example, "Many Americans hire private investigators to spy for them and gain information about someone else. Just as the CIA violated the rights of citizens in poor countries around the world, private investigators violate the rights of anyone they spy on."

+ **false cause** (also called *post hoc, ergo propter hoc*, assuming that just because one thing happened after another, it is caused by the first event), for example, "After people lost respect for government authority in the 1960s, violent crime rose all across the country."

+ **hasty generalization** (also called "sweeping generalization"), for example, "Recent polls about attitudes toward government funding of health care confirm that Americans will never accept a single-payer medical insurance system."

+ **non sequitur** (making no apparent logical connection), for example, "If other stress factors lead to the weakening of their willpower causing binge eating, all of the diet centers have counseling sessions."

+ **reverse reasoning** (confusing cause for effect), for example, "The more knowledge teenagers have about sex, the more likely they are to engage in premarital sexual activities."

+ **slippery slope** (inaccurately predicting a causal chain), for example, "If human cloning research is permitted, the next steps will be designer human beings and then the elimination of handicapped people, and end with the killing of people who aren't perfect or whom we don't like."

+ **spurious causation** (treating things with a common cause as though they cause each other), for example, "Poor people with bad nutrition commit more violent crime than those with healthy diets."

For a fuller description of logical errors, see David Hackett Fischer, *Historians' Fallacies: Toward a Logic of Historial Thought* (1970. New York: Harper & Row). Even though written specifically for historians, it is very useful for all writers.

TWO FORMATS OF LOGIC AND STRUCTURE

We suggest here two formats of logic and structure that are common in sociology papers. There are, of course, other formats that may be appropriate for specific assignments. If the paper assignment does not specify an explicit format requirement, it is often helpful to talk over your format ideas with the instructor.

The Three-Part Essay Format

This type of paper is most commonly structured in terms of a major thesis (that answers a question) and three supporting "points."

There is nothing magical about the number three; it is a convenient number of points for the length and scope of papers typically written for course assignments. Each of the three points should logically support the thesis. You should be able to say "if point A (or B, or C) is true, the thesis is true." More precisely, in terms of formal logic, you need to be able to maintain that "if point A (or B, or C) were *not* true, the thesis would probably not be true."

Take as an example the thesis "Over the last hundred years, educational opportunities in America have opened up the American social structure to more upward mobility."

Point A could be: Educational achievement is more closely connected to high-status jobs than it was a hundred years ago.

Point B could be: Education is more equally accessible to all members of the society than were earlier means of determining people's status.

Point C could be: The content of education relates more to job skills than it did a hundred years ago.

The paper itself is structured around an introduction, discussion of point A, discussion of point B, discussion of point C, and a conclusion. The introduction presents the question that is being answered, the general thesis, and usually a plan of the body of the paper. Each point is discussed in turn. Each section usually starts with a claim—a statement of its main point. Often the next sentence is an example of this claim, followed by an explanation of how the example illustrates the point. Then you can elaborate on this point, identify its implications, take issue with some aspects, or provide other types of evidence. Finally, you need to tie it back in with your general thesis and with the argument so far.

You will need at least one paragraph for each discussion section, because that's what a paragraph is—a logical section with one main point. You may need more than one paragraph to deal with each main point, especially if the point is complicated or if you are presenting elaborate evidence. If you do, allocate separate paragraphs to each subpoint or aspect. This often happens when you want to analyze a particularly revealing example and explain to what extent it does, but also does *not,* illustrate a point you want to make. In other words, the discussion gives evidence and reasoning for why the point is true; the discussion also explains the logical connection between that point and the general thesis.

The conclusion then summarizes the overall argument and often offers your personal thoughts about the issue you have discussed.

A modified version of the essay format is also appropriate for a paper based on ethnographic research. If that is the kind of paper you're preparing, follow the structure described in this section, replacing the thesis and supporting claims with three major themes, or three points about a single theme, gleaned from your data. See Chapter 7 for details on this modified application.

The Journal Format

This is the format often found in articles in major academic journals such as the *American Sociological Review* and the *American Journal of Sociology*. The journal format is not the same as "journalistic style." The term "journalistic style" is sometimes used to describe the easy and fluid style of writing in popular magazines such as *Time* and *Newsweek*. The journal format refers to a particular way that a paper or article can be organized. One would almost never use the journalistic style of writing in a paper organized according to the journal format. The journal format follows the procedural logic of the "hypothesis testing" mode of conducting research, in which you formally test a specific hypothesis through systematic research. The journal format, although usable for projects other than formal hypothesis testing, is best suited to projects that include some sort of systematic data collection and analysis. Its structure follows this order: introduction (including the literature review and the statement of hypothesis), methods, results, and discussion. (See Chapter 6, on the quantitative research paper, for more detail.)

The introduction specifies the question that is being answered in your paper. In this section, a "review of the literature" summarizes what other people have written about the topic, explaining why it is an important issue to study and what their answers are. It is important that the literature review not be a laundry list of "he said, she said" but a logical assessment of what is known and not known about your question. This section should also formally state your hypothesis (for example, "A greater proportion of men today hold higher-status jobs than their fathers did a hundred years ago") and justify why you expect it to be true.

The methods section reports your research procedure, detailing where you got the data, how the variables were measured, and what sort of analysis you conducted on the data. A reader should be able to replicate your study by following the "cookbook" of your methods section.

The results section reports in literal terms what the study shows. For instance, "30 percent of men a hundred years ago were in higher-status jobs than their fathers, while 29 percent of men today are in higher-status jobs than their fathers," which is virtually no change. (These numbers are made up for this book. They are not accurate.)

The discussion section draws the conclusions and reflects upon the result—for example: "The hypothesis must be rejected. The occupational structure has not opened up. The American promise of an equal chance for all is not yet fulfilled."

The essay and journal formats are illustrated by sample student papers in this book. The sample paper on quantitative research (see Chapter 6) follows the journal format. The other three sample papers—one based on library research (see Chapter 4), one based on textual analysis (see Chapter 5), and another demonstrating ethnographic field research (see Chapter 7)—are modified versions of the essay format. See the relevant chapters for details on organizing your paper.

THE PROPOSAL

A *proposal* (sometimes called a "statement of intent" or even, misleadingly, an "abstract") is a preview of your paper. Instructors assign a proposal to get you started on your paper by framing a question and making a commitment to answering it with evidence from either library research, textual analysis, quantitative research, or ethnographic research. Obviously, your proposal can't describe your intended paper in much detail because at this stage you often don't know much about the topic. However, you can frame your question and provide a context for it. As such, the proposal is a quick introduction, usually only one or two pages long, to what you want to do. On the basis of this information your instructor can advise you about possible leads to follow up or alert you to problems that may snowball as you prepare your paper.

Your proposal should feature your research question; for example, "To what extent is homelessness in Los Angeles attributable to mental illness?" In addition, it may include any of the following, depending on what you already know or hope to find out:

+ **an academic justification for studying this topic;** that is, why it interests other researchers. Does it provide an opportunity to illustrate, test, or compare one or more sociological theories? Or does the topic have substantive, practical, or policy implications? For example, "What does the increasing problem of urban homelessness mean for policymakers, for providers of social services, for public health and recreation, for tourism, and for others in addition to the homeless people themselves?"

+ **related questions** triggered by your main question, such as: "What counts as 'mental illness'?"; and "Who counts as 'homeless'?" These questions must be considered when operationally defining your variables in a quantitative paper. The question "Which comes first: the illness or the homelessness?" is related to the causal order you specify in a quantitative paper. "What drives people onto the streets?"; "How do people survive in these conditions?"; "Where do homeless people go for help?"; "Why do some people get off the street while others don't?" These are alternative questions you may want to investigate rather than the one you originally set out to answer.

+ **a provisional answer** to your question; in other words, your thesis (or hypothesis, if you're doing a quantitative research paper). An example of a thesis might be: "Many older homeless people behave eccentrically, but increasingly children and families are being made homeless and they are not necessarily mentally ill, at least not before becoming homeless." An example of a hypothesis might be: "As unemployment rates increase, the number of homeless increases." These provisional answers may be just hunches or "educated guesses" based on course materials. You will definitely refine your thesis or hypothesis as you learn more about your topic, and in the process you may change it entirely.

+ **a method for answering the question:** if you are doing a library research paper, you need to state what you will find out first and where you will start looking for it; for example, statistics on how many homeless people live in Los Angeles as published by other researchers in academic books and journals. If you are doing a quantitative research paper, your instructor will want a detailed methodological blueprint with a step-by-step plan listing variables, or, if you are doing a qualitative research paper, a description of the ethnographic site where you will be doing your observations. In any case, you need to demonstrate that what you plan to do will provide an adequate answer to your question. This sometimes will also require acknowledging the limitations of your answer; for example, we really don't know exactly how many homeless people there are because they are so difficult to identify. Moreover, some types of mental illness, such as paranoid schizophrenia, are easier to detect than equally debilitating forms, such as severe depression. What all this means is that you need to do some preliminary reading and thinking before you write your proposal.

A SAMPLE STUDENT PROPOSAL

Here is a sample proposal for a quantitative research paper, using a journal format, that student Christina De Roulhac wrote for an Honor's Thesis. The assignment was to identify a research question, set it within an academic context, and outline a way to answer that question. One of the admirable qualities of this proposal is that she is taking a very controversial issue in which emotions often overshadow information and identifies a question that can be answered by research. She does not claim to have no opinion, and she alerts the reader that her family has been very active in the church. The structure of this proposal is very straightforward. Christina states a question that nearly everyone can relate to, specifies it in sociological terms, offers a hypothesis of what she thinks the answer is, cites the sociological basis of that answer, describes a method for answering the question, gives a caveat about her personal involvement in the study, and reminds the reader why the issue is important. Not all proposals have to fit this model, but it is a useful template.

The question is inspired more by a topical issue than sociological theory, but it is framed in a way that empirical research will provide an objective answer. Empirical research is based on the collection of data using methods such as structured observation, archival analysis, survey, or experiment.

The two major concepts, *liberalism* and *conservatism,* are defined.

This is a clear hypothesis stated in a way that can be tested to find out if it is true, though there is a hint of tautology. *Tautology* is a statement that is true by definition. The key words in this sentence that carry the heavy analytical load are "desired," "leads," and "pastors and churches." All human action is motivated by some desire. Motives are notoriously hard to pin down. The study would be tautological if Christina used their support or condemnation of homosexuality as evidence of what their desire was.

The hypothesis is drawn from sociological theory, not her own preconceptions about why liberal or conservative ministers would advocate any particular opinion on homosexuality. She might have clarified how the theory might have to be reevaluated if the hypothesis does not hold up. Would it have to be slightly modified or reconsidered as an entire theory?

Christina De Roulhac
Sociology 191
January 9, 2006

PROPOSAL

In the present debate over homosexuality, some pastors and churches actively uphold traditional Biblical interpretations regarding same sex relations, while others challenge these teachings and welcome gay, lesbian, bisexual, and transgender individuals as well as advocate for their rights. Using the current controversy over homosexuality in American Baptist Churches (ABC) USA, a mainline protestant Christian denomination, I will study when and how pastors and churches encourage liberalism and when and how pastors and churches promote conservatism. Liberalism is a Protestant movement that favors free intellectual inquiry, stresses the ethical and humanitarian content of Christianity, and de-emphasizes dogmatic theology. In contrast, conservatism is a theological orientation that aims to maintain the existing or traditional order. This issue is particularly salient in the ABC because the Pacific Southwest, an ABC region of about 300 churches, decided on May 11, 2006 to sever ties with the ABC over irresolvable differences in Biblical interpretation, particularly in regards to homosexuality.

My hypothesis is that a mutual and reciprocal influence between Biblical interpretation and a church's desired niche in the Christian marketplace leads a number of pastors and churches to encourage liberalism and other pastors and churches to promote conservatism.

My hypothesis builds upon the economic and sociological model of the Christian marketplace that "views churches and their clergy as religious producers who choose the characteristics of their product and the means of marketing it. Consumers in turn choose what religion, if any, they will accept and how extensively they will participate in it." (Finke and Iannaccone 1993:28). In this model, pastors and churches must meet consumers' demand in order to survive, but also play a role in creating new niches and markets. The "niche" is also an important concept because it is "a way of specifying competitive processes and environmental

1

This is a clear description of her sample. If the proposal had been longer, she might have added more detail about how they would be found and recruited.

What the proposal needs at this point is specification of how the interview data would be used to accept or reject her hypotheses. How would she know whether the pastors were sensitive to niches and whether their knowledge of niches affected their attitude toward homosexuality? How would she reject a more conventional explanation that ministers preach what they believe and that parishioners either stay or leave depending on whether they agree?

Although the larger social implications of this topic are obvious, it is a good idea to always point out what the larger implications are.

dependencies" in an environment, such as the Christian marketplace (Hannan, Carroll, and Polos 2003:309).

My hypothesis also builds upon N.J. Demerath's (1995) "Cultural Victory and Organizational Defeat in the Paradoxical Decline of Liberal Protestantism" which asserts that fulfilling a niche in the Christian market is important, especially for liberal churches. Demerath argues that the liberal Protestant values of individualism, freedom, pluralism, tolerance, democracy, and intellectual inquiry are related to decreased membership relative to more conservative, strict churches. To offset their disadvantage, Demerath (1995) suggests that the liberal churches that thrive fill particular niches because they are "groups that have coalesced successfully around distinctive liberal political agendas (whether pro-civil rights, antipoverty, or antiwar), and those strict liberal congregations whose solidarity derives from a bold identification with a distinctive lifestyle – e.g., gay and lesbian" (p. 466). Both liberal and conservative pastors and churches make decisions and act in a way that preserves their place in a desired niche, and these decisions influence and are influenced by Biblical interpretation.

For this study I will interview 10-16 pastors from the ABC, who represent different points in the homosexuality debate. Half the pastors will be liberal and welcoming and affirming of gays in the church, and the other half of the pastors will be more conservative in their views. I will ask how they got involved in the homosexuality debate, how their Biblical interpretation effects the decisions they make for the church, and why they think people choose to join their church. The interviews with pastors will be supplemented by interviews with new members of the represented churches. In these interviews I will ask why they joined this particular church and what they think of their church's stance on the issue of homosexuality.

My family's involvement in the ABC is both a strength and limitation of this research. It is a strength because I have connections to many pastors, but a weakness because I have my own views in this debate. My views will not influence my research because I will not be studying the arguments of each side of the debate, but instead studying the factors which precipitate and fuel pastors' and churches' decisions and actions. This research is important because the issue of homosexuality is a wide spread controversy

2

According to the most recent edition of the *American Sociological Association Style Guide* (2007), references to journal articles should include the issue number after the volume number.

Again, references to journal articles should include the issue number after the volume number.

in many mainline Protestant denominations as well as politics in the
United States.

REFERENCES

Demerath, N.J. 1995. "Cultural Victory and Organizational Defeat in the
        Paradoxical Decline of Liberal Protestantism." *Journal for the Scientific
        Study of Religion* 34:458-69.
Finke, Roger and Laurence Iannaccone. 1993. "Supply-Side Explanations
        for Religious Change." Pp. 27-39 in *Annals of the American Academy
        of Political and Social Science.* Vol. 527, *Religion in the Nineties,*
        edited by W. C. Roof. Newbury Park, CA: Sage Publications.
Hannan, Michael, Glenn Carroll, and Laszlo Polos. 2003. "The
        Organizational Niche." *Sociological Theory* 21:309-340.

The Writing Process

THE SECRET TO WRITING IS REWRITING

All the steps that go into a final paper or textbook chapter or journal article are invisible. Usually we only see someone else's impressive final product, while our own efforts look to us like an unflattering photograph. However, no one ever sits down, thinks, and then types an "A" paper all at once as their ideas flow into their fingertips. Writing is definitely *not* a delivery system of ready-made ideas; it is a process of approximation. Every good writer goes through a process of getting something down on paper or in a computer file—doodles, an outline, a provisional question or list of questions, a thesis or hypothesis, an easy paragraph, or whatever. Then the writer looks at it, likes some aspects, and considers a way to develop those; or considers what kind of additional information is needed and does some more reading; or sees logical gaps and works to make the argument more coherent; or dislikes the way some sentences sound and rewrites them, or moves paragraphs around to make more sense; and in so doing gets more ideas to jot down, and so this recursive process continues.

There is no One Right Way or One Right Direction to move through these stages. For example, some people like to begin by writing down everything that occurs to them in association with the general topic; they may even turn off their computer monitor and simply keyboard in everything they can think of; then they print this out, search through it for threads of thought and rich possibilities, and then outline some sequence of the previously jumbled, buried ideas. Other writers work out a highly structured outline first because the logical subdivisions help them spot and understand potential relationships between ideas. Then they compose a draft, possibly beginning to write sentences and paragraphs about ideas somewhere in the middle or at the end of their outline. The very act of writing triggers more ideas, so you may find that outlining comes more easily after you've written some ideas or after your first rough draft.

Different people have very different ways of getting started. Some need to sharpen two pencils and make a cup of coffee; some can only write in the morning, others late at night; some can only type and others compose only in longhand. One of the authors of this book writes best while shoeless! None of these things matter, as long as the writing gets done. Students sometimes feel that there is a correct way to go about sitting down to write and that any personal quirks should be "cured." But they forget that writing can be an emotionally risky venture and that people often need little rituals to ease the tension. Just like the basketball player who caresses the basketball before shooting a foul shot, the baseball player who always knocks the mud off his shoes before stepping into the batter's box, or the ballerina who sits in the middle of the stage for five minutes before the curtain goes up, anything (provided it's legal and nondestructive) necessary to get ready for writing is appropriate as long as you don't do it *instead* of writing.

We therefore are not recommending any one particular way to move through the stages in this writing and rewriting process. However, we would like to share with you some suggestions about drafting your paper— particularly the value of outlining and revising—and about the nature of writing styles.

A computer tip. As you keyboard your paper, embed a symbol system that you can use later to locate passages easily with the "Find" command in Microsoft Word. This means use something like XXX to identify a place or places that you will want to find later, for example, to illustrate a point, explain an illustration, or complete a thought. Always refer to tables and figures by writing out the number ("Table One"). In that way you can use the universal "Find" and "Replace" functions later to renumber them if necessary.

THE PERSONAL VULNERABILITY OF WRITING

Although we usually think of writing as an intellectual activity, a lot of personal feelings are at stake, especially when writing in college. When you write for a class, the writing is evaluated and most students feel that *they* are being evaluated, that somebody they barely know and have not had the opportunity to develop personal trust with is telling them whether they are worthy to be in college. That can be very scary. It's not surprising that students want to avoid such a risky activity. It is not made any easier by the common style of grading that tells students more about what is wrong with their work than what is good about it. For an excellent personal account of struggling with these feelings, see "Risk" by Pamela Richards in Howard Becker's *Writing for Social Scientists*.

We can offer no easy solutions to the anxiety of writing or being evaluated. Few individuals, even professional writers, are ever entirely free of it. It may help to talk to your fellow students, teaching assistant, or instructor about your concerns. You will probably find that they (even the instructor) share the same feelings. The counseling centers at many colleges and universities have writing workshops designed to help alleviate your anxieties. In extreme cases where "writer's block" prevents you from completing assignments or hurts the quality of your work, professional counseling may be appropriate.

GETTING IDEAS

Review your class notes. Reread the relevant parts of your textbook or other assigned reading. Talk to others in your class or study group about your general plans. Visit your instructor during office hours. Even formulating one or more questions to raise with them will trigger thoughts. Browse a free online encyclopedia like Wikipedia to get an overview of the issues involved. Note the linked key words that identify related major concepts that you may need to clarify in your own mind.

OUTLINING

Writing an outline can provide at least two benefits at different stages in the writing process: it can give birth to ideas and it can describe the connections between ideas that are already articulated. The first kind of outline is glorified doodling; the second kind of outline is a blueprint or a road map that tracks the relationship and sequence of main ideas in your paper. The first kind, to use C. Wright Mills's distinction in *The Sociological Imagination*, is private; its purpose is discovery, not presentation to others. The second kind can very usefully be shown to an instructor long before the paper's due date, to make sure you're on target. It is much easier to revise this second kind of outline (by adding, eliminating, or shifting main parts) than it is to repair a completed paper.

DISCOVERY OUTLINES (private, just for your eyes)

1. Freewriting. This is brainstorming or free association. Just write nonstop for 5–15 minutes with no censoring of your ideas. If you are keyboarding on a computer, dim the screen so you're not distracted, and at the end of 15 minutes scroll back to find some key words or phrases you like, underline them, and then immediately use the "Insert" command to add 5–10 more minutes' worth of thoughts.

2. Lists. Make up a shopping list of all the ideas or questions that you can think of that you associate with or might need in any way for your paper, just as if you were going to the store for groceries. Then group them into families.

3. Reporter's Notebook. Consider the famous journalism questions "Who?" "When?" "Why?" "Where?" "What?" and "How?" and try to create information related to the general topic for each question.

4. Diagrams. Some people are visually oriented and like to see their ideas emerging as pictures on the page. Here are several different kinds of diagrams you can try:

+ *Clustering.* Write one key word or phrase (for example, a person's name, an issue, a term) in the middle of a sheet of paper. Circle it and then write down related concepts and examples in their own circles elsewhere on the page. Draw lines between the circles to indicate various logical relationships between all these items.

+ *Branching.* Build a tree from a key word or phrase. Analyze it into its branch ideas and then into the twig and leaf ideas. Your tree can be vertical, horizontal, or upside down.

+ *Columns.* Set up a compare-and-contrast table in two columns. Include in each column the information that fits under the things you are juxtaposing.

+ *Flow chart.* Put your major concepts (variables) in boxes with causes (independent variables) on the left side of the page, effects (dependent variables) on the right, and mediating processes (intervening variables) in between. Draw lines and arrows between the boxes to show causal relationships. This is an excellent technique to get straight in your mind just what causes what.

A computer tip. Most word-processing programs, such as Microsoft Word, have outlining capabilities. If your own word processor has such an outlining function, learn how to use it. You may want to use it later to begin drafting your paper by inserting material. Open two files so you can access and move information between two corresponding windows: (1) your notes and/or outline and (2) your developing draft of the paper. Most writers move back and forth between their outline and rough draft as work on one modifies the other. Alternatively, most word-processing programs allow you to insert text beneath each outline item, where you can write the body of your paper, then hide the outline itself.

PRESENTATION OUTLINES (public, to show to others)

This is a completed set of ideas, arranged in a specific sequence. As such it's a map or blueprint of the paper itself. It can be a topic outline composed of words and phrases like a table of contents, or it can be a sentence outline. In either case, a proper presentation outline signals the order and relationship of ideas through visual layout (headings and indentations) and through a symbol system, either an alternating number–letter system (roman numeral, capital letter, arabic numeral, lowercase letter) or a number system (1, 1.1, 1.1.2, and so on).

For example, student Dana E. Knickerbocker began with this question: "How does gender impact capital-punishment sentencing?" Dana's next step was to outline three alternative answers:

1. The "chivalry" theory indicates that gender bias in capital sentencing works to a woman's advantage.
2. The "evil woman" theory proposes that the relatively few women who do receive capital sentences have violated norms of "ladylike" behavior. In other words, these women "killed like men."
3. Because women commit such a small fraction of the kinds of murders that qualify for the death penalty, "gender-neutral" rather than "gender-based" factors account for women's experiences with capital punishment. Current law holds that killing strangers for private gain is more heinous than killing intimates in anger. Men are more likely to kill for gain; women are more likely to kill intimates.

Dana then began to fill in this structure with evidence, for instance, listing these subpoints under the first answer:

+ Cite current number of men versus women on death row.
+ Brief historical view of how infrequently women are executed compared to men.
+ Give a couple of examples showing that women can be as heinous as men when murdering yet do not receive the death penalty.
+ The "femininity loophole," or why women can't be executed: "She had PMS," "She was emotionally overwrought," "She was dominated or abused by a man," She's a mother," "She is not a threat."
+ Cite petition from male San Quentin inmates pleading to spare the life of a condemned female or to be killed in her place.
+ Cite statistics indicating reversal or commutation of death sentences for women who have effectively been remolded into traditional womanhood during prison: sewing, religion, and the like.

At this point, Dana can reorder points or subdivide them further, or leave them and move on to developing the second and third answers into a complete outline.

A SAMPLE STUDENT OUTLINE

Here is Tanaya Burnham's complete outline for a paper on Multiracial Identity in the United States. It answers the question "How do multiracial individuals develop a positive self-identity when society, as well as members of their own racial groups, often reject them?"

   I. Introduction: In the United States, people tend to be classified by their race, but what about those whose parentage is not monoracial?
  II. Laws that forbade interracial marriage
      A. History of anti-miscegenation laws
      B. Consequences of anti-miscegenation laws
 III. Interracial families and multiracial identity
      A. Who is likely to marry outside their race?
      B. Implications of multiracial identity
         1. Group rejection
         2. Multiracial identity
 IV. The multiracial baby boom
      A. The 2000 U.S. Census
  V. Conclusion

WRITING A FIRST DRAFT

Paragraphs are the major building blocks of a paper. Whatever kind of outline or plan you have for organizing your paper, your goal in writing your first draft will be to create a group of paragraphs in an appropriate order. In a first draft, these paragraphs may be incomplete. You may later eliminate some of them entirely. You may split some paragraphs up or move some paragraphs around to different places. However, at this initial stage you should try to make the leap from your outline to a logical sequence of major points and subpoints, each of which is developed in paragraphs, that is, in groups of related sentences. The sentences in each paragraph will have different purposes, for example, to explain, to illustrate, to qualify, to connect, to demonstrate, to announce, or to summarize the main point of that paragraph. You should be able to encapsulate the theme and purpose of each paragraph in a phrase or short sentence. Everything in the paragraph should be directly related to this theme. Don't worry about the shape or style of your sentences now. Aim at a logical order of points that are developed in related groups of sentences. Resist the temptation to revise individual bits of your paper as you write your draft, or you may spend too much time fiddling with a small part instead of getting a complete draft done.

    Notice in the paragraph below, how Tanaya builds two paragraphs around one main point from her outline. Following her outline that had already discussed racial discrimination and multiracial identity, Tanaya begins with the heading, "Group rejection," and makes this general point, "Qualitative research on biracial and multiracial individuals showed that these individuals often experienced more discrimination by their own racial groups than by groups outside their racial heritage." She then develops two paragraphs for this point, one paragraph about the main idea of discrimination experienced by children within their own families and one paragraph about the main idea of discrimination of such children by members of their own racial groups.

SAMPLE STUDENT PARAGRAPHS

Multiracial children can also experience prejudice within their own families as well. The birth of children to an interracial couple experiencing tensions within their extended family could either bring the family together, proving blood ties are stronger than racial barriers, or could even tear the family further apart (Root 2001). Some grandparents have been known to disown their own children and the interracial family altogether, leaving the multiracial children feeling a sense of abandonment from their extended families (Root 2001). Tensions between one side of the family and a parent can cause the multiracial child to have questions of loyalty (Root 2001). Multiracial children can also feel abandoned by their own parents as well, for instance in situations where a parent shows preference to monoracial siblings (Brown 2001).

Multiracial individuals often experience more discrimination by their own racial groups than by groups outside their racial heritage (Stephen and Stephan 1991; Root 2001). Multiracial children were taunted with racial terms like "Oreo," "mutt," "wannabie," etc., from children of their own race (Tizard and Phoenix 2002). Young adults of Korean and white ancestry recount how they were excluded by the white community for being Asian and excluded by the Korean community for not being Korean enough (Standen 1996). They were also criticized for not knowing how to speak Korean fluently or for being too Americanized (Standen 1996). Multiracial individuals are subjected to a higher standard of cultural competence compared to monoracial children of the same immigrant generation (Standen 1996). I, too, have a similar experience because even though all of my American-born full Korean cousins and I are not fluent in the Korean language, my fellow biracial cousins and I are more criticized by my family for our inability to converse in Korean. Multiracial individuals also run the risk of being considered cultural traitors. Especially if one parent is white, there seems to be a fear by the minority race that their culture will be left behind and the multiracial children will choose to perpetuate the dominant culture over their ethnic one (Root 2001). This fear also brings concern about whom the multiracial child will marry and how they will raise their children. Some multiracial children from Asian families were encouraged to marry someone of their same Asian ethnicity (Winters and DeBose 2003).

REVISING

Once you have written a more or less complete draft of your paper, your next step is to revise it. Revising can greatly improve the logic and structure of your argument (these two features of your paper are discussed at length in Chapter 1). You need the "big picture" of a complete draft on which to work. Revising includes inserting new ideas and deleting or modifying old ones, rewriting sentences or paragraphs to improve clarity or logic, moving sentences or paragraphs around to strengthen organization, and adding transitions to enhance the flow of your writing and accentuate the relationships among your ideas. For example, examine the two paragraphs above, one paragraph about discrimination within families and one about discrimination from one's own racial group. Do you think any of the sentences in the second paragraph would be more appropriate in the first paragraph and should be moved up? This is the kind of question to ask yourself at this stage. Setting your draft aside for a few days between revisions helps you see its strengths and weaknesses, and possibilities for revision, more easily.

Once you are satisfied with the logical order of your paragraphs and with the order and adequacy of the sentences in each paragraph, you need to look closely at each sentence. At this stage, most writers rely on three revision techniques: *eliminating wordiness, adding details and examples,* and *adding transitional expressions.* Following is a sample paragraph from a student's draft proposal for a paper on stress management. The paragraphs come in the right order in the paper, and the sentences come in the right order in the paragraph, but the writing is not very graceful. This paragraph is grammatically correct but is not well written. Notice how the student has applied each of these three revision techniques to improve the paragraph.

Original draft paragraph:

From the readings I did for the course on stress, I have found that there have been many studies done to try to find the single most common cause of stress. Some stress scholars believe it is the major life changes that provoke stress. Others believe that it is the everyday hassles and annoyances of life which bring about stress. Despite the conflicting viewpoints in the causality of stress, all scholars agree that when stressful stimuli can be recognized and regulated early there seem to be less damaging effects on the body. At this point I have a confident feeling that I will be able to locate good, current information on the questions of stress management, which I intend to research. (121 words)

1. Eliminate Wordiness. The following can lead to wordiness in writing:

- Redundant pairs ("everyday hassles and annoyances")
- Inflated phrases ("At this point")

- ✦ Intensifiers ("single most common")
- ✦ Action in a noun rather than a verb ("a confident feeling")
- ✦ Passive voice ("be recognized and regulated")
- ✦ Expletives ("it is")

Paragraph revised to eliminate wordiness:

According to my readings about stress, many studies have tried to find its most common cause. According to some scholars, major life changes provoke stress; for others, everyday annoyances cause it. Despite conflicting explanations, all agree that early recognition and regulation lessen bodily damage. I feel confident now that I can locate good, relevant information on stress management. (58 words)

2. Add Details and Examples. Details answer the journalistic questions "Who?" "When?" "Why?" "Where?" "What?" and "How?" Examples can be illustrations that you create or evidence that you cite.

Paragraph revised to add details and examples:

According to my readings about stress, many studies have tried to find its most common cause. *Loss and Trauma: General and Close Relationship Perspectives* (2000) includes 24 chapters by different social scientists. According to some scholars, major life changes provoke stress; others argue that everyday annoyances cause it. Two paradigms predominate: the "stress model," especially in medical sociology and psychology, and the "normative development" model, especially in life-span development research. Despite conflicting explanations, all agree that early recognition and regulation lessen bodily damage. I feel confident now that I can locate good, relevant information on stress management. (98 words)

3. Add Transitional Expressions. Transitional words function like traffic signals, directing the reader from one sentence to the next by identifying the logical relationship between these sentences.

- ✦ *To show addition:* again, also, and, and then, besides, equally important, further, furthermore, moreover, next, similarly, too, what's more
- ✦ *To show time:* after, afterward, as, at length, at once, at the same time, by, earlier, eventually, finally, first, formerly, gradually, immediately, later, next, once, previously, second, soon, then, thereafter, while
- ✦ *To make the reader stop and compare:* after all, although, at the same time, but, conversely, for all that, however, in contrast, in the meantime,

meanwhile, nevertheless, nonetheless, notwithstanding, on the contrary, on the other hand, still, whereas, yet
+ *To give examples:* as an illustration, for example, for instance, in other words, to demonstrate, to illustrate
+ *To emphasize:* as a matter of fact, clearly, in any case, in any event, in fact, indeed, more important(ly), obviously, of course, that is
+ *To repeat:* as I have said (demonstrated, argued, noted), in brief, in other words, in short
+ *To draw a conclusion:* accordingly, as a result, at last, consequently, hence, in brief, in conclusion, in sum, on the whole, so, therefore, thus, to conclude

Paragraph revised to add transitional expressions:

According to my readings about stress, many studies have tried to find its most common cause. For example, *Loss and Trauma: General and Close Relationship Perspectives* (2000) includes 24 chapters by different social scientists. According to some scholars, major life changes provoke stress; however, others argue that everyday annoyances cause it. Two paradigms predominate: first, the "stress model," especially in medical sociology and psychology, and, second, the "normative development" model, especially in life-span development research. Despite conflicting explanations, all agree that early recognition and regulation lessen bodily damage. I therefore feel confident now that I can locate good, relevant information on stress management. (104 words)

Note that this final, revised paragraph still includes fewer words than the original draft. However, every word adds meaning. The result is clear, concise, logical writing.

When revising, think carefully about your paper's key concepts and terms. Define them as you introduce them (usually in the opening paragraphs) and use them accurately throughout the paper. Be especially cautious when using terms originated by sociologists that have become part of everyday language and yet retain special sociological meaning (for example, "stereotype," "status," "self-fulfilling prophecy"). Dictionaries are written to reflect the ordinary usage of words, which are often different from sociological definitions. Thus you should avoid using dictionaries to define sociological concepts. If you are unsure, we recommend that you consult one of the following specialized dictionaries in the reference section of your college library: *A New Dictionary of the Social Sciences, A Modern Dictionary of Sociology,* or *Dictionary of Modern Sociology.* Several such dictionaries are now online. The Online Dictionary of the Social Sciences is at <http://socialsciencedictionary.nelson.com/ssd/main.html>. It's often helpful to write out sociological definitions of your central terms on scratch paper—in language you can understand—in order to foster clear and accurate use of them as you revise. When dealing with words that do not have special sociological meaning, a good dictionary and a thesaurus can help you both to locate the most precise word that expresses what you want to say and to find synonyms for varying your word choice.

An Internet tip. References such as the *American Heritage Dictionary of the English Language* and *Roget's Thesaurus,* as well as other references, such as collections of quotations, are available online; such resources are useful at this revising stage. Examples of online sources are <http://www.bartleby.com/>, <http://www.dictionary.reference.com>, and <http://www.thesaurus.reference.com>.

The revising stage is also the time to troubleshoot your draft for biased or sexist language. Have you inadvertently used sexist language (such as used the masculine pronoun "he" exclusively)? Although most writers prefer to use nonsexist language, repeating "he or she" (or "she or he") every time a singular pronoun is required can sound awkward and repetitive. An occasional "he or she" sounds fine; but two in one sentence or, say, three in one paragraph are distracting. Do not use "he/she." Sometimes writers solve this problem but create another by following a singular noun or pronoun with the non-gender-specific, but plural, pronouns "they" and "their." If you are unsure, check with your instructor or teaching assistant to see how she or he prefers that writing be made gender neutral.

WRITING STYLES

The second edition of the *Style Guide* from the American Sociological Association (1997:1) explains, "Obviously an author's ideas are important, but almost as important is *how* the author expresses those ideas." "Style" refers to *"how* the author expresses those ideas." "Style" has two main meanings. First, "style" can refer to the impression your writing creates about you. Your writing will automatically make you sound like someone, for example, friendly and informal, pompous, careless and sloppy, emotionally involved, or scientifically detached. We all have different writing styles for different occasions. "Style" can also refer to professional standards about the expected format for displaying your paper on the page and for identifying and citing the information you borrow from sources.

Just as people dress differently, speak differently, and behave differently in different social situations, so, too, writers choose different words and sentence structures depending on the writing situation and their readers. Therefore, writers do not have only one style, and no style is automatically better than any other. It is true, though, that, like dress and behavior, one style may be more appropriate than another for some specific occasion. You will address a classmate in a personal Instant Message differently from the way you write when you e-mail a question to your instructor. One will likely be more informal than the other. Assigned papers will be even more formal. Good writers learn to vary their linguistic wardrobe and behavior to the occasion and to adjust their styles to their readers.

One special problem about academic style in assigned papers is worth noting. Some people try to compensate for uncertainty with verbal bravado: using big words and complex sentence structures to sound intelligent. Sociologists have been frequently criticized for using too much jargon and writing in a convoluted style that is difficult to comprehend. Some students try to copy that style, thinking that it will make their writing seem "academic." That defeats the purpose of writing, which is to communicate. The best writing is usually easy to read and understand. The intelligence is in the ideas, not the vocabulary. Students too often think that if they sound intelligent they will get a better grade than if they write intelligently. Occasionally an instructor will give a higher grade to papers with fancy words, but most look more closely at the ideas.

So remember these tips:

+ Don't use a big word where a small one will do.
+ Use contractions (for example, "it's," "don't," "you're") as you draft your paper if they feel more natural to you than writing the words out ("it is," "do not," "you are"). Before you revise your final draft, however, ask if your instructor objects. If you have waited until the last minute and do not know your instructor's preference—which may vary according to the type of assignment—then play it safe and avoid contractions (for example, they are not appropriate for the journal format).
+ Use specialized sociological terms only to be precise about the concept you are discussing.
+ Each sentence should include only one thought or idea.
+ Try to use active rather than passive verbs wherever possible to ensure that both writer and reader know *who* is "doing the doing." Too much use of the passive voice can create ambiguity about the social processes under discussion.
+ Try to avoid using too many prepositional phrases, which can fill sentences with modifiers of modifiers and make them difficult to read.
+ Use adverbs and adjectives carefully. Some people think that good writing means filling your text with flowery adverbs and adjectives. Make sure that the modifiers you use add meaning and not just filler to your text.
+ Remember that reading your paper should be a pleasure, not a chore.

What your writing looks like on the page. It is a good idea to locate a manual of style—which presents standards and examples of grammar, punctuation, usage, and typography—to answer specific questions that may arise during the writing process. If your paper includes tables and graphs, choose a manual that also provides guidelines on how such information should be arranged and labeled. (The style manuals we recommend below include such guidelines and are available in many libraries and bookstores.) Early in the quarter/semester, before the almost inevitable end-of-the-term crunch, ask your instructor to recommend a manual; you can put it aside until you need it. If your instructor doesn't have a preference, you may choose the inexpensive, very useful, but brief (108 pages) paperback *ASA Style Guide* (2007) now available from the American Sociological Association (1307 New York Avenue NW, Suite 700, Washington, DC 20005-4701) or from the ASA Online Bookstore at <http://www.e-noah.net/asa/asashoponlineservice/>. *The Chicago Manual of Style* is long and comprehensive; it is available both in print and online (for a subscription fee) <http://www.chicagomanualofstyle.org/home.html>; however, you can get a one-time only 30-day free trial. If you only need help with citations, you can use the *Chicago-Style Citation Quick Guide* <http://www.chicagomanualofstyle.org/tools_citationguide.html> for free. We also recommend the inexpensive, popular paperback edition of Kate L. Turabian's *A Manual for Writers of Term Papers, Dissertations, and Theses,* which recommends many of the same style standards suggested by *The Chicago Manual of Style.* If anxiety about standards and rules impedes your writing, don't even think about a manual until you have generated at least one draft.

A NOTE ABOUT ACADEMIC E-MAIL

You may be expected to use an electronic class mailing list, bulletin board, or chat room, or even have e-mail assignments, like the Proposal in Chapter 1. Remember that academic e-mail is "academic." Your e-mail style should make you sound like you are talking to your instructor in office hours, not having a conversation with a friend from MySpace. u no wot we mean.

You don't have much screen space. Most screens are smaller than a sheet of paper, and readers do not like to scroll down. Virtual real estate is precious. Every word must be calculated strategically (1) to send the clearest possible message and (2) to send the best possible impression of you. Be aware of your choices and the trade-offs involved. E-mail is more formal than a telephone conversation and less formal than a business letter. If in doubt, be more formal. Be friendly but polite. Be considerate. Have manners. Don't use emoticons like ;) or abbreviations like "u" for "you." Don't write in ALL CAPITAL LETTERS (which sounds like shouting), and don't write in all lowercase letters (which makes you look peculiarly like the poet e. e. cummings).

+ **Consider Alternatives:** Why write an e-mail message at all? Why not instead go to office hours, telephone, or leave a voice mail message? You don't want to annoy readers by sending "junk mail."
+ **Your Audience:** Visualize who will be reading your e-mail. Be sensitive to pronouns. Create the information in terms of "you" and "your," or "we" and "us," not "I" and "mine." For example, if you are e-mailing your instructor, instead of starting "**I** am sending **my** draft thesis," write "**You**

asked **us** to send **you** a draft thesis before class tomorrow" or "Here is the draft thesis that **you** assigned in class yesterday." If you are e-mailing your class mailing list, write "Did Professor Hamilton say that Chapter 6 would be on the midterm?" instead of "Hey, I slept in today. Did I miss anything important in class?"

+ **Your Nickname:** The first visible part of your message will be your name in your reader's e-mail in-box. Avoid using a cute or possibly offensive nickname. For example, what kind of impression are you creating if you write as "vietqueen21@gmail.com" or "nite-elf@hotmail.com"? If in doubt, use your college ID: "Khanh.Nguyen@uci.edu".

+ **Subject Line:** This is the second visible part of your message in your reader's e-mail in-box, and it is extremely important. It should describe what the message is about so that your reader knows whether to open it up and read it now, wait for later, or simply delete it unread. The subject line has the same function as a thesis or a title in a paper—an umbrella idea for the main point. Make it meaningful (especially when abbreviated in an in-box list) and specific, not "assignment" but "Draft thesis for Paper 2 in Soc 222." Consider providing a new subject line for a message in a continuing thread if the old one is no longer relevant, putting the old one in parentheses (Was ". . . . . .").

+ **Addresses:** Consider the order of recipients if you are e-mailing more than one person. Consider whether one person should be addressed, with others "cc'ed."

+ **Attachments:** Limit their use. Some readers' mailing programs do not handle attachments, and they resent receiving them. Attachments can also carry viruses. If you must send an attachment, explain what the attachment is about.

+ **History:** Include only enough of one or more previous e-mails that you are answering in order to remind the reader(s) of the context. Don't automatically include a complete copy. Cut off irrelevant parts. For example, don't just write back "yes," but cut and paste the relevant part(s) from the original:

> > So can you bring a draft to my office at 12:30 on Wednesday?
> Yes

In this way, the reader will remember what the message is about.

+ **Salutation:** A salutation is polite and reassures the reader that the message is addressing the right person, but it does take up space. An alternative to a salutation is a heading (but don't just repeat the subject line).

+ **Message Length:** Do not write anything longer than two screens without a good reason. Keep your paragraphs short.

+ **Drafting the Message:**
  + Consider composing the text of your message offline in your word processor and then importing it. This will give you more time to reflect on your message, to use a spellchecker, and to proofread carefully and correct any errors.

- Use headings and an outline format if the message has several components.
- Identify specifically what you want the reader(s) to do with the information in the message.
- E-mail usually has a shelf life, so identify a time frame for the reader's requested action.
- Don't write anything in an e-mail that you would not want to see on the front page of the newspaper tomorrow morning. E-mail is stored indefinitely by third parties. Recipients can forward your messages to whomever.

- **Web Links:** If you refer to Web pages, type out or paste in the entire URL. In that way, the reader can usually just click on the URL to visit the linked site automatically.
- **Use a Signature File:** Identify who you are with your full name. You can add your affiliation and a contact phone number if you want your reader(s) to have it. A signature file is your virtual business card. A motto is OK if it's not too cute. Don't include long graphics made out of letters, which might entail the annoyance of printing an extra page. Remember that some "free" e-mail services carry advertising, and consider the trade-offs in the impression your message will accordingly make with its commercial endorsement of Yahoo or whatever.
- **Answering Your E-mail:** Readers expect a prompt response. Delay will annoy. If a delay is unavoidable, explain it and apologize.
- **Use the Postpone Command:** A message about an awkward, sensitive, or painful subject should be postponed overnight for valuable further thought and revision.
- **Managing Your E-mail:** Try to deal with and clear your messages promptly each time you open your in-box by replying, saving, or deleting them.
- **A Vacation Message:** If you will be away from your e-mail and unable to answer it, leave a vacation message with an alternative means of contact or a date of earliest possible reply.

Working with Sources

If I have seen a little further it is by standing on the shoulders of Giants.
ISAAC NEWTON
In a Letter to Robert Hooke
February 5, 1676

The generation of knowledge is a group activity. Scholars build on and re-spond to each other's data (concepts, insights, theories, statistics), which cir-culate from one scholar to another through conference papers, articles, and books. When you write your paper, you are engaging in this process. Even if you are not assigned to read beyond your textbook, you will probably want to learn more about the topic anyway, just to become more informed yourself. Obviously, you will write a better paper if you know more about the subject. Like Newton, you will see more by standing on the shoulders of others. At the very least you will want to get an overview of related concepts and theories from a general text or reference source, such as *21ˢᵗ Century Sociology: A Refer-ence Handbook* edited by Clifton D. Bryant and Dennis L. Peck (2007) and pub-lished by Sage Publications. Later in this book you will find detailed information about searching for and evaluating print and electronic sources in the chapter on how to write a research paper, where you are expected to build your argument from evidence that you find in the library or on the Internet (see Chapter 4). This chapter is a basic orientation on keeping track of what you learn from reading sources. It includes several sample assignments of an annotated bibliography entry. An annotated bibliography entry is a short writ-ing assignment based on reading a source. It is an exercise in critical thinking and, like the proposal, is often assigned to get you started on a paper.

TAKING TWO KINDS OF NOTES

As C. Wright Mills explains in his appendix "On Intellectual Craftsmanship" in *The Sociological Imagination* ([1959] 2000), "You will have to acquire the habit of taking a large volume of notes from any worth-while book you read"

(p. 199). Taking notes is a personal skill that varies somewhat from student to student. Specific techniques include any or all of the following: writing notes in word-processed files opened up for that specific purpose, writing in the margins of your own copy of the text or on the back of photocopied pages, attaching Post-it notes to specific passages in the text, or writing notes on separate note cards or sheets of paper. Regardless of where they are physically recorded, careful notes provide two benefits.

1. "A Prod to Reflection."   As Mills explains, "the mere taking of a note from a book is often a prod to reflection. At the same time, of course, the taking of a note is a great aid in comprehending what you are reading" (p. 199). The first kind of note, what Mills calls "a prod to reflection," can take the form of annotations: definitions, cross-references, examples, questions, or other ideas that are triggered in your mind as you read. Whether or not this noted information ends up in your paper is not the point with this kind of note. Taking this kind of note exercises your skills of critical reading. It makes you interact with the author, and thereby it helps you understand and learn what you are reading so that you are able to write about the subject.

2. A Summary of Borrowed Information.   In the second kind of note, according to Mills, "you try to grasp the structure of the writer's argument" (p. 199). This second kind of note is more objective. It is a systematic analysis of all or part of the author's argument. This summarizing kind of note outlines the author's main points and the interrelationships between the points and the evidence on which they are based. Your notes should summarize the main points or thesis, not just specific facts. That is, you should make note of the forest, not just the trees. In general, you should paraphrase the author's original words rather than quote them. You should quote only in a few special instances:

1. When the original is worded so elegantly, memorably, or powerfully that you do not want to change its effect.
2. When you just can't paraphrase it and do justice to the meaning, even though you have tried.
3. When the original is provocative or unusual, and you want to borrow the prestige of the original author to run defense for yourself, in case your reader disagrees with this point. The epigraphs we've used in this book illustrate the power of a distinguished author's exact words to enhance an argument.
4. When you want to do an extensive analysis on one small passage (an *exegesis*).

When you want to use the author's exact words, be sure to mark them as a quotation in your notes so that you will properly cite the source in your paper. You must also document paraphrases.

SAMPLE ANNOTATED BIBLIOGRAPHY

Your instructor may assign one or more annotated bibliography entries at the beginning of your paper project. This assignment is intended to get you started. Writing your annotation will prod you into thinking about how you will answer your question, and it will help you begin to accumulate evidence. An annotated bibliography entry is a special kind of note taken on a source.

Some instructors give very simple instructions for the annotation: "Write several sentences describing one source from a library database or the Internet about your topic." Here, for example, is a student's informal annotation about a report from the National Community Investment Fund: "Talks about the direct benefits of Employer Assisted Housing programs and how they treat the problem rather directly and have more positive effects than just giving workers a place to live, such as how it makes it so they can afford to live closer to where they work, helping them to maintain a stable job."

Other annotated bibliography assignments are more formal. One common assignment requires you to analyze a source, looking for specific kinds of information about the source, and then to write a short paragraph that notes these specific kinds of information. These different kinds of information can include a complete identification of the publication, the authority and credentials of the author, the author's thesis, the author's evidence, the author's purpose in writing, and the author's audience.

EXAMPLE OF AN ANNOTATION FOR A PRINT SOURCE

Ocampo, Beverly Weidmer, Gene A. Shelley, and Lisa H. Jaycox. 2007.
"Latino Teens Talk About Help Seeking and Help Giving in Relation to
Dating Violence." *Violence Against Women* 13(2):172–89.

Esteemed social scientists Ocampo, Shelley, and Jaycox analyze dating violence among Latino youth. They assert that teens subjected to dating violence may be more likely to seek help and support from friends than from medical professionals. Unfortunately, the type of help and support that friends provide may lead to negative consequences. For example, friends may tend to blame the victim for the abuse and thereby result in the victim staying in the abusive relationship. Through survey and focus data on 1,655 Los Angeles teens, the researchers show that Latino youth are, indeed, more likely to confide in their friends rather than medical professionals. The authors argue that teens must be taught skills about how to help friends experiencing dating violence because it is likely that victims will continue to mistrust health care professionals.

EXAMPLE OF AN ANNOTATION FOR A WEB DOCUMENT

Cohen, Charles I. 2004. "Statement of the U.S. Chamber of Commerce on 'Employee Free Choice Act–Union Certification'." U.S. Chamber of Commerce. Retrieved March 9, 2007 (http://www.uschamber.com/ issues/testimony/2004/040716employeefreechoiceact.htm).

In his presentation to the Senate subcommittee on labor, Charles I. Cohen, a Senior Partner of Morgan, Lewis & Bockius LLP, argued on behalf of the United States Chamber of Commerce that the Employee Free Choice Act is flawed because it grants too much power to labor unions. Cohen compares the provisions of the bill to the legislation that it is amending (the National Labor Relations Act [NLRA]) to show that many of the changes are unlawful. His purpose is to persuade the Senate to reconsider the bill and perhaps re-fine it so that the changes are not as dramatic. Cohen's audience is the senate subcommittee on labor, which is in charge of researching the bill.

AVOIDING PLAGIARISM: WHEN AND WHAT TO CITE

Because research is a collective effort, academic conventions have developed to keep track of whose ideas are being borrowed, or used and reused, so that accuracy can be checked and credit for this valuable information given to the proper authors. You, too, as an apprentice scholar are engaging in this re-search process when you write a paper; and you, too, are expected to follow these conventions for identifying what you borrow from others. By acknowl-edging your sources in proper citations and references, you avoid plagiarism.

Plagiarism is an academic offense. It is theft of intellectual property, of someone else's ideas and words. It is cheating that presents another writer's words or ideas as if they were your own. Plagiarism is taken very seriously in colleges and universities and can be grounds for expulsion. Professional scholars are similarly bound to avoid plagiarism, by such guidelines as those in the American Sociological Association's *Code of Ethics.*

Instructors can usually detect intentional plagiarism. Their years of study have made them familiar with the articles, books, and textbooks in their fields. When a student copies this writing into a paper, instructors recognize the sound and shape of the prose. Even if they can't immediately tell what page it comes from, they know it is not the student's original work. Also, pla-giarized papers usually do not resemble the student's authentic writing style, which the instructor has read before, for instance, on midterm examinations. Moreover, special software has now been developed to catch dishonest copy-ing of online sources. Your instructor may ask you to submit an electronic version of your paper to a plagiarism-detecting service on campus, such as

Turnitin.com, which will automatically match up parts of your paper against comparable texts in countless databases on the Internet.

You can avoid unintentional plagiarism by making careful notes that respect the integrity of the sources you use and by identifying exactly where you got these borrowed words or ideas that you later use in your paper. The rule goes this way: you don't need to cite common knowledge, but you must acknowledge any author's private intellectual property—any presentation of information that is uniquely the author's. *You must cite such borrowing whether you quote it directly or paraphrase it.*

When you cite borrowed information, beware of two problems: (1) borrowing too much of the original language without quoting it, which is plagiarism, and (2) distorting the source and thereby paraphrasing it inaccurately. Following are examples of these two kinds of problematic citations from a source.

The original source:

The relationship between socioeconomic status and health has long intrigued social scientists. However, since its inception this research tradition has been plagued by questions of causal directionality. Namely, individuals may be sick because they are poor; alternatively, it may be their ill health itself that plunges them into poverty (e.g., through job loss due to illness).

Conley, Dalton and Neil G. Bennett. 2000. "Is Biology Destiny? Birth Weight and Life Chances." *American Sociological Review* 65(3):458–67.

1. Too much of the original source:

The relationship between socioeconomic status and health has interested social scientists for a long time. Conley and Bennett (2000), the authors of "Is Biology Destiny? Birth Weight and Life Chances," state that ". . . since its inception this research tradition has been plagued by questions of causal directionality. Namely, individuals may be sick because they are poor; alternatively, it may be their ill health itself that plunges them into poverty (e.g., through job loss due to illness)" (p. 458).

In the first sentence of this paragraph, too many words from the source are used without quotation marks even though the second sentence is a quotation. This is therefore an example of plagiarism.

2. An inaccurate distortion of the original source:

According to Conley and Bennett (2000), there is a causal relationship between sociological status and health: the higher an individual's socioeconomic status, the better their health (p. 458).

This statement misrepresents the source's position.

Here is a good way to cite borrowed information from this source:

Although researchers are interested in the relationship between socioeconomic status and health, Conley and Bennett (2000) point out that it is difficult to determine whether low socioeconomic status leads to poor health or poor health leads to low socioeconomic status (p. 458).

Do not worry that your paper will be unoriginal if you include many citations. Precise and full citation is one of the features that instructors look for when assigning quality grades; it shows that you have done some real work. *If you are in doubt, always cite your sources.* Err on the side of overdoing it.

Students often have difficulty determining whether an idea is common knowledge (which doesn't need to be cited) or an author's unique insight (which needs to be cited). The term "anomie," for instance, was coined by Durkheim. Does that mean that if you write the word "anomie" in a paper about the contemporary urban underclass, you are borrowing Durkheim's idea and word and must therefore cite him? No, not necessarily. You might want to mention Durkheim to invoke his authority, but the term doesn't belong exclusively to Durkheim any more. Over the years "anomie" has become part of every sociologist's working vocabulary; the concept is common knowledge and therefore doesn't need to be cited. However, let's say that you read a book or article about the urban underclass in which the author makes an important point using the concept of anomie. If you borrow that author's point for your own paper, then you must cite him or her (but not Durkheim) as your source. Remember, too, that you must cite your sources when you borrow anything unique to those authors: their words when you quote exactly and their ideas when you paraphrase.

IDENTIFYING YOUR BORROWED WORDS OR IDEAS

Every time you weave a borrowed idea into your paper you have two alternatives, depending on how you recorded this information originally. First, you can quote or paraphrase the borrowing. Second, you can rely on a parenthetical citation alone to identify the source of the borrowing, or you can name the source in the text of your paper.

Quoting a source directly means extracting a word, phrase, sentence, or passage and inserting it into your own paper. Quoted information should be enclosed within double quotation marks or, if lengthy, indented as a block quote. Quote only when the original words are especially powerful, clear, memorable, or authoritative. Otherwise, paraphrase.

There are two minor changes you may make in a quotation, neither of which changes its meaning. These legitimate changes are illustrated in our own quotation from C. Wright Mills's *The Sociological Imagination* ([1959] 2000):

> Every individual lives, from one generation to the next, in some society; . . . he [or she] lives out a biography, and . . . he lives it out with some historical sequence. By the fact of his living he contributes, however minutely, to the shaping of his society and its history; even as he is made by society and by its historical push and shove. (P. 6)

First, notice that we omit some of Mills's sentence, again without changing the meaning, and we indicate this omission by a punctuation mark called an "ellipsis," three spaced dots. If the ellipsis points came at the end of the sentence, they would be preceded by a period—hence, four dots. Second, we are uneasy about Mills's use of "he" to refer to all humankind and want to make the language inclusive, so we add our own words "[or she]," inserting them within square brackets into Mills's quotation.

Another possible addition within square brackets is the Latin word *sic,* meaning "so," which you can use when you want to quote original words that contain an error.

Paraphrasing means condensing the author's meaning and translating a passage into your own words. This is a perfectly acceptable practice and, in fact, an important skill to develop. Paraphrasing forces you to think through and actively understand what you have read. But if you use another's idea when writing, you must give that person credit with a citation, even if you are presenting the idea in your own words.

There are good and bad ways to paraphrase. Here is an original passage from Emile Durkheim's *Suicide* (1951), followed by examples of good and bad paraphrasing:

> The term "suicide" is applied to all cases of death resulting directly or indirectly from a positive or negative act of the victim himself, which he knows will produce this result. . . . This definition excludes from our study everything related to the suicide of animals. Our knowledge of animal intelligence does not really allow us to attribute to them an understanding anticipatory of their death nor, especially, of the means to accomplish it. . . . If some dogs refuse to take food on losing their masters, it is because the sadness into which they are thrown has automatically caused lack of hunger; death has resulted, but without having been foreseen. . . . So the special characteristics of suicide as defined by us are lacking. (Pp. 44–45)

Following are two examples of bad paraphrasing. In the first, the writer has shifted words around in the sentences and replaced individual words by plugging in synonyms. The writer has not genuinely condensed or translated the author's meaning into her or his own words; this problem is usually compounded by a failure to cite the source (in this case, Durkheim):

> When some pets stop eating because their owners have left, this is caused by the unhappiness into which they have fallen, which necessarily makes them lose their appetite: the final end that ensues, however, was not anticipated. Therefore, the unique features of suicide as described by our definition are missing.

In the second example, the writer has changed the order but kept the words the same. Again the writer has not condensed the passage or translated it into her or his own words; and, again, this problem is usually compounded by a failure to cite the source:

> Lost masters cause their sad dogs, refusing food, to lack hunger. The dogs die, not foreseeing this result. What is lacking is our special characterization of suicide as we define it.

A good paraphrase boils down the original idea and puts it in your own words. Here is a good paraphrase:

Example
According to Durkheim (1951:44–45), animals, such as abandoned dogs who starve themselves, do not commit suicide because they do not understand the connection between death and the means of causing death.

Remember that even good paraphrasing requires citing the source of the borrowed *idea* being presented.

CITATIONS IN THE TEXT

Let's say that you are writing a paper on some aspect of suicide and that you want to use this insight from Durkheim. You have a choice of four legitimate ways of weaving it in. Study these four examples:

+ Animals do not commit suicide (Durkheim 1951:44–45).
+ Suicide necessarily involves knowledge of the consequences. "This definition excludes . . . everything related to the suicide of animals" (Durkheim 1951:44).
+ According to Durkheim (1951:44–45) animals do not commit suicide, because committing suicide involves understanding the consequences.
+ Durkheim (1951) argues that suicide involves knowledge of the consequences. In his words, "This definition excludes . . . everything related to the suicide of animals" (p. 44).

Note that the first two examples rely entirely on the citation within parentheses to identify the borrowed idea. The last two examples put some of that parenthetical information in the text of the paper itself, in what is called "a running acknowledgment" (it "runs" in the paper, and it "acknowledges" the source).

When you *paraphrase*, all the information (name, date, and page number) goes inside one parenthesis at the end of the paraphrased idea, unless you name the author in a running acknowledgment, in which case the date and page number go inside one parenthesis immediately after you name the author.

When you *quote*, all the information (name, date, and page number) goes inside one parenthesis at the end of the quoted idea, unless you name the author in a running acknowledgment, in which case the date goes inside one parenthesis after the author's name and the page number goes inside another parenthesis at the end of the quotation.

When you use a running acknowledgment, don't always rely on "states," as in "Durkheim states that. . . ." ("Feels" is even worse.) Instead, experiment with some of these verbs and other similar examples: "argues," "contends," "maintains," "claims," "reports," "charges," "concludes." You can also use various phrases for a running acknowledgment; for example, "according to Durkheim" or (for a quotation) "in Durkheim's words."

How do you choose among these four citation options? Consider the reader. How important is it for the reader to know immediately, in an emphatic way, where the idea comes from? Is it the idea itself (as in the first two examples above) or is it the source (as in the last two examples above) that is most important?

FORMAT

The following format guidelines from the American Sociological Association (ASA), as published in the *ASA Style Guide* (2007), describe how you should cite borrowed information in your paper, whether paraphrased or quoted. (Your instructor may want you to use some other standardized format, such as the published guidelines of the American Psychological Association [APA] or of the Modern Language Association [MLA].)

In the ASA format, authors' names used in the text are followed by the publication date in parentheses. The page number follows the date; or in the case of a direct quotation, follows the quotation.

Example

Goffman (1981:180) disputes the notion that mentally ill patients are hospitalized primarily for treatment. Instead, he believes that they are institutionalized so that they can be controlled.

Example

Goffman (1981) claims that the goal of hospitalization "is not to cure the patient but to contain him in a niche in free society where he can be tolerated" (p. 180).

If you don't name the author in the text of your paper, enclose the last name, year, and, if appropriate, page number(s) within parentheses at the end of the borrowed thought:

Example

The treatment of the mentally ill in this country can give the impression that the goal of hospitalization "is not to cure the patient but to contain him in a niche in free society where he can be tolerated" (Goffman 1981:180).

When you write a textual analysis (see Chapter 5), you might use only one source—the book or essay that you are analyzing. In this case, you need to give the publication date only once—the first time the author's name is mentioned.

Example (first mention of author in textual analysis)

Durkheim (1951) claims that suicide is not only an individual event but also a social phenomenon.

Example (after second mention of author in textual analysis)

Durkheim describes the role of social factors in suicide.

Note that the page number of quotations, or of specific claims or evidence, should be indicated even after the first mention of the author.

Example

Durkheim (p. 44) defines suicide in a way that leaves all animal deaths out of his study.

Full publication information on the text you use for your analysis should be included in your list of References (discussed later in this chapter).

At times you may want to cite several authors who discuss a single idea. Then you will have a series of citations that should all be enclosed within parentheses. The way you should order them depends on which style system you are using. Some systems prefer date order; others prefer alphabetical order. Still others list authors in order of their contributions. According to the *ASA Style Guide* (2007), authors should be listed in alphabetical order by first author.

Example

Family researchers have discovered that within the first year of divorce, mothers and children undergo as much as a 30 percent decrease in family income, whereas men experience up to a 10 percent increase (Bianchi, Subaiya, and Kahn 1999; Kulik 2005; Manting and Bouman 2006).

For dual authorship, give both last names. For more than two authors, give all last names the first time you refer to the source; in subsequent citations to that source, use the first author followed by "et al." (But include all the authors' names in the References at the end of the paper.) For sources with four or more authors, use the first author followed by "et al." throughout.

Example

Employment opportunities that offer low salaries, provide no benefits (such as health insurance or pensions), have little to no job stability, and are not protected by unions or labor laws are considered of dubious benefit to workers (Ferber and Waldfogel 1996; Kalleberg et al. 1997; Mischel, Bernstein, and Schmitt 1999).

For authors with more than one publication in the same year, designate each work by adding an "a," "b," and so on to the year of publication, in the order mentioned in your paper.

Example

Individuals' subjective estimates of their life expectancy influence their morale (Mirowsky 1999a).

The impact of economic hardship on subjective life expectancy is moderated by the recency of the hardship (Mirowsky 1999b).

If the quotation is longer than five lines, present it in block-quotation form. Indent all lines five spaces from the left margin (leave the right margin as it is throughout the text) and single-space. Quotation marks are unnecessary, since the indented left margin tells your reader that the material is quoted. The quotation from Durkheim, discussed earlier in this chapter under "Identifying Your Borrowed Words or Ideas," is an example of a long quotation.

In rare cases, you may also use the block-quotation format when you want to emphasize especially important or interesting quoted material.

NOTES

In some disciplines, sources are cited in footnotes (which appear at the bottom of the paper's pages) or endnotes (which are grouped together at the end of the paper). In sociology, however, source citations are incorporated into the text. Notes, if there are any, follow the text and relay information that may be of interest to the reader but is not directly relevant to the paper's thesis. Avoid using notes as a way out of organizing your paper by making them a "dump" for materials you are not sure how to integrate. Add notes sparingly, only to express a tangential comment that you feel you *must* make.

REFERENCES AND BIBLIOGRAPHIES

The text of your paper is followed by a list of the source materials you used in writing it. Some instructors prefer that you list all materials you consulted in developing your paper, whether or not they are directly incorporated into your paper; in this case the list is entitled "Bibliography." Others prefer you to follow the format of most sociology journals, listing only those materials actually cited in your paper; in this case, the list is entitled "References." Check with your instructor to see which type of listing is preferred, but remember that in *both* cases you must list your sources for all borrowed ideas, whether they are directly quoted or paraphrased.

Listing sources you found online (as we tell you how to do in Part 2) presents special problems, because electronic databases are often updated frequently, making it impossible to locate your exact source later on. The *ASA Style Guide* (2007:76–80) provides several examples of the correct format for different kinds of online sources.

When you are compiling your Bibliography or References section, list all sources alphabetically by the author's last name. Under each author's name, list works according to the year of publication, beginning with the earliest date. Do not separate the list into sections for "articles," "books," or other sources; a single list is sufficient. In the examples that follow, note the order of the information and how it is punctuated, underlined (or *italicized,* which is equivalent to underlining), and abbreviated. When formatting this section, place the heading at the left-hand margin, type it in all capital letters, and triple-space between the heading and the first source listed.

When the source you have cited has more than one author, all authors' full names should be included, in the same order in which they appear on the book's title page or after the title of the article. Alphabetize under the first author's name. The first author should be listed last name first, and the other author(s) should be listed first name first.

If no author is named for a source, then list the information in alphabetical order according to the organization responsible for publishing it.

Examples of Sources with No Named Authors

Los Angeles Times. 2007. "Black Activists Search for a Constituency." February 13, p. B1.

U.S. Department of Justice's Task Force on Intellectual Property. 2006. *Progress Report of the Department of Justice's Task Force on Intellectual Property.* Washington, DC: Department of Justice.

Use the following examples of various kinds of source materials as models for capitalization, spacing, indentation, and punctuation. For additional models, check the format of citations and reference entries in any issue of *American Sociological Review.* Here are some general tips.

1. Is the work a *book* whose entire main text is written or edited by the same author or authors? If so, note that in this format titles of books are underlined (or italicized) in the References or Bibliography list. If a book was first published many years ago, include the original publication date in brackets before the more recent date. For more than one book published in the same year by the author(s), identify each work by adding "a," "b," and so on to the year of publication.

Examples of Listings for Books

Durkheim, Emile. [1897] 1997. *Suicide.* Translated by John A. Spaulding and George Simpson. Glencoe, IL: Free Press.

Elias, Norbert. [1939] 1978a. *The Civilizing Process.* Vol. 1, *A History of Manners.* Translated by Edmund Jephcott. New York: Urizen.

———. 1978b. *What Is Sociology?* Translated by Stephen Mennell and Grace Morrissey. New York: Columbia University Press.

———. 2006. *Early Writings.* Translated by Edmund Jephcott. Dublin: University College Dublin Press.

Fetchenhauer, Detlef, Andreas Flache, Abraham P. Buunk, and Siegwart Lindenberg, eds. 2006. *Solidarity and Prosocial Behavior: An Integration of Sociological and Psychological Perspectives.* New York: Springer.

Seidler, Victor J. 2006. *Transforming Masculinities: Men, Cultures, Bodies, Power, Sex and Love.* New York: Routledge.

Vohs, Kathleen D. and Eli J. Finkel, eds. 2006. *Self and Relationships: Connecting Intrapersonal and Interpersonal Processes.* New York: Guilford Press.

2. Is the work an *article* published in a *journal*? Give the volume number and the issue number of the journal in which the article appears, followed by a colon and page numbers to help your readers locate the article.

Examples of Listings for Journal Articles

Rosenfield, Sarah, Julie Phillips, and Helene White. 2006. "Gender, Race, and the Self in Mental Health and Crime." *Social Problems* 53(2):161–85.

Cheng, Simon and Brian Powell. 2007. "Under and Beyond Constraints: Resource Allocation to Young Children from Biracial Families." *American Journal of Sociology* 112(4):1044–94.

3. Is the work found in an edited *collection of articles* or in an *anthology*? If you are referring to a specific article in the collection, the citation goes under the name of the author of the article and includes the name of the anthology and the editor(s) within the reference.

Examples of Listings for Collections

Preissle, Judith. 2007. "Feminist Research Ethics." Pp. 515–32 in *The Handbook of Feminist Research*, edited by Sharlene Nagy Hesse-Biber. Thousand Oaks, CA: Sage Publications.

Krause, Neal. 2006. "Social Relationships in Late Life." Pp. 182–98 in *Handbook of Aging and the Social Sciences.* Vol. 6, edited by Robert H. Binstock and Linda K. George. San Diego: Academic Press.

4. Has the information been communicated during a *class lecture*?

Example of Listing for Lecture Notes

Lopez, David. 2007. Class lecture. July 21.

5. Does the information come from an online source?

Examples of Listings for Online Sources

Mansnerus, Laura. 2006. "Small Cities Hit Hard in Crime Report." *New York Times,*
     June 15, 2006. Retrieved June 15, 2006 (http://www.nytimes.com/2006/06/
     15/nyregion/15crime.html?_r=1&oref=slogin).

Moreno-Riaño, Gerson, Mark Caleb Smith, and Thomas Mach. 2006. "Religiosity,
     Secularism, and Social Health. A Research Note." *Journal of Religion and Society* 8.
     Retrieved June 15, 2006 (http://moses.creighton.edu/JRS/2006/2006-1.html).

U.S. Bureau of the Census. 2002. "Questions and Answers for Census 2000 Data
     on Race." Public Information Office. Retrieved June 4, 2006 (http://www.
     census.gov/Press-Release/www/2001/raceqandas.html).

6. Does any information in your paper come from *machine-readable data files (MRDFs)?* If so, you must also identify the source of this kind of survey data. Note in the following example that you must describe it as an MRDF, and identify its producer and distributor, author, date, title, and place of origin, as well as the organization responsible for it. The codebook accompanying a data file often contains an example of a bibliographical reference for it. Look for this example on the back of the codebook's title page.

Example of Listing for Machine-Readable Data Files (MRDFs)

American Institute of Public Opinion. 1976. *Gallup Public Opinion Poll #965*
     [MRDF]. Princeton, NJ: American Institute of Public Opinion [producer]. New
     Haven, CT.: Roper Public Opinion Research Center, Yale University [distributor].

BIBLIOGRAPHIC SOFTWARE

Some writers prefer to use bibliographic software to simplify keeping track of sources, formatting them in papers, and preparing bibliographies. Packages such as *Endnote* and *ProCite* are available at college bookstores or through software vendors, while those such as *RefWorks* are subscribed to by some institutions, usually through their libraries. These packages enable you to create your own dataset of books and articles, which you can enter by hand or download titles from online sources, including many college or university library online catalogs. Often the same books or articles are used in different papers for different courses, so you can gradually build up a useful list, meaning that you don't have to start from scratch on each paper. When you are writing the paper itself, you can enter a code for a book or article, typically the author's last name and year of publication. For example, your paper might include a direct quotation from Hochschild's *The Second Shift:* "Even for the most exceptional women, the contradictions between work and family are very real" with the citation "(Hochschild 1990:263)." Often the format for entering sources is a slight variation of this. The bibliographic software interfaces with the word-processing software to read the citations from your paper and make the bibliography. When the paper is completed, the software can construct your bibliography according to whatever format you select, alphabetize it, and place it at the end of your paper. If you have the appropriate information for each source, there is little worry about how to handle different kinds of sources, such as anthologies, unpublished dissertations, or Web sites. It does the hardest work for you. Such software does require an investment of time to learn, especially at the beginning. But if you learn the basics and add books and articles as you go along, then the tedious work of creating bibliographies, when you are often pressed for time at the end, is greatly relieved.

PART

2

Writing from Various Data Sources

As to Holmes, I observed that he sat frequently for half an hour on end, with knitted brows and an abstracted air, but he swept the matter away with a wave of his hand when I mentioned it. "Data! data! data!" he cried impatiently. "I can't make bricks without clay."

DR. WATSON IN ARTHUR CONAN DOYLE'S
"Adventure of the Copper Beeches"

The goal of a sociology paper is to frame an interesting sociological question that you will answer with data. But where will the data come from?

There is no one answer. As we indicated earlier, sociology is diverse. Data may be gathered from many sources and by several methods. The next four chapters present guidelines for writing papers based on four data sources: library and Internet (Chapter 4), textual analysis or article critique (Chapter 5), quantitative research (Chapter 6), and ethnographic field research (Chapter 7). They reflect the most typical writing assignments in sociology classes, and they use or modify the formats described earlier: essay and journal (see Chapter 1).

Depending on the type of paper you are assigned, you may be expected to formulate a thesis or hypothesis. Although there are differences between the two, both basically refer to the answer you expect to find to your sociological question. You develop a *thesis* if you are writing a library/Internet research paper, a textual analysis paper, or an article critique; you formulate a *hypothesis* if you are writing a quantitative research paper; and you do neither if you are writing an ethnographic research paper. Unlike other paper types that start with a thesis or a hypothesis, ethnographic papers end with *themes* you derive from your observations.

When you are writing a library/Internet paper, your job is to find literature consistent with your thesis. The literature you review constitutes your data; it determines whether your *thesis* is substantiated. If you are writing a textual analysis (or article critique) paper, the quality of your summary, analysis, and evaluation determines whether your *thesis* is verified. On the other hand, if you are writing a quantitative paper, the numerical data you collect determines whether your *hypothesis* is supported. Finally, if you are writing an ethnographic research paper, the quality of your field observations determines whether your *themes* adequately characterize the social world of your participants.

The information you learn in early chapters can help you to write later chapters. That is, unless you are given a text or journal article to review, you must begin the writing process by searching for sources in the library or on the Internet; Chapter 4 shows you how to do this. After you find a text or journal article to review, you need to know how to analyze and evaluate your source(s); Chapter 5 gives you guidelines for accomplishing this task. If you are writing a quantitative research paper (see Chapter 6), you can synthesize a series of textual analyses and/or article critiques to form the basis of the literature review section.

Therefore, we begin with how to write a general research paper. Although you may be familiar with this type of paper from your previous English classes, you may not know the best strategies for searching for sociological sources. In Chapter 4 we show you how to search for sociological books and journal articles using online library catalogs and specialized databases (such as *CSA Sociological Abstracts*) as well as Internet search engines (such as *Google Scholar* and *Google Book Search*). We also discuss how to manage and organize the large volume of scholarly sources you will encounter when you do such a search.

Next we describe what to do when your writing assignment requires you to do more than search for, and review or summarize, books and articles in response to a sociological question. In Chapter 5 we explain how to write a textual analysis of a book or a critique of a journal article. Both involve the process of explication—summarizing, analyzing, and evaluating your source(s)—a process that requires and strengthens critical thinking skills.

In Chapter 6 we explain how to write a quantitative research paper. Unlike the general research and textual analysis papers that use the three-part essay format (see Chapter 1), the quantitative paper uses the journal format (see Chapter 1), and, therefore, is divided into four sections. In writing the first section, the literature review, you use the same techniques described in Chapters 4 and 5. That is, you search for appropriate sources using the library and the Internet, you critically analyze those sources, and finally you synthesize them to create a literature review. The literature review sets the stage for the development of your hypothesis, and lays the foundation for the other three sections of your paper: methods, results, and discussion.

In Chapter 7 we discuss how to do an ethnographic research paper. Ethnography is just one type of qualitative method. As with other types of qualitative methods, you use an inductive rather than a deductive approach to study social phenomenon. Your goal in writing an ethnographic research paper is to describe the social world through the eyes of the participants in everyday settings. This type of paper uses a modified three-part essay format.

To help you in writing all these papers based on different data sources, we include an annotated sample paper, written by an undergraduate sociology student, at the end of each chapter in Part 2. The sample papers illustrate our guidelines. You can match them up with your own papers and use our marginal comments to check what you have written yourself. Because no paper is perfect (not even published ones!), when reading the sample student papers, it's important to pay special attention not only to what was done correctly but also to what was done *incorrectly*. It is the best way to avoid repeating common writing mistakes.

The General Research Paper Based on Library or Internet Data

A general research paper based on library or Internet data requires you to consult these data for two purposes: first, to refine the question that you will address in your paper (if a specific question hasn't already been assigned); and, second, to collect the information that you will use to support your paper's thesis. This information can be found both in print on paper and online electronically. Both kinds are increasingly interchangeable. The daily editions of the *New York Times*, for instance, originally emerge on paper but can also be read simultaneously online at the *New York Times* Web site. Then they are archived in libraries on microfiche or microfilm. *CSA Sociological Abstracts*, a reference source published in annual printed volumes generally shelved in the reference section in libraries, is also available in a computerized version on the Internet if your library has a license. Many scholarly articles published in professional journals that are shelved in library periodical rooms or library stacks can also be retrieved electronically through online library catalogs and read on screen. Not only are the boundaries among these different media increasingly blurred, but our Information Age presents us with mountains of data.

Students often feel overwhelmed by so much information. For example, the student who was assigned a research paper on the topic of single-parent families began by entering "single-parent family" in her college's online library catalog and found references to 102 books, while the search engine *Google Book Search* returned over 3,433 entries. (A search for journal articles on this same topic using the library's subscription to the electronic database *CSA Sociological Abstracts* yielded 1,239 additional sources, while the search engine *Google Scholar* produced 24,100 hits.) To make matters worse, the research process, although in principle straightforward—determine what information you need, search for it, locate it, and record it—is rarely so simple. Instead, it is usually more a matter of lucky, imaginative guesses about keyword search terms and persistence in following clues to potentially good sources down branching paths. These branching paths will sometimes turn into frustrating dead ends after much wasted time, but they also can change and enrich your understanding of the question addressed in your paper and what is involved in answering it. Finding your own path enables you to make your paper uniquely your own.

Several strategies and techniques can help you with this general research process: determining where to start, searching efficiently for potential sources with keywords, evaluating the quality of potential sources, and keeping track of your sources. We will present these techniques in roughly sequential order, but the research process is inevitably messy. Once you are immersed in your topic, you must expect to have to circle back in order to search for and locate additional sources. You will evaluate their usefulness with criteria that will change and become more refined as you become more expert. You should resist any temptation to begin a general research project by starting to read through a mountain of hundreds, if not thousands, of available sources. Instead, begin by spending some time and thought on developing a good question and on preparing a record-keeping system.

BEFORE YOU START: CHOOSING A TOPIC

You often start a library research project not knowing much about your topic. How, then, do you begin to develop a good question?

First, you must select a general subject area—an area that is relevant to the concerns of your course and of interest to you. One way to find a topic is to skim your syllabus and course readings. Be sure to consider the entire syllabus, since a topic that will be discussed later in the course might be the basis for a good research question. Your instructor can help at this stage by letting you know if your topic is too broad or too far afield.

Next, even before searching the online library catalog or the Internet, construct some provisional questions. For example, let's say you want to study the feminist movement in the United States. Ask yourself why this topic interests you. Your personal interest in a subject not only motivates you during the research and writing process; it can also guide you to ask a good question. Also ask yourself what specific aspect of the subject you want to investigate for this particular class assignment and what specifically you want to know about it. In the case of feminism, for example, you may want to focus your research on differences in wages ("Are women's wages lower than men's?"), on power differences ("What determines the relative power of men and women inside families?"), or on ways people learn to fill the gender roles expected of them ("How are males and females socialized to enact sex-role stereotypes in their daily lives?").

Remember to maintain a sociological perspective on the subject. The examples given in the previous paragraph are sociologically relevant because they are concerned with differences between groups of people (men and women) and because they focus on patterned relationships in the social world. A review of Chapter 1 will help stimulate the sociological imagination you need to ask a good question. '

DETERMINING YOUR FIRST SOURCE(S)

Quality, not quantity, is what counts in a good research paper. Finding *enough* sources is usually easy, given the problem of information overload. Finding the *right* sources can be a challenge. Should you start with a newspaper, a professional journal or magazine article, a general or specialized encyclopedia article, a government Web site, a book, or what? If you have an appropriate destination in mind, you are more likely to have a successful journey and to avoid detours and dead ends. Planning your initial search for the best sources involves several factors: how recent the information that you need is, how much you already know about the topic, and the type of general research paper that's been assigned. A general research paper can have different objectives such as: (1) summarizing the scholarly literature on a topic, (2) comparing and contrasting the opinions of sociologists and the general public about a long-term social problem, (3) applying sociological theories and concepts to current events, or (4) analyzing sociohistorical change by examining magazine and newspaper archives.

Different sources contain information from authors with varying degrees of professional expertise. Here is an example illustrating how the student researching the topic of the single-parent family would look in different sources for different kinds of information.

Newspaper: immediately newsworthy current events and local coverage; for example, City Council budget provisions for day care or stories about single parents on welfare. Most newspapers now have Web sites, though many charge for displaying items in their archives.

Magazine: recent current affairs and enduring popular topics; for example, a cover story on the state of marriage in the United States or a profile ranking Fortune 500 companies with the best day care programs. While most magazines have Web sites, many do not post the full content of their paper editions.

Journal: scholarly research results of specialists' studies conducted in the last few years; for example, case studies of economic and educational prospects of children growing up in single-parent homes. Most scholarly journals have electronic editions, though you may need to access them through a university computer or they may require that your browsing program have a university proxy setting. Your library can tell you how to set that up.

Book: in-depth coverage of a topic or collections of scholarly articles compiled over the last few years; for example, a history of family structure in the United States or a long-term study of single-parent families in Canada.

Encyclopedia: the big picture of what is known about a topic; for example, ways in which parents influence the social development of children or the forms of family organization in different cultures. There are general encyclopedias online, such as Wikipedia, but they should be used cautiously and cannot substitute for more serious academic scholarship.

Internet: spans the range above; for example, information obtained from instantaneous chat room discussions for single parents to archived statistical government information from the U. S. Department of Health and Human Services.

These sources represent layers of information processed over time. Consider, then, which layer you will probably need most, especially at the beginning of your search. For example, a student researching the legalization of same-sex marriage would need to rely on newspapers, magazines, and the Internet in order to read up on recent developments in the Hawaii and Vermont legislatures. A student investigating the disappearance of the gift economy in South Pacific societies would consult books and scholarly journal articles. Aiming in the right direction will make finding what you need more likely.

Consider, too, how much you know about your topic. If you don't know much, you may need to begin with an overview in a general or specialized encyclopedia, either online or in print. If you have already been studying the topic in class and are therefore able to understand the details, you may want to begin with a recent professional journal article.

A sociological principle can also guide you in your selection of sources: there are strong relationships between the quality of the information and the social setting of the source. Some journals and magazines, some book publishers, and some authors are more reliable than others. Most students would intuitively know that tabloid magazines are not appropriate for college research papers (unless they were the topic being researched), but they are an extreme example. In general, we can identify a few guidelines for choosing reliable sources:

- ✦ Academic journals are more reliable than popular magazines. Some academic journals, such as *American Sociological Review,* may be difficult for undergraduates to read, especially the articles with complex statistics. But you can get the gist of such articles and consult the bibliographic references at the ends of the articles. Although popular magazines should not be excluded altogether, you should be cautious of their contents.
- ✦ University presses (such as the Cambridge University Press or the Harvard University Press) are generally less likely to print poorly researched books than are commercial presses (such as Doubleday Books or Penguin Books). For commercially published books, those written by academics are usually

more reliable than those written by journalists. Again, the point is not to ignore books by journalists, but to approach them with a critical eye.

+ Articles and books that carefully cite their sources of information are generally more reliable than those that don't. While some students find a heavily footnoted article or book daunting, carefully cited references provide the reader with the means to follow up on the author's assertions.

ADVANTAGES AND DISADVANTAGES OF LIBRARY AND INTERNET SOURCES

Once you feel ready to consult some sources, consider whether to begin with those available through the library (either in print or electronically) or those available exclusively through the Internet. Some students may be tempted by the convenience and familiarity of the Internet to rely solely on it, ignoring the rich resources that may be available only on paper in the college or university library. The Internet may be easier and in some ways better to use, but it may also be worse! Library sources are subjected to quality control and professional review by librarians, while information available exclusively through the Internet can be useless and misleading. Library sources are also available over any time period, while Web sites often only make recent information available.

One of the principles students learn in college that they often are not taught in high school is that all knowledge is not created equal. Some sources of knowledge are much more reliable than others. The print and electronic information made available through a library usually is trustworthy. Professional librarians have judged it worth the cost of storing the print sources or of acquiring the electronic sources. Information available exclusively through the Internet is different and more challenging. Some information obtained from the Internet is excellent, but much of it is undependable. At first glance it may look authoritative, but further scrutiny reveals it to be incomplete, commercially or otherwise biased, out of date, or just wrong. Or, at first glance, Internet information may not itself look worthwhile, yet may include links to other valuable data. How can you determine the value of a potential research source? Where exactly should you look in a source for features that determine its quality? What specific features of a source reveal its worth and allow you to evaluate its usefulness?

CRITERIA FOR ASSESSING WEB PAGES

Clearly, filtering out useful from useless information on the Internet is essential. We recommend applying the following five criteria for assessing Web pages:

1. Credibility of Local Origin.   Where does the information come from? Before you link to a WWW data source, check its electronic address (its uniform resource locator or URL). If the address includes the abbreviation *edu* or *gov* (which identifies its association with an educational institution or government agency), you may find more reliable information there than if the source's URL has the abbreviation *org* (organization) or *com* (commercial). Other less common abbreviations, such as *net,* also exist. On some search engines, such as *Google,* you can specify the domain by adding "site:edu" or "site:gov" (without the quotation marks) after your initial keyword. For example, if you were looking for government Web sites with information about single parents, you could search "single parent* site:gov" (without quotation marks).

Examples

<http://www.ccnsus.gov/>	(the U.S. Census Bureau)
<http://www.soc.qc.edu/>	(the Sociology Department at Queens College, CUNY)
<http://www.aclu-sc.org/>	(American Civil Liberties Union of Southern California)
<http://www.singleparentcentral.com/>	(A resource site for single parents)

We are *not* suggesting that organizational or commercial Web sites are automatically inferior. The American Civil Liberties Union of Southern California, for instance, provides texts of legislation, starting with the Bill of Rights, and updates about the progress of pending legislative initiatives from the organization's liberal point of view. Similarly, Single Parent Central offers a broad variety of books and articles about being a single parent, though most are written to be useful to single parents rather than being scholarly studies. It also includes "quick facts" on single-parent families, mostly taken from government sources. However, you should be aware of any source's origin and judge its reliability.

2. Accountability.   Is there an author or sponsor identified on the Web page, with an e-mail link? Is there a link on the page back to its "home"? Useful sources provide this information about their data.

3. Timeliness.   When was the Web page last updated? Is the information still accurate? Online information quickly becomes obsolete.

4. Scope and Coverage.   Does the information on the Web page seem well researched? Are useful links embedded in the page? How does the online information compare with what you have found on paper? Are the graphics worth the time it takes to download them? Be a thoughtful consumer of online information and beware of electronic junk mail.

5. Reputation.   Is the Web site sponsored by or linked by an organization you know to be reputable? Ask your instructor, teaching assistant, or librarian about sources you are not sure of.

SEARCHING ONLINE INFORMATION WITH BOOLEAN OPERATORS AND KEYWORDS

Most colleges and universities have an online library catalog as well as subscriptions to electronic databases (such as *CSA Sociological Abstracts*) needed to search for scholarly publications. Whether you are using the online library catalog, a library-sponsored electronic database, or the Internet, you will search electronically for sources for your research paper. Many searches can be based on single keywords, but students will generally want to use more than one word so that they can be more specific. Using electronic search engines through the library or on the Internet both require a basic knowledge of what is known as *Boolean logic,* the rules for combining words in a search. Although different reference sources use somewhat different terms, the principles are the same. Boolean operators are logical relationships between the words being searched. Most undergraduates use only three Boolean operators when they search online sources: OR, AND, and NOT. These Boolean operators allow you to use a computer to search for data sources tailored specifically to your own topic.

Online library catalogs and electronic databases as well as the Internet allow you to combine concepts using Boolean operators and to search for them simultaneously. For example, the University of California has over 100,000 books on the subject of Los Angeles, 11,970 books on mental illness, and 4,253 books on homelessness, but it has only three books in its collection about all these subjects combined: mental illness among the homeless in Los Angeles.

To search online sources available through the library or on the Internet, you must know exactly what terms to look for, such as keywords, words in titles, authors' names, Library of Congress subject headings, or descriptors. In this example, the online library catalog found these three books by looking for words in titles (*mental illness, homelessness, Los Angeles*). Second, you can enlarge or shrink the scope of the search by using the Boolean operators OR, AND, or NOT. In this example, the online library catalog search combined title words with AND (*mental illness* AND *homelessness* AND *Los Angeles*). Usually when you put several words in a search, the computer implicitly is treating them as though they had AND between them. If you entered "mental illness homelessness Los Angeles" it would return only sources that included "mental" AND "illness" AND "homelessness" AND "Los" AND "Angeles." You would not want the computer to treat this search as though the terms were linked by OR. That would give you all hits about any illness, all homelessness, and everything about Los Angeles, not a very useful collection.

You are probably already familiar with using two categories to find library information: (1) authors' names and (2) the subjects they have written about.

Online searching provides you with the opportunity to search with at least two more categories: (3) titles of sources, as in the example specified previously, and (4) keywords associated with sources. Online library catalogs and many other academic search engines such as *CSA Sociological Abstracts,* unlike general search engines such as *Web Google,* require that you search in specific fields. Searching on "Durkheim" in an author field would give you books written by Durkheim, while entering "Durkheim" in the subject or title fields would return books about him. Some will have spaces for any keyword. If you put "Durkheim" in a general keyword field, it will return both books by him and books about him.

Technically, a keyword is a word that may be located in the title of the source, or in the Library of Congress subject heading for the source, or even in the abstract of the source if that database provides abstracts. For example, an online search in a library catalog for articles, combining the keywords *mental illness, homelessness,* and *Los Angeles* with the Boolean operator AND, found this electronic library resource titled "An Assessment of Mental Health Needs Among Homeless People in Central Los Angeles" published by the USC Keck School of Medicine (Figure 4-1). The keyword *mental illness* appears only in the article's note. A search by title words alone would not have found it. Although not all databases use keywords, keywords are particularly useful, and we recommend that you start an online search with them.

In contrast, the Boolean operator OR *enlarges* a search. As shown in the following diagram, a search for online data sources about the controversy over tribal rights in Indian adoption should use the term *Indian adoption* with the Boolean operator OR plus the term *Native American adoption* (that is, *Indian adoption* OR *Native American adoption*).

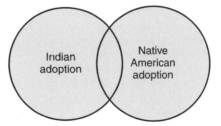

Boolean operators can also be combined. For instance, the student looking specifically for online information about Indian adoption in California could search with this command:

Indian adoption OR *Native American adoption* AND *California*

The problem with this search is that it would include sources about adoptions involving people from India in California. Luckily this can be fixed with the

Figure 4-1 **SAMPLE OF INFORMATION OBTAINED FROM AN ONLINE LIBRARY CATALOG.**

Melvyl® The Catalog of the University of California Libraries

Sign In (optional)
Quit Help
Article Database & E-journal Lists
Other Catalogs
Basic Search   Advanced   Command   Browse   Most Recent Search   Previous
Searches   Saved Items

Search results: 3 Item(s) [Modify Search]   **Display:**   Full   MARC

[Print / Email] [Save] [Save Across Sessions] [Request]   ◉ Previous   Next ◉

Item 1 of 3 Total

Return to Search Results List

Title An assessment of mental health needs among homeless people in central
Los Angeles [electronic resource].

Publisher Los Angeles, Calif.: Division of Community Health, USC Keck School
of Medicine, 2004.

Note Title from PDF title page (viewed May 31, 2005).

Note Includes bibliographical references.

Note This report offers an "in-depth view of the mental health needs of the
homeless in central Los Angeles and the system that is designed to
provide for their care." The report presents an overview of mental illness
and homelessness; explores the current mental health service capacity in
downtown Los Angeles; identifies barriers and gaps; and presents
conclusions and recommendations.

Language English

Subject Homeless persons -- Mental health services -- California -- Los Angeles.

Homeless persons -- Mental health -- California -- Los Angeles.

Homeless persons -- California -- Los Angeles.

Homeless Persons -- Los Angeles.

Mental Health Services -- Los Angeles.

Mental Disorders -- Los Angeles.

Health Services Accessibility -- Los Angeles.

Added Entry Keck School of Medicine.

Format Book

Computer file

Online

Library UC Los Angeles   All

Library	Call Number	Availability	Notes
UC Los Angeles			
		Available online	
Online	HV4506.L67	Circ status	Online access

◉ Previous   Next ◉

Basic Search   Advanced   Command   Browse   Most Recent Search   Previous
Searches   Saved Items

CDL   Comments and feedback
Melvyl® is an initiative of the California Digital Library
© 2006 The Regents of the University of California

NOT operator. NOT (sometimes designated with a minus sign) is especially useful if you are searching for a word that has a common meaning you want to exclude or is often found with another word you want to exclude. For example, if you were studying adoption among Native Americans, you might want to use the keyword *Indian* without getting all the hits for people in India. You could enter *Indian adoption* NOT *India* or *Indian adoption* —*India*, depending on which search engine you are using.

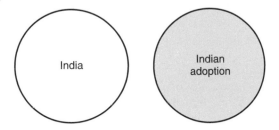

USING A TRUNCATION SYMBOL

A useful technique when using Boolean operators is to introduce a *truncation symbol*. Although different databases use different truncation symbols, the most common of these symbols are # and *. A truncation symbol stands for letters in a word, such that *adopt#* would stand for *adoption, adoptive, adopting*, as well as *adopt*. So, too, *legal** could stand for *legality* or *legalization*. The computer searches for any word beginning with the letters up to the truncation symbol. To be sure of finding all the potential good, relevant data sources, the student searching for online information about Indian adoption should use a truncation symbol; in the case of the University of California's online library catalog it is a #:

Indian adopt# OR *Native American adopt#*

USING THE LIBRARY TO REVIEW THE SOCIOLOGICAL LITERATURE

Begin your work in the library by getting an overview of the sociological research that has already been conducted on your question. (The following section on locating references will help you do this.) This overview of research published in books and journal articles is called "a review of the literature." ("Literature" in this sense, of course, has nothing to do with fiction and poetry.) "Reviewing the literature" in sociology involves discovering whether scholarly research has been published on the question you tentatively have in mind, how the question was formulated, and what answers have been suggested.

Reviewing the literature will help you in two important and interrelated ways. First, a review of the literature helps you to refine your question. How has the question been framed before? Has more than one plausible answer been suggested as a result of empirical or theoretical research? As you fine-tune your question, remember that you must be able to find sufficient evidence to support the answer you will propose, and that it must be specific enough to be researchable within the time frame of your assignment. Second, reviewing the literature helps you to identify those books and journal articles that contain reports of research into the question you will address in your paper. The quality of your paper will depend on how thoroughly you locate such research; it is the "data" you will use to support your thesis. Once you locate relevant books and articles, you will take in-depth notes on them.

USING THE LIBRARY TO LOCATE SPECIALIZED SOCIOLOGICAL REFERENCES

While many students are tempted to complete research papers entirely in the comfort of their home or workspace, it is important to visit the college or university library since not all sources are available in electronic form, at least not yet. The key to the library is the reference section, where you can get help from reference librarians. Reference librarians are there to answer your questions and to help you find the most appropriate books, articles, journals, and abstracts for your project.

If your course textbooks include lists of "Recommended Readings," often located at the ends of chapters, you can start with those references, choosing suggested books and articles that seem most appropriate. Start with the most recently published sources because they include references to earlier works.

Be aware that, for a college research paper, unlike most papers for high school, you will be expected to consult articles in specialized professional journals. (An annotated list of select journals and other resources used by sociologists is given later in this chapter.)

In addition to any references you find in your textbooks, you should begin your research with the following six library resources on which sociology students rely:

+ Specialized dictionaries and encyclopedias, and review articles
+ Online library catalog
+ Journals often used by sociologists (print and electronic versions)
+ *CSA Sociological Abstracts* (electronic version)
+ *Social Sciences Citation Index* (electronic version)
+ Other computerized bibliographic sources

SPECIALIZED DICTIONARIES AND ENCYCLOPEDIAS

These references explain key terms and concepts, and provide background information on the life and times of key historical figures:

Johnson, Allan G. 2000. *The Blackwell Dictionary of Sociology: A User's Guide to Sociological Language.* Malden, MA: Blackwell Publishers.

Ritzer, George. 2006. *Blackwell Encyclopedia of Sociology.* Boston, MA: Blackwell Publishers.

Some sources on the Internet include:

Sociology Dictionary <http://www.webref.org/sociology/sociology.htm>

Online Dictionary of the Social Sciences <http://socialsciencedictionary.nelson.com/ssd/SocialDict.jsp>

The advantage of beginning with specialized dictionaries or encyclopedias is that they can give you a quick overview of a subject. However, they are often not the most up-to-date sources.

If you know something about the topic, a better starting point may be a review article published in the *Annual Review of Sociology.* These articles are written by experts in various sociological specialties on recent developments in their fields, allowing readers to learn about the state of the art on a variety of topics. Each article includes an extensive bibliography on the topic, so the articles are valuable both as a summary of recent scholarship and as a source for finding books and articles on your topic. It can be found in paper versions in college libraries or online at <http://arjournals.annualreviews.org/loi/soc>, though like many of the other most useful sources, the Web site is restricted, so you need to access it through your library or with a college proxy.

ONLINE LIBRARY CATALOG

Use the online library catalog to find suitable books. The books are organized according to author's name, title, and subject. Finding information by searching the catalog by author and title is relatively straightforward. But if you look for books by subject and don't find any information, it may be because the subject you are looking under is not an official subject category. For example, if your paper is on the implications of regulating handguns, and if you search the online library catalog using the subject "Handguns" or "Handgun Control," you will not find anything. "Handguns" and "Handgun Control" are not official topics. In this case, you must consult a special reference book to find official topics, called "subject headings." This special reference book, a large, red multivolume set called *The Library of Congress Subject Headings,* is usually at the reference desk. For example, if you look up "Handguns" in *The Library of Congress Subject Headings,* you will find this instruction: "See Pistols." If you look up "Handgun Control" in *The Library of Congress Subject Headings,* you will find "See Gun Control." You will also be told that "Works on legal aspects of gun control are entered under 'Firearms—Law and legislation'." Finding books by subject often requires this kind of detective work in order to find the right subject heading (for example, "Firearms—Law and legislation").

However, when searching electronically, you can usually find books by searching for terms you think are in the title and then looking at the subject keyword. For example, when you search for books with the word "handgun" in the title, you will find that the subject keyword is "pistols." You can then search using the subject heading "pistols" to find books, regardless of whether the word "handgun" is included in the title. Many online library catalogs are designed so that the term in the subject field is a link to a list of all books within that topic.

JOURNALS OFTEN USED BY SOCIOLOGISTS

Scholars rely on journal articles, as well as books, to keep up with new research and professional opinion. But journals aren't a trade secret. Undergraduates, as apprentice scholars, can also use journal articles. Most college libraries have a quiet, convenient place where current issues of major journals are kept before they are bound and shelved, like other books, in the main sections of the library. We recommend that you find this reading area, often called "Current Periodicals," and browse through some of the journals in the following list. This experience will give you a dramatic sense of the discipline's ongoing research tradition, which is only hinted at in textbooks. It may also trigger some ideas about possible topics for your future papers. Although the articles in these journals are intended primarily for a trained scholarly audience, rather than the general public, and sometimes employ sophisticated statistical techniques, you will find many articles easily accessible to undergraduates.

The following list of periodicals related to sociology is not exhaustive. For more references to specialized journals and governmental sources, ask your reference librarian.

American Journal of Sociology Published bimonthly by the University of Chicago Press, this influential journal includes theoretical and research articles, book reviews, and commentaries on articles published previously. <http://www.journals.uchicago.edu/AJS/home.html>

American Sociological Review Published bimonthly by the American Sociological Association (ASA), this review covers diverse areas of sociology, often with a statistical and empirical orientation. A cumulative index appears every three years. <http://www2.asanet.org/journals/asr/>

City and Community Published quarterly by the ASA Section on Community and Urban Sociology, this journal publishes theoretical and empirical articles about communities and places, both urban and rural. <http://www.blackwellpublishing.com/journal.asp?ref=1535-6841&site=1>

Contemporary Sociology Published bimonthly by the ASA, its special feature is to review books, journals, articles, and films that cover a wide range of areas, such as historical and comparative sociology, social psychology, gender, education, and stratification. The review essays are especially useful for learning about new publications and sociologists' evaluations of them. <http://www.asanet.org/page.ww?section=Contemporary+Sociology&name=Homepage>

Contexts This non-technical magazine published quarterly by the ASA covers timely sociological ideas and research about society and social behavior. <http://www.contextsmagazine.org/>

Criminology Published quarterly, this interdisciplinary journal emphasizes research in the social and behavioral sciences about crime and deviant behavior, and presents articles on the theoretical and historical components of crime, law, and criminal justice. <http://www.blackwell-synergy.com/loi/crim>

Demography This interdisciplinary journal, published quarterly by the Population Association of America, includes research studies on developing countries as well as developed countries. <http://muse.jhu.edu/journals/dem/>

Gender and Society Published quarterly, this interdisciplinary journal is sponsored by Sociologists for Women in Society. It aims to advance the study of gender, as well as racial, ethnic, cultural, and national diversity. <http://www.sagepub.com/journalsProdDesc.nav?prodId=Journal200793>

Journal of Aging Studies This quarterly publication highlights innovative research approaches, critiques of existing theory, and empirical work related to age and aging <http://www.elsevier.com/wps/find/journaldescription.cws_home/620198/description#description>

Journal of Contemporary Ethnography Published quarterly, this journal presents ethnographic studies based on qualitative interviewing and participant observation. <http://jce.sagepub.com/>

Journal of Gerontology: Social Sciences The social science edition of this journal is published bimonthly by the Gerontological Society of America. This interdisciplinary journal seeks to promote the scientific study of aging and the life course. <http://psychsoc.gerontologyjournals.org/>

Journal of Health and Social Behavior Published quarterly by the ASA, this journal uses a sociological perspective in understanding health-related issues; for example, organizational aspects of hospitals or class characteristics of sufferers from various illnesses. <http://www.ingentaconnect.com/content/asoca/jhsb;jsessionid=d09q75k4gsi4.alice>

Journal of Marriage and the Family Published quarterly by the National Council on Family Relations, this journal covers such diverse research areas as family planning, family structure, theories of the family, and cross-cultural studies on fertility. Each issue also features a book review section. <http://www.blackwellpublishing.com/journal.asp?ref=0022-2445>

Journal of Personality and Social Psychology Published monthly by the American Psychological Association (APA), this journal is divided into sections on attitudes and social cognition, interpersonal relations and group processes, and personality processes and individual differences. <http://www.apa.org/journals/psp/>

Qualitative Sociology This quarterly journal publishes research based on qualitative research methods, such as interviewing, participant observation, ethnography, historical analysis, and content analysis. <http://springerlink.metapress.com/link.asp?id=105337>

Sex Roles: A Journal of Research Published bimonthly, this journal presents empirical and theoretical examinations of the underlying processes of gender role socialization. <http://www.springerlink.com/link.asp?id=101600>

Social Forces Published quarterly, this international journal for social research and methodology is associated with the Southern Sociological Society. It presents articles on such topics as mobility, class, ethnicity, gender, and education. Each issue includes book reviews. <http://socialforces.unc.edu/>

Social Problems Published five times yearly, this is the official journal of the Society for the Study of Social Problems. <http://www.ucpress.edu/journals/sp/>

Social Psychology Quarterly Published quarterly by the ASA, this journal covers empirical and theoretical studies related to social interaction, socialization, labeling, conformity, and attitudes. <http://www.asanet.org/cs/social_psychology_quarterly>

Sociological Forum This official journal of the Eastern Sociological Society, published quarterly, contains articles that link subfields of sociology to other disciplines. <http://www.blackwellpublishing.com/journal.asp?ref=0884-8971&site=1>

Sociological Inquiry Published quarterly for the chapters of Alpha Kappa Delta (the undergraduate sociology honors society), it covers a wide range of sociological topics. <http://www.blackwellpublishing.com/journal.asp?ref=0038-0245>

Sociological Methodology Published annually by ASA, this journal covers qualitative and quantitative methodological issues in the field of sociology. <http://www.blackwellpublishing.com/journal.asp?ref=0081-1750&site=1>

Sociological Perspectives The purpose of this quarterly journal, which is sponsored by the Pacific Sociological Association, is to advance research and theory in sociology and related disciplines. <http://www.ucpress.edu/journals/sop/>

Sociological Theory A quarterly publication of the ASA, this journal is devoted to discussions of new and old sociological theories, theory construction, and theory synthesis. The journal also includes a section for debate and comment on recent theoretical controversies. <http://www.blackwellpublishing.com/journal.asp?ref=0735-2751&site=1>

Sociology of Education Published quarterly by the ASA, this journal contains papers on human social development as well as on relations among educational institutions. <http://www.asanet.org/page.ww?section=Sociology+of+Education&name=Homepage>

Symbolic Interaction Published quarterly by the Society for the Study of Symbolic Interaction, this specialized journal presents empirical and theoretical articles that take a symbolic interactionist perspective. <http://ucpress.edu/journals/si/>

The Sociological Quarterly Sponsored by the Midwest Sociological Society, this journal presents research on recent theoretical, methodological, and empirical developments in the field of sociology. <http://www.blackwellpublishing.com/journal.asp?ref=0038-0253&site=1>

CSA SOCIOLOGICAL ABSTRACTS

Although you could search for articles by going to the Web site of each journal, this method is not efficient. Further, many of these sites charge a fee to access journal articles. A more efficient and inexpensive way to search for journal articles related to sociological topics is to take advantage of your library's subscription to the academic database *CSA Sociological Abstracts.*

This database includes articles in several thousand sociology journals, with brief descriptions of the articles' contents. Published both as a set of annual volumes and as a computerized database, *CSA Sociological Abstracts* includes references to sociological publications since 1952 and is by far the best resource for finding sociological articles. However, use of this database and others like it (see below) is restricted to colleges and universities that have purchased a subscription. Therefore, to access these databases, you must use the computers at your college or university library or log in from a remote access site using your library's proxy server. Ask your librarian if your library has a subscription to the online version of *CSA Sociological Abstracts* and, if it has, whether you can access this database from home or another location using a library proxy server.

CSA Sociological Abstracts gives more than bibliographic information. It also provides abstracts of articles published in major sociological journals. (An abstract is a summary of an article.) Learning to use *CSA Sociological Abstracts* will save you much time, since these summaries will allow you to decide whether the sources themselves are relevant to your topic. In this way you can weed out some without having to locate and read them. You can get more information at <http://www.csa.com/factsheets/socioabs-set-c.php> but will need to access it through a university computer or proxy server.

To use the library's electronic version of *CSA Sociological Abstracts,* check first with your instructor or librarian. We cannot tell you exactly what syntax you will need to use because there are different software "shells" for accessing the computerized version. However, your instructor or librarian can help you get started. Figure 4.2 presents search results from the CSA Illumina platform.

If you searched with the keyword "Firearms," you would find that there are 443 items (at the time of this writing), more or less with the most recent items given first. Figure 4-2 shows the search results. Notice the tabs indicating that of the 443 items, 326 are journal articles (260 of which are from peer-reviewed journals), 25 are from conferences, and 8 are from books. Notice also that for each article listed, the database provides several links, some of which provide you with the full text of the article (entry 1), the full list of references for the article (entry 2), or other articles that cite the current article (entry 3).

For all items listed, there is a link telling you how to find the publication online or in the library. If you click the "View Record" link or the title of an entry, you obtain more in-depth information. (Note that some software shells will show only some fields unless you ask for a complete display; others will allow you to select which fields you want displayed.)

After you check the boxes for the items you are interested in, save the information to a storage device, print it, or e-mail it to yourself; otherwise, make a note of the author(s), title, year of publication, and journal, and paraphrase the abstract in your own words.

Figure 4-2 SEARCH RESULTS FROM COMPUTERIZED VERSION OF *CSA SOCIOLOGICAL ABSTRACTS*.

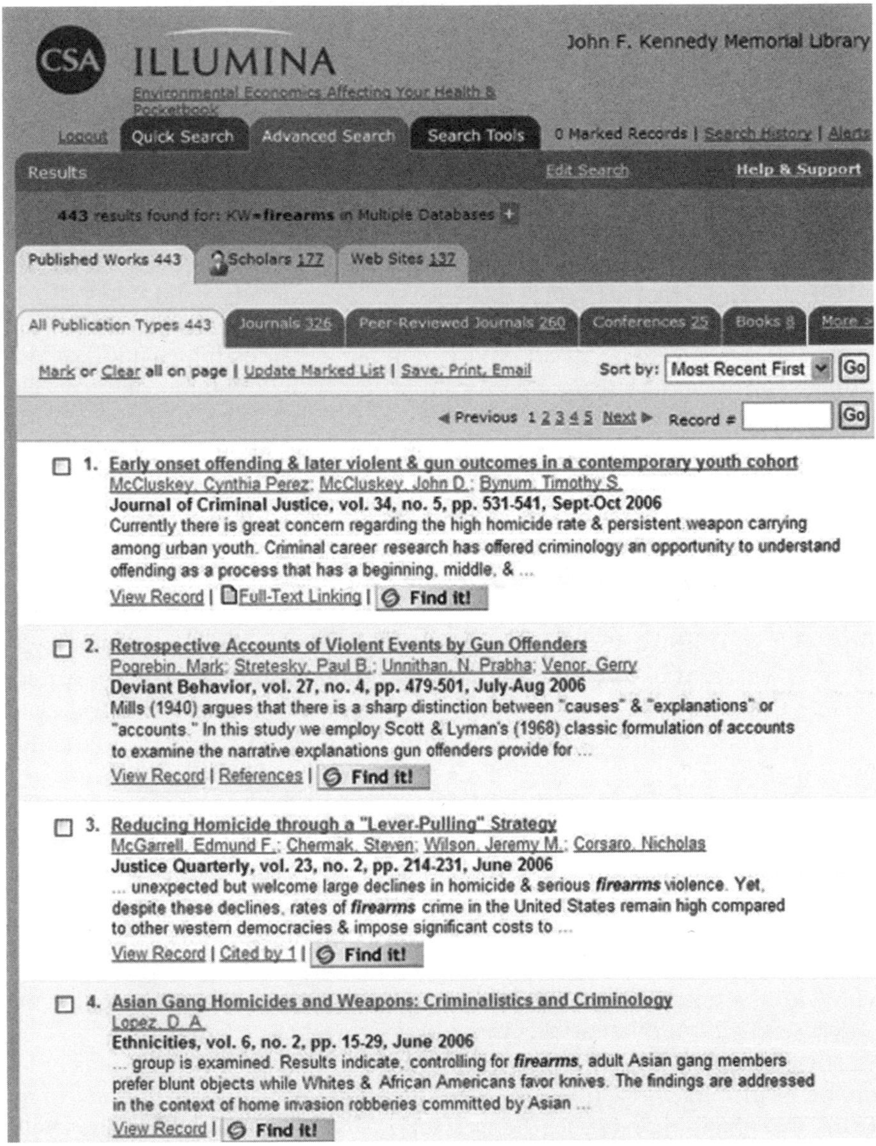

SOCIAL SCIENCES CITATION INDEX

Like *CSA Sociological Abstracts,* this valuable source of bibliographic information comes both in printed annual editions and as an electronic database. *Social Sciences Citation Index* identifies the references that authors cite in their articles (hence, the word "citation" in its title). This feature allows scholars to trace the interconnected network of a research tradition and see which scholars' work influenced which other scholars by clicking on the "cited references" or the "times cited" links. Figure 4-3 reveals that the article by Lizotte and Bordua published in the leading sociological journal *American Sociological Review* was cited by other scholars 64 times.

Figure 4-3 SEARCH RESULTS FROM COMPUTERIZED VERSION OF *SOCIAL SCIENCES CITATION INDEX.*

ISI Web of Knowledge^{SM}   Web of Science   GO   HOME   LOG OUT

Web of Science®

WELCOME ? HELP GENERAL SEARCH CITED REF SEARCH SEARCH HISTORY ADVANCED SEARCH

Full Record

◄ Record 13 of 16 (Set #6) ►   ▲ SUMMARY

Title: FIREARMS OWNERSHIP FOR SPORT AND PROTECTION - 2 DIVERGENT MODELS
Author(s): LIZOTTE AJ, BORDUA DJ
Source: AMERICAN SOCIOLOGICAL REVIEW 45 (2): 229-244 1980
Document Type: Article
Language: English
Cited References: 29   **Times Cited:** 64   FIND RELATED RECORDS (i)
Addresses: LIZOTTE AJ (reprint author), EMORY UNIV, DEPT SOCIOL, ATLANTA, GA 30322 USA
UNIV ILLINOIS, URBANA, IL 61801 USA
Publisher: AMER SOCIOLOGICAL ASSOC, 1722 N ST NW, WASHINGTON, DC 20036-2981
Subject Category: Sociology
IDS Number: JQ770
ISSN: 0003-1224

◄ Record 13 of 16 (Set #6) ►   ▲ SUMMARY

Acceptable Use Policy
Copyright © 2007 *The Thomson Corporation*

Reprinted by permission of Thomson Scientific.

Providing information about citations was once the unique purview of *Social Sciences Citation Index*. However, now other electronic databases, such as *CSA Sociological Abstracts* and *Google Scholar* (see below), also include this type of information, although less comprehensively.

OTHER COMPUTERIZED BIBLIOGRAPHIC SOURCES

Your library may have other computerized bibliographies like *CSA Sociological Abstracts,* but in other academic disciplines, such as PSYCHINFO (the computerized version of *Psychological Abstracts*), ECONLIT (the computerized version of *Economic Abstracts*), and ERIC (the Educational Resources Information Center, a national information system sponsored by the U.S. Department of Education that collects educational documents and makes them available to teachers, administrators, students, and other researchers). You can also consult computerized bibliographies on a variety of particular topics, such as the Chicano Database, PAIS (the Public Affairs Information Service), and Population Index on the Internet. Ask your librarian which of these are available at your college or university and for help on how to use them. They can be very useful for finding books and articles on the topic of your paper.

GENERAL BIBLIOGRAPHIC SOURCES

In addition to the specifically sociological or social science sources, there are several excellent general sources with information about scholarly work in all disciplines including humanities and sciences. These are available at most university libraries and through their Web sites. Most are restricted, so you will need to use a university computer or proxy.

JSTOR

JSTOR enables you to download from academic journals articles that are between one to five years old. This includes the most academically respectable journals in many disciplines but not very many specialty journals.

LEXISNEXIS

LexisNexis is a very extensive data set of news, legal, government, and medical sources. It includes an extensive library on public opinion polls, which is very useful for sociology papers.

PROQUEST DIGITAL DISSERTATIONS

This site has information on doctoral dissertations from 1861 to the present, with abstracts since 1980. Doctoral dissertations are especially useful for very detailed or esoteric information. If you have enough lead time, paper copies can be ordered. Dissertations are also in the library at the university where they were written.

WORLDCAT

WorldCat is a very useful catalog of books, Web resources, and other material worldwide. It includes citations for books, journals, manuscripts, maps, music scores, sound recordings, films, computer files, newspapers, slides, and video-tapes in a variety of languages.

MELVYL

Melvyl, the catalog system for the University of California library, has a facility called SearchLight that links you to specialized search engines in many disciplines, including *CSA Sociological Abstracts*. When you get the results in SearchLight, if the number is underlined, click on the number, not on the name of the resource. <http://melvyl.cdlib.org>

GOOGLE SCHOLAR AND *GOOGLE BOOK SEARCH*

Google Scholar <http://scholar.google.com/> and *Google Book Search* <http://books.google.com/books?q=&btnG=Search+Books&as_brr=0> work like basic *Google* but return articles and books on the topic rather than Web sites. Many of the items listed are links to the articles or books themselves, though some may be restricted and require access from a library or university proxy. They are much more reliable than results from the regular *Google* search engine because they are confined to academic research. They are two of the most powerful and convenient general search engines for academic research. A search on "single-parent families" in *Google Scholar,* for example, returned almost 15,000 hits when the "Recent articles" option was selected (Figure 4-4 shows the first page of the response) and over 18,000 hits when the "All articles" option was se-lected (not shown). *Google Book Search* located nearly 4,000 books (not shown).

Like other electronic academic databases listed above, for each reference listed, *Google Scholar* tells you how many scholarly books and articles have cited it. You click on that link to see exactly what those books and articles are, a valuable way to learn both how it has been received and find more recent references on similar topics. Many of the hits can be accessed directly. The link for "Library Search," seen here on the fifth entry, takes you to a site where you can enter your zip code and it will list libraries close to you that have the item (in this case a book).

OTHER GENERAL SEARCH ENGINES

While many students begin a search with general search engines such as *Google, Yahoo!,* or *Alta Vista,* we recommend that you try these after you have tried the more scholarly and specialized resources unless you are specifically looking for journalistic articles. As we emphasized above, these search en-

Figure 4-4 *GOOGLE SCHOLAR* RESULTS FOR "SINGLE-PARENT FAMILIES."

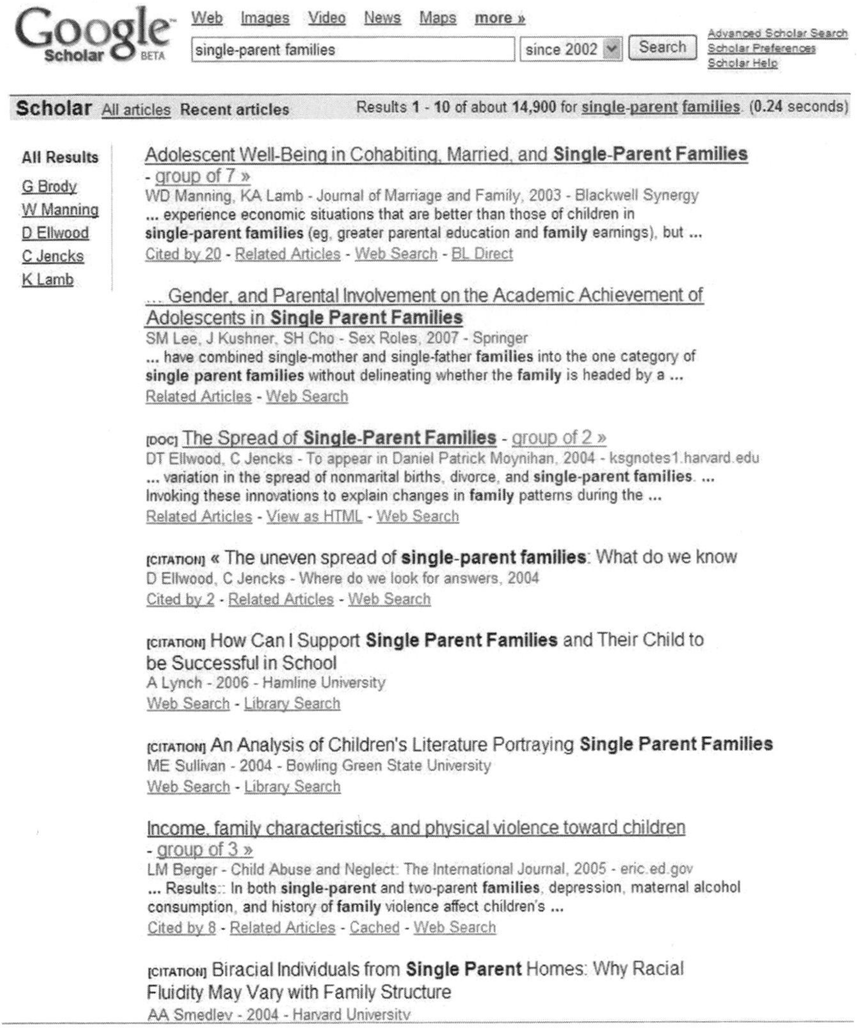
Google Scholar BETA
Web Images Video News Maps more »
single-parent families | since 2002 | Search
Advanced Scholar Search
Scholar Preferences
Scholar Help

Scholar All articles Recent articles Results 1 - 10 of about 14,900 for single-parent families. (0.24 seconds)

All Results
G Brody
W Manning
D Ellwood
C Jencks
K Lamb

Adolescent Well-Being in Cohabiting, Married, and **Single-Parent Families** - group of 7 »
WD Manning, KA Lamb - Journal of Marriage and Family, 2003 - Blackwell Synergy
... experience economic situations that are better than those of children in **single-parent families** (eg, greater parental education and **family** earnings), but ...
Cited by 20 - Related Articles - Web Search - BL Direct

... Gender, and Parental Involvement on the Academic Achievement of Adolescents in **Single Parent Families**
SM Lee, J Kushner, SH Cho - Sex Roles, 2007 - Springer
... have combined single-mother and single-father **families** into the one category of **single parent families** without delineating whether the **family** is headed by a ...
Related Articles - Web Search

[DOC] The Spread of **Single-Parent Families** - group of 2 »
DT Ellwood, C Jencks - To appear in Daniel Patrick Moynihan, 2004 - ksgnotes1.harvard.edu
... variation in the spread of nonmarital births, divorce, and **single-parent families**. ... Invoking these innovations to explain changes in **family** patterns during the ...
Related Articles - View as HTML - Web Search

[CITATION] « The uneven spread of **single-parent families**: What do we know
D Ellwood, C Jencks - Where do we look for answers, 2004
Cited by 2 - Related Articles - Web Search

[CITATION] How Can I Support **Single Parent Families** and Their Child to be Successful in School
A Lynch - 2006 - Hamline University
Web Search - Library Search

[CITATION] An Analysis of Children's Literature Portraying **Single Parent Families**
ME Sullivan - 2004 - Bowling Green State University
Web Search - Library Search

Income, family characteristics, and physical violence toward children - group of 3 »
LM Berger - Child Abuse and Neglect: The International Journal, 2005 - eric.ed.gov
... Results:: In both **single-parent** and two-parent **families**, depression, maternal alcohol consumption, and history of **family** violence affect children's ...
Cited by 8 - Related Articles - Cached - Web Search

[CITATION] Biracial Individuals from **Single Parent** Homes: Why Racial Fluidity May Vary with Family Structure
AA Smedley - 2004 - Harvard University

Reprinted by permission of Google.

gines have no quality controls and return the useful as well as the useless, the reliable as well as the shoddy.

Figure 4-5 shows the results of a search for "single-parent families" using *Google Web*. First, notice that instead of the 14,900 hits for recent articles on *Google Scholar*, itself a rather unmanageable number, on regular *Google*, there were more than one million hits, more than anyone could read in a lifetime. This page also demonstrates some of the kinds of sites returned. The first site is a list of interesting but undocumented facts about single parenting. There is

Figure 4-5 *GOOGLE WEB* RESULTS FOR "SINGLE-PARENT FAMILIES."

Sign in

Google™   Web   Images   Video   News   Maps   **more »**

single-parent families   [Search]   Advanced Search
                                             Preferences

Web   Results 1 - 10 of about **1,240,000** for single-parent families. (0.11 seconds)

PWP - Facts About **Single Parent Families**
58% of **single parent** male **families** and 49% of **single parent** female **families** own or are
buying their homes. · The proportion of custodial parents in ...
www.parentswithoutpartners.org/Support1.htm - 10k - Cached - Similar pages

Growing Up In **Single Parent Families**, HYG-5291-95
Single parents and their children constitute a rapidly increasing population. More recently,
single fathers, unwed teenage mothers, other singl.
ohioline.osu.edu/hyg-fact/5000/5291.html - 7k - Cached - Similar pages

Being a **Single Parent**
While different than a nuclear **family**, **single-parent families** have their own ... **Single
parent families** become more interdependent, finding that working ...
www.metlife.com/Applications/Corporate/WPS/CDA/PageGenerator/0,4132,P988,00.html -
33k - Cached - Similar pages

Single parent - Wikipedia, the free encyclopedia
Many factors influence how children develop in **single-parent families**: ... [3] About 1 out of 4
families with dependent children are **single-parent families**. ...
en.wikipedia.org/wiki/Single_parent - 25k - Cached - Similar pages

Single-parent families
Single-parent families in today's society have their share of daily struggles and long-term
disadvantages. The issues of expensive day care, ...
www.pineforge.com/newman2studyfamilies/essays/single_parent.htm - 11k -
Cached - Similar pages

Single-Parent Families
Census Bureau projections indicate that at least one-half of all American children will spend
part of their growing years in a **single-parent family**.1 This ...
www.joe.org/joe/1986winter/rb2.html - 6k - Cached - Similar pages

Jacqueline Kirby, M.S.
Ninety percent of **single-parent families** are headed by females. ... The rate of poverty is
even higher in African-American **single-parent families**, ...
hec.osu.edu/famlife/bulletin/volume.1/bullart1.htm - 11k - Cached - Similar pages

Montana State University Extension Service
Research shows that successful **single-parent families** have the following ... The same
characteristics that make **single-parent families** strong are found in ...

no way to know how reliable or unreliable any of the information may be.
The second one is an academic source, a fact sheet from Ohio State University
Extension. "Being a Single Parent" is a Web site sponsored by a commercial
insurance company. While probably reliable information, the reader would
want to remain mindful that the sponsor has a business interest in the topic.

Skipping down, the next to the last document is an academic paper by a scholar. It is probably dependable, but there is no way to know if it has been peer reviewed, that is, reviewed by other scholars. Although this search could have led to useful sources, it would have been much more efficient and reliable to use the university library, specifically sociological search engines like *CSA Sociological Abstracts,* or *Google Scholar.*

However, the Internet can be an excellent source of data. The demographic data on the U. S. Census Bureau's Web site <http://www.census.gov> provide a good example of a valuable source. This site, sponsored by the U. S. Department of Commerce, provides information about all kinds of population issues in various graphic and tabular formats: maps and statistics. The Census site also provides downloadable software for census and survey processing, and access to Census Bureau online roundtables, which are forums where the public can read and then post follow-up comments. So, too, the capacity of the search engine *Google* <http://www.google.com/ig/usgov> to identify specialized U. S. Government Web sites can provide up-to-date government information that would be much harder to locate elsewhere, if at all.

Other links that give you access to data that you can download but require some knowledge of quantitative techniques, though it may be as elementary as reading a cross-tabulation table, include:

General Social Survey (GSS) Resources (programs and data may be downloaded; surveys are available for the years 1972–1998; a searchable index of papers utilizing GSS data includes full citations and short abstracts). For an introduction to the data set and how to use it, see their Web site <http://webapp.icpsr.umich.edu/GSS/>

FEDSTATS This is a portal to 70 federal, state, and local government agencies that collect and report statistics. <http://www.fedstats.gov/>

The Gallup Poll Results of public opinion polls on a broad variety of topics. <http://www.galluppoll.com/>

SETTING UP A RECORD-KEEPING SYSTEM

Whether you record information in a word processor, on paper, or index cards, the principles are the same. Keep track of where information comes from. Record the information in your own words. Keep your records organized so you can synthesize it and use it effectively.

A record-keeping system will keep you from feeling as if you are drowning in a sea of information and will enable you later on to create a formal bibliography for your paper. (See "References and Bibliographies," pages 56–59.) We recommend bibliographic software. If you obtained articles through online databases like *CSA Sociological Abstracts,* you can use *Ref Works* to put your bibliography or reference section together. *Ref Works,* like other bibliographic software, allows you to choose the formatting style you would like to use, such as that of the American Sociological Association, or the American Psychological Association, etc.

If your library's shell for *CSA Sociological Abstracts* does not include biblio-graphic software such as *Ref Works,* and you do not own such software, you may use an index card system, one index card for each source. Put biblio-graphical details on cards as you go along. Have some blank index cards always with you. Then, when you come across the details about a promising source, in the library or on the Internet, you can record these details on an index card:

Author: all authors of the source, with only the first author's surname and first name in inverted order

Title: article, chapter, book, Web site

Facts of publication:

For journals: journal name in full, date of publication, volume number, issue number, inclusive pages

For books: city and state of publication, publisher's name, publication date

For a Web site: URL, sponsoring organization if named, date of publica-tion, date of access

Of course, you can also open a special computer file for this information, but you may not always have your laptop or a storage device with you when you come across a likely source. Later, you can simply arrange your cards in alphabetical order by author and keyboard the reference page (or bibliography, if required) for your paper. Recording this information is es-pecially important for online sources that you cut and paste into your own files of notes. Recording this information will enable you to reconstruct it later when you may no longer know what the original source was or have access to it.

TAKING NOTES

Taking notes is one of the most challenging and personal parts of the writing process. Especially in the early stages, a student may not know exactly what the paper's main argument will be. There is the fear of neglecting to record information you will need and the danger that you will become bogged down in recording sources that will have no relevance to the final paper. There is no single correct way to take notes, but there are some general principles.

First, always keep in mind the question you are addressing, the answer that you expect to offer, and alternative answers that you will be arguing against. Ask what answer the book or article might offer, what information is available to support your answer (or make you rethink your answer) or rebut other answers, and why sources on the topic might be addressing some other answer. Some people prefer to take a lot of notes when first reading; others prefer to take note of general points and a reminder of what is in the source so that they can go back later and take more detailed notes later. In either case, it is important to make a note of keywords or topics they can find quickly, perhaps at the top of the document or page. These might include any keynotes in the source that you used to find the book or article or your own terms that you might use to organize your paper. For example, if you are writing about homelessness and expect to organize the paper into sections on causes, effects, and solutions, you might use those terms in your subject headings. Having subject headings will make it much easier to organize your notes when you sit down to write.

Second, summarize the book or article in your own words. When taking notes, the biggest temptation is to copy information word for word. Not only is this very inefficient, but you are less likely to really comprehend the material unless you put it in your own words. And it very easily slides to plagiarism, the theft of other people's words and ideas. Even if it is inadvertent, it is a serious scholarly offense. Cutting and pasting is very tempting when you are reading things on the Internet and taking notes in a word processor. It should be done very selectively when you think you might actually quote the material. Otherwise, read the material, switch back to the word processor, and write the information in your words.

Third, as mentioned above, pay attention to the forest as well as the trees, making note of the main points of what you are reading as well as the specific pieces of information. The main points are usually summarized in a book or article's opening and closing sections.

Fourth, read with an eye toward other things you have read. Can you see patterns or debates in a field? For example, some work on homelessness focuses on the characteristics of the homeless themselves, emphasizing substance abuse, mental illness, or family background. Others emphasize the structural forces, such as housing costs, lack of services, or welfare reform. Alternatively you may notice that some articles use quantitative methods and others use qualitative methods. It is especially important if you notice that some books or articles explicitly disagree with others. After reading a few pieces, you should begin to see patterns.

Finally, write your own reactions as you take notes. This can be a positive comment like "A very valuable source," an observation about the relation to other sources, such as "A useful rebuttal to Garcia," or a more extensive analysis that might be text for the paper itself. Some people like to mark their own reactions with a symbol such as an asterisk (*).

Many students find that once they begin the research process they quickly accumulate piles of photocopies and printouts. Because such copying is expensive, you will want to be selective and not reproduce everything on your topic. While you look over the material to check its usefulness, you can also use the following strategy for sorting out important information from material that is irrelevant. It will not take much more time, and will help you manage the information and clarify your plans. (Don't forget to record the bibliographical details about your photocopies or printed-out sources.)

You are probably already in the habit of underlining or highlighting important statements when you read your textbooks. You can do the same thing with copied source material. You will find this process more helpful if you have at hand pens in several different colors, one for each of various subheadings. As you scan the copy, you can key a particular color to a particular subheading. For example, the student researching single-parent families used one color for statistical data, another for information about legal resources and regulations, and still another for information about children in such families. The result may be a page that resembles a rainbow, but you will have separated the subheadings visually. Write your color-coding key on something you can locate readily. (One suggestion is to write this key on the back of the bibliography card you've made for this photocopied source.)

As you read and highlight, take advantage of having your own copy to write notes in the margins. Jot down your responses to this reading. These annotations may be as brief as a subheading, or they might contain a brief summary of your opinion or a reminder to yourself for later. Unlike many of the notes that you take in a textual analysis (see pages 119–126), which attempt to outline and restate the text's main argument, the notes that you take in a research project are carefully selected to become evidence in your own paper. As C. Wright Mills explains in "On Intellectual Craftsmanship," his appendix to *The Sociological Imagination* ([1959] 2000):

> rather than read entire books, you will very often read parts of many books from the point of view of some particular theme or topic in which you are interested. . . . Therefore, you will take notes which do not fairly represent the books you read. You are *using* this particular idea, this particular fact, for the realization of your own projects. (P. 199)

Of course, Mills is not saying that your notes can be inaccurate or that they can misrepresent the original author. He is suggesting that the note-taking purpose is different. For more information, review "Taking Two Kinds of Notes," in Chapter 3, pages 45–46.

In addition to your notes, be sure to write the author's name or the title of the article somewhere on the page you have highlighted and annotated. You will already have collected the full set of bibliographic information in one location, but this shorthand on the photocopy will enable you to match up the two. Doing this will mean that you will not have to keep the entire article if you are only using a page from it.

If you decide to highlight and annotate a great deal of photocopied material, you will eventually end up with many loose pieces of paper that seem to have no organization. Two techniques can solve this problem. They may seem to involve a lot of reshuffling and arranging and labeling, but they are part of a logical, as well as a logistical, process. It is closely related to the other techniques of outlining described on pages 32–33. Shuffling your pages will automatically help you to think about your topic and its various problematic aspects, one or more of which will be possible directions for you to develop. Indeed, as Mills explains, this "re-arranging" process is "one way to invite [the sociological] imagination. . . . You simply dump out heretofore disconnected folders, mixing up their contents, and then resort them" (p. 212).

1. If you have a number of photocopies and printouts that contain information about one subheading (for instance, the effects of recent welfare legislation on single mothers), you can group these copies together alphabetically by author or by the first letter of the title and put them into a folder labeled with that subheading.
2. If you have a number of photocopies or printouts that contain information about two or more subheadings, you can at least alphabetize the pages by author or the first letter of the title. On the label of the folder, you should write the subheadings contained inside. You will know automatically that a folder with two or more subheadings is arranged alphabetically.

Again, we want to emphasize the value of Mills's advice that writers play around with their files, rearranging them and developing new file headings. This leads to new insights about your question. For example, your files on divorce might originally have been labeled "strain of modern life," "financial stress," "disagreement over raising children," and "adultery." But when you read through the files, you may find that the material clumps together in categories like "class differences," "attitudes toward women's roles," "legal changes," and "demographic change." At this point in the research process, not only will you better understand the significance of your collected data, but you will also be better prepared to organize your paper. For more information on various techniques of outlining your first draft, see pages 32–35 in Chapter 2.

A SAMPLE STUDENT PAPER

The following sample general research paper on country music was written by Mayank Chawla for an undergraduate course in sociology. She supports her thesis with information she obtained from library books, journal articles, and a few newspaper articles. Mayank's paper follows a variation of the three-part essay format as discussed in Chapter 1.

Mayank should have included a title page because her paper is more than five pages in length (see Part 3 for how to prepare a title page). She should have also included the date she turned in the paper.

Mayank opens with a personal observation but quickly, in paragraph two, connects it to sociological issues, telling us about the conventional wisdom in the literature and how she is adding to it. Sociology is a way to learn new things about society we didn't know and to see in a new way things that are very familiar to us. She does the latter, taking a very common observation—that country music is "white" music—and seeks to understand how this is so. As such, her paper answers the question, "What exactly is the connection between country music and white identity?" Her paper answers this question by explaining how country music, which she argues is "for and by white people," necessarily expresses various social, political, and economic relationships.

This paragraph tries to say too many things, talking about authenticity, narrative, musical features of country music, the similarities to other genres, and its relationship to its audiences.

Mayank Chawla
Professor Roy

WHITE NOISE: COUNTRY MUSIC AND WHITE IDENTITY

The first thought that struck me was that it looked like Hitler's fantasy: a dozen happy, patriotic, rosy-checked, innocent, light-haired, blue-eyed, *white* children. At the least, I expected a token, light-skinned (most likely biracial) black girl (or two), sprinkled among the white kids. In the midst of public controversy over the lack of representation of people of color in the media, I recently saw a KZLA commercial that seemed suspiciously white and strategically patriotic, mentioning the word "American" multiple times in the advertisement. I dismissed my thought as racially hypersensitive, until I found other friends randomly pointing out the obvious whiteness of the advertisement.

Studies of race and music have exhaustively focused on people of color and their music in an institutionally racist society. In this paper, I invert the scholarly lens of observation to examine the presence of white identity in what we commonly hold as the quintessential music of white America: country music. Sociologically, historically, and politically, I explore how we have come to associate country music with whiteness, and the overall validity of this correlation. Most authors of extensive scholarly studies on country music are long-time country fans; their bias is reflected in a generally inadequate treatment of race and country music. Any mention of correlation between whiteness and country music is dismissed, justified, or minimized. In this paper, I argue that there exists a strong relationship between country music and whiteness. Although I am not personally a fan of country music, I do not seek to vilify the genre and its fans, but rather, to examine it as both a product and agent of white identity.

Masked behind a façade of "authenticity," country music, like all genres, is fabricated (Peterson 1997), making any essentialist characterization of country music difficult. However, a few general characteristics pervade all or most country music. A "storytellers medium," country songs have a strong sense of narratives, like mini, musical soap operas. The songs generally have simple chord structures, regular rhythm,

1

This paragraph expresses two separate ideas. It tells us both something about the audiences and about an exception to the generalization that country music is white music. Accordingly, it should be split up into two paragraphs. At the least, the references to Charlie Pride, one of the few African American country music performers, would be better later in the paper, as a qualification to its main argument.

Following the *ASA Style Guide* (2007), Mayank does not capitalize the words "black" or "white" when designating racial groups but does capitalize the names of racial and ethnic groups that represent geographical locations (e.g., African American). She also capitalizes references to regions of the United States (e.g., South).

One of Mayank's themes is the historical process by which country music became associated with whiteness. She might have offered the reader a sign-post that this section is about historical background. Offering an apparent paradox is a very effective device for getting the reader's attention. The fact that country music has strong roots in African American music is the kind of anomaly that begs for sociological explanation.

and small melodic range. This simple musical structure highlights the narrative lyrics of country songs (Peterson and McLaurin 1992). Folk and pop songs, however, often possess the same elements, but do not fall within the genre of country music. Country music is not simply a genre defined by essential musical characteristics, but rather a reflection of the people and region from which it originated and the nation that consumes it.

"Participants in country music culture behave something like a vast extended family at an endless church supper in a rural American small town" (Ellison 1995:xvii). Country is a genre defined by the performers who produce it and the loyal fans who consume it. The audience is strikingly homogeneous: almost exclusively white, Christian, middle-aged, Republican, working class, and Southern (Danker 1991). The few blacks that enjoy country music generally grew up in the South. The performers are overwhelmingly white and 80% were born in the South (McLaurin 1992). Most of the country music studies I encountered are quick to mention Charlie Pride, the first and only successful black country singer. He came to the country music stage in 1961 and performed at the Grand Ole Opry in 1967 (Lawler 1996). As Barbara Ching points out, "Pride may well have suffered greatly from hard times, but the character he presents to the world is an unquestionably successful one who suffers no incurable unease" (Ching 2001:31). Pride's non-confrontational demeanor allowed for his incorporation into country music. He regularly ameliorated tension at his concerts by opening with some version of "I guess you're surprised to see me comin' out here wearin' this permanent tan and singing country music" (Ching 2001:31). Although Pride achieved moderate success in country music, no other black performer to date has achieved similar success. Pride himself once said, "I don't think of myself as the Jackie Robinson of country music . . . I'm just trying to be myself" (Lawler 1996:109). As a black man, Charlie Pride's break into the white genre was a unique exception, not the norm (Lawler 1996).

Paradoxically, country music, a supposedly authentically white genre, has its roots in African American musical forms. In fact, Bill C. Malone, the eminent country music scholar, argues that black or (blackface) musicians dominated music in the South, and it was not until later that rural white music gained prominence in the South (Malone 1993). Black (and

2

The detailed examples (names of artists and the titles of their songs) are very effective. Good writing is specific.

She completes telling us about the apparent paradox the paper is addressing and begins the explanation by telling us that the white connotations of country music are not accidental. *Creating Country Music* will be one of her main sources of information, so it is useful for her to cite it by title in the text. She also tells us in this paragraph who the actors were. The white connotations of country music did not just happen but were the result of actions by specific people. But the transition into the paragraph that begins "Poor rural whites" could be made smoother. The text jumps from a statement that record company executives shaped the music's identity to a discussion of the racial dynamics of poor rural white people.

blackface) minstrelsy had a profound influence on country music. Malone argues that minstrel songs, like "Old Zip Coon," "Away Down on the Old Plantation," and "Dixie" (Malone 1993) "lost their original 'Negro' connotations as they became part of the repertoire of country music" (Malone 2002). Prominent country singers like Jimmie Rodgers, Bob Wills, and Roy Acuff even worked as blackface performers early in their career (Tosches 1985). In fact, in 1953, the year before the landmark desegregation of public schools, the Grand Ole Opry's number-one tent show starred Jamup and Honey, two blackface performers (Malone 1993).

Blues and jazz, decidedly African American musical forms, have also had a penetrable influence on country music. Many major white country music performers were influenced and inspired by black blues and jazz musicians and their instruments. Richard A. Peterson, a prominent country music scholar, points out that although Jimmie Rodgers (Malone 1968) has a clearly white Southern twang, blues and jazz dominate in his music (Peterson 1997). The fiddle and the banjo, landmark instruments of rural white Southern music, were actually used by Southern blacks before being taken up by Southern whites (Malone 1968). In fact, white country performers have commonly used the phrase "nigger picking" to refer to the most complex guitar styles in country music (Malone 1968). As Malone (1968) points out, "[a]lthough Negro songs and styles have moved freely into white country music, Negroes have not" (p. 27). Paradoxically, black influence has been completely ignored in the "pure" white genre of country music, even by country artists who were inspired by black musicians. The Country Music Hall of Fame and Museum in Nashville fails to acknowledge any of the black performers who originated the style for which many early white country stars were famous (Peterson 1992). Country music has co-opted black musical forms and disseminated them as "purely white."

Connotations of country music as a white genre are not accidental. In *Creating Country Music: Fabricating Authenticity,* Peterson (1997) details the deliberate separation of white and black music in the South, as a strategic decision by record company executives. Industry competition led to segregated markets for country music. In the 1920's, Okey Record Company specifically marketed country music to poor whites. The opposite of "hillbilly music" was "race music," the wide range of music created by

3

Although Mayank has been careful with her citations, here she forgets to include the page number for this quote.

The discussion of the movement of country music from rural areas into cities seems to jump ahead of the story. If Mayank had thought about the major point of the two paragraphs on this page, she might have realized the transition was a bit awkward. Even though the last sentence of the paragraph that ends "a venue of expression for poor white identity" and the first sentence of the next paragraph seem to flow smoothly, the overall theme of the two paragraphs could be more logical.

and marketed to blacks (Green 1965). Country music did not accidentally or coincidentally evolve into a white genre; it was deliberately crafted and institutionalized as an assertion of (rural) white identity.

Poor rural whites have historically suffered class oppression at the hands of upper middle class whites. Because of this oppression, poor whites (including European immigrants) have repeatedly appealed to claims of whiteness to elevate their condition and avoid being equated with blacks. Eighteenth century rural songs, including "I'd rather be a nigger an' plow ol' Beack,/Dan a white hill-billy wid a long red neck" and "Oh poor olde hillbilly, oh, where do you stand,/while the Dark Tobacco Planters Association is forming its clan?" illustrate the fear of poor whites (Green 1965). This attitude continued into the twentieth century. The lyrics of Merle Haggard's song "I'm a White Boy," written in 1975, say "I'm proud and white. Daddy's name wasn't Willie Woodrow; I wasn't born in no ghetto" (Tosches 1985). After the Civil War, poor whites felt threatened by newfound black freedom (Peterson 1992). Minstrel shows, says whiteness scholar David Wellman (1997), "reassured white men who they were not: not black, not slave, not gay" (p. 312). Rural whites had a personal, social, and political interest in distancing themselves from blacks and identifying as white (Roediger 1994). Country music provided a vehicle for defending this interest. In asserting their whiteness, poor rural whites maintained a sense of working class pride. Throughout time, country music has reflected white working class woes. From sharecroppers to factory workers to truck drivers, country music has provided a venue of expression for poor white identity (Peterson 1991).

Country music originated in a region rooted in a rural economy and rural identity. The inherently conservative rural nature of country music protects white identity in the face of urban threats. Country music was constructed and marketed as a rural (white) music opposite urban (black) genres of blues and jazz. The rural nature of country music has adapted, retaining its increasing urbanization. Where rural people and cowboys once dominated the country music scene, truck drivers, or "eighteen-wheel cowboys" (Gregory 1989:242) epitomize the modern country music man. "Rural music did not die when it moved into the cities; it merely adapted itself to changed conditions." Rural settings symbolize "pure,"

4

When Mayank quotes journalist Bruce Feiler, she makes a point of explaining that he wrote in the *New York Times*. Is identifying the *New York Times* useful for the reader to understand the point of the quotation? Possibly, because the *New York Times* is a national newspaper and reflects a journalist's opinion for a national audience. But a journalist usually is not as credible a source of evidence as a scholar, for example, David Wellman, the whiteness scholar quoted in the previous paragraph. Moreover, the citation should say "(as cited in Ware and Back 1992:266)" so that the reader does not think that Ware and Back are the authors of this quotation.

The paragraph above about the Southern heritage would have fit better before she began to talk about the shift from rural to urban contexts. Also, because she has already described her main thesis as paradoxical, using "paradoxically" again to describe a secondary point of the paper weakens the effect. But the larger point is effective. Here she is elaborating on the theme introduced earlier that country music grew out of Southern white culture. Elaboration of a basic point is one of the more challenging tasks of writing this sort of paper. To get legitimate length without repeating yourself, ask and then answer the questions taught in journalism classes: "Who, Where, How, When, Why, Which, What?" This paragraph provides details answering the questions "How," "Which," and "Why": Q. How does country music present itself as quintessentially American? A. By presenting itself as anti-foreign. Q. Which songs illustrate this anti-foreign quality? A. Patriotic anti-Japanese and anti-commie songs. Q. Why do these songs illustrate this quality? A. They reflect poor whites' desires to enter mainstream white American society.

wholesome white identity, while urban settings represent change, moral degeneration, and the infestation of non-whites. In fact, Bruce Feiler wrote in a New York Times article, "[Country music] has become the de facto sound track of white flight" (Ware and Back 1992:266). In a nation moving towards urbanization, country music has glorified rural arrested development, and consequently, preservation of white purity (Malone 1968).

Country music represents the ideology of the white South—an ideology rooted in slavery and segregation. Southern pride continues to be a strong force in country music. For example, "most country music continues to be produced in Nashville, the capital city of a former Confederate state" (McLaurin 1992:24). Country songs throughout time repeatedly allude to a sense of place, often mentioning names of specific Southern towns, cities, and states. Historian Tom Connely calls country music "The great modern expression of the Lost Cause mentality" (McLaurin 1992:15). "Lost Cause mentality" implies that white Southerners have an inferiority complex, due to the defeat of the Confederate army, and continue to hold a renewed sense of pride in the (Confederate) South. Country music is, hence, a manifestation of this renewed white Southern pride.

Paradoxically, country music is intensely patriotic, given that Southerners once wanted to secede from the Union (McLaurin 1992). In fact, Southern pride in the courage of Confederate fighters lends itself well to a virulent American patriotism (McLaurin 1992). The dualism inherent in country music has easily translated into pro-American sentiment. In repeatedly presenting itself as the quintessential American genre, country music is anti-foreign. During World War II, a good number of patriotic country songs contained a "get the dirty little Jap" type of racism. Similarly, in the era of McCarthy and the Cold War, patriotic, anti-commie songs were popular, including, "They Locked God Outside the Iron Curtain," "The Red That We Want is the Red We've Got in the Old Red, White, and Blue," and "Korea, Here We Come" (DiMaggio, Peterson, and Esco 1972:45). The strongly anti-foreign, patriotic nature of country music reflects poor whites' desires to enter mainstream white American society. As McLaurin notes, "Since the Civil War and Reconstruction, Southerners have struggled to remove the stigma and prove themselves truly loyal Americans" (McLaurin 1992:28).

Like much recent sociological writing, here she is introducing gender dynamics to complement the analysis of race. Yet this paragraph is too brief to be very convincing. The sentence "Masculine obligation to the family is not simply a personal, but a *racial* obligation" is an excellent insight but needs more evidence than provided here. This is one of the tough decisions that writers must face—to make an important point that skeptical readers may not swallow, to add even more to a fairly long paper, or to omit a point that most readers would not miss if it were not included. There is no correct answer that everyone would agree on. She then returns to the theme of gender at the bottom of the page.

Note how Mayank provides a smooth transition from the end of this paragraph to the beginning of the next paragraph, echoing the concepts in each (". . . national image of country as an authentic, purely white genre" and "The 'pure' white image of country music").

Mayank should have included the page number for this quote.

White patriarchy is a central focus of country music. Country music constructs white masculinity as the "gendered and racialized obligation to paternal protection of the white family" (Lipsitz 1998:75). Implicit in Southern notions of white masculinity is an obsession with the protection of white womanhood. Historically, white Southerners have viewed white women as innocent and vulnerable to the predatory tendencies of black men. Masculine obligation to the family is not simply a personal, but a *racial* obligation. As a product of a region where white womanhood is sanctified, country music is racially patriarchal.

Epitomized as a "pure" and "authentic" white form, country music has been widely used by white supremacist groups. A well-distributed 1925 poster of famous fiddler John Carson shows Carson standing in front of a KKK sign, at the Mountain City, Tennessee Old Time Fiddling Contest, sponsored by the KKK (Peterson 1997). During the Korean War, white supremacist groups distributed underground racist country recordings, like "Move Them Niggers North," "Kajun Klu Klux Klan," and "Nigger, Nigger," by the Coon Hunters, which talked about tarring and feathering Martin Luther King Jr. (Malone 1968). Some of these recordings were sold over the counter at an Atlanta F. W. Woolworth until 1967 (Peterson 1992). The appeal of country music to white supremacist groups was due to the national image of country as an authentic, purely white genre.

The "pure" white image of country music developed as the nation became interested in finding and reclaiming a pure, untainted white male identity. This search for an authentic white identity propagated the "widely shared belief that the Appalachia preserved the nation's genes, culture and values of the original white settlers" (Campbell 1999). The nation was obsessed with recovering untainted "Anglo-Saxon" roots and the Appalachia seemed like a treasure-chest. There was a widely-held belief that the West was America's last frontier. This fear of the vanishing frontier coincided with a fear of the feminization and weakening of the pure, rugged, individualistic white man (Slotkin 1992). Hence, began the nation's glorification of the American cowboy.

Rugged, courageous, violent, and white, the singing cowboy became an American idol and sex symbol. Hollywood played a crucial role in the romanticization of America's cowboy past and the national popularization of

6

Once again, it is important to include page numbers for any quote.

Having discussed race and gender, the paper now addresses class. Many readers would have appreciated an explicit signpost that reflected the order and movement of major ideas in her outline. A clear signal phrase or transitional sentence would have helped the reader understand that the paper is now going to talk about class, perhaps a statement like "This rugged white Western singing cowboy, like his fans, is a marginalized member of a distinctive poor white culture."

country music (Malone 1968). America's most famous singing cowboy, Gene Autry, symbolized white America's obsession with reclaiming what it perceived as vanishing white male hegemony and red-blooded Americanism (Horsman 1997). As Gavin James Campbell notes in his dissertation, "The perceived loss of mastery over African Americans, women, lower class whites, and the fear that urban life had feminized white men to the point of helplessness . . . made both the mountaineer and the old-time fiddler more attractive than ever" (Campbell 1999). Nineteenth-century complications of race-relations propagated the nation's nostalgia for simpler times in a "racially-pure mountain South in which blacks simply vanished" (Campbell 1999). The theme of "ethnic pluralism" in the 1960's gave whites further permission to glorify and romanticize our white Western cowboy past (Gregory 1989). Country singers gladly accepted and played into stereotypes of the rugged singing cowboy (Malone 1993).

Country music's current conservative, right-wing leanings are ironic, given the initial populist leanings of the genre (Malone 2002). The "hillbilly" was once the white counterpart of the black "sambo" (Peterson 1992). The development of a distinct poor white culture was in fact prompted by marginalization. Shunned by mainstream white society, poor Southern whites clustered in neighborhoods and developed and maintained a distinct identity and culture (McLaurin 1992). With its strongly conservative leanings, country music continued to express the concerns of the urban white working man through the 1970's and 1980's. Johnny Paycheck's "Take This Job and Shove It!" gained popularity in the early 1970's, while Dolly Parton's "9 to 5" described working class concerns of the 1980's. Today, a major theme in country music is the working truck driver (Peterson 1992).

Country music swung towards the right when folk music broke away from the genre. Country music, as the music of the "common man," was at some point used by left-wing radicals and reformers to challenge capitalism (Malone 1968). Consequently, urban folk music broke off from country music. While country music is inherently conservative and sought to preserve the status quo, folk music advocated change and criticized the status quo. As Jennifer Lawler astutely points out, "folk and country had the same heritage . . . the split was political." While the music remained similar the message was radically different, to the point where "soon fans of one

Mayank's paper is well organized. The beginning of almost every paragraph tracks a new main idea that is then developed with explanation and examples.

Note the use of ellipses (. . .) to indicate one or more words deleted from a quotation. For more information about the use of ellipses, see Chapter 3.

Stating that Jimmy Carter, a democrat, also liked country music weakens Mayank's argument that only right-wing politicians supported this music genre.

could not very easily be fans of the other" (Lawler 1996:23). Folk music has a strong protest element, while anti-protest themes pervade country music. While folk represented left-wing progressives, country came to represent right-wing conservatives.

From the 1960's, country music and the neo-conservative right-wing had a mutually reinforcing relationship. Right-wing politicians adopted country music for political ends, and country artists willingly catered to the right-wing to bolster their popularity. Gregory interestingly notes, "northern blue-collar constituencies which thirty years before had been at the very heart of New Deal liberalism were changing political coloration . . . Threatened by the civil rights agenda of liberal democrats...they were moving towards a politics of racial and patriotic conservatism" (Gregory 1989:242). Racist Alabama governor George Wallace adopted country music to the point where every Wallace rally incorporated country music (Malone 2002). Wallace's overwhelming appeal to the country music community reflects the genre's interest in protecting white privilege. Threatened by the counterculture of the 1960's, right-wing politicians gained an even broader conservative following by the 1970's. Richard Nixon called Merle Haggard's conservative song, "Okie from Muskogee," the "true voice of the silent American majority" (McLaurin 1992). Jimmy Carter publicly showed an affinity for country. Both Ronald Reagan and George Bush used Lee Greewood's popular "God Bless the U.S.A." in their second presidential campaigns (Ellison 1995). In the late 1980's, George Bush proclaimed country music to be his favorite (Malone 2002). In fact, Naomi Judd and Tanya Tucker performed at the Republican convention where Bush was nominated. Late in the campaign, Bush sprinkled campaign speeches with phrases from country song lyrics.

The new right's objective was to dismantle political gains of the Civil Rights movement. Since it could not explicitly reverse these gains, it had to rearticulate their goals in the context of asserting a positive white identity and wholesome American values, like "defense of traditional values, opposition to 'big government' and patriotic, [religious] and militaristic themes" (Omi and Winant 1944:124). The close relationship between a neo-conservative agenda and the country music community, although paradoxical, is not difficult to see. The values that the new right defended

8

One of the methodological challenges of interpretive analysis is how to make a case that a cultural form connotes a meaning when there is no explicit reference. Here Mayank makes a case that country music expresses a white identity even though it never mentions whiteness. This is the conclusion her paper has been building up to, so the discussion on page 109 is becoming more abstract, relating to the broader social dynamics of how race works. And here she offers her own opinion more explicitly. The reader would have intuited her general attitude toward the white identity in country music, but at the end of this paragraph she says outright that "Country music, as a symbol of an authentic white America, has troubling implications for our nation's future."

Note the punctuation in this paragraph for the two main ways of integrating quotations correctly into a sentence:

1. a phrase with a signal verb plus comma: As Richard Dyer astutely notes, "White power . . ."
2. a signal verb with a "that" clause and no comma: Ian Haney-Lopez explains that "celebrating whiteness . . ."

aligned almost perfectly with the country music community, and both groups had a strong interest in reinforcing the existing racial hierarchy. As Malone (1998) suggests, "the national mood of conservatism may have inspired a rediscovery of the mythic South as a region of contentment, stability, and bucolic values" (p. 117).

Although country music reinforces white identity, it manages to do so without explicit references to white racial identity. Ironically, in a genre shaped by race relations, explicit mentions of race are virtually absent in country music. Country music is not called "white" music, but it is called purely and authentically "American." As Richard Dyer astutely notes, "White power secures its dominance by seeming not to be anything in particular" (Lipsitz, 1998:1). Transparency is a key component of white power. Transparency allows white identity to be neutral, universal identity, when it is really white identity. However, "the assumption that white people are just people, which is not far off from saying that white people are people whereas other colors are something else" (Dyer 1997:2). Country music's assertion of *white* American identity is unnecessarily redundant, since "American" is generally short for "white American." The assertion of a white identity can be problematic, even in the midst of ethnic pluralism. Ian Haney-Lopez (1992) explains that "celebrating whiteness even with the best of antiracist intentions, seems likely only to entrench the status quo of racial beliefs" (p. 72). Country music, as a symbol of an authentic white America, has troubling implications for our nation's future.

Once the "language of a subculture" (Gregory 1989), country music has penetrated the mainstream. The proliferation of country artists in popular American culture continues to intensify. Country performers, like LeAnn Rimes, Shania Twain, and Faith Hill have enormous success crossing over into popular music, while retaining loyal country followers. Country music has transformed from the music of "plainfolk Americanism" (Gregory 1989) into the music of mainstream materialism. The positive aspect of the mainstreaming of country music is that it brings a more diverse audience to the genre. The aforementioned artists have a larger proportion of non-white fans than artists before them. Played repeatedly on mainstream popular radio stations, people of color have been exposed and warmed up to country music. The negative facet of country mainstreaming is that it popularizes a

9

Here she qualifies her indictment of country music, noting there are voices of dissent from within country music, adding a measure of optimism to an otherwise highly critical paper.

"Finally" is a helpful signpost to the end of a list. Mayank uses many skillful transitional expressions throughout her paper, for example, "consequently," "however," "in fact."

genre, reinforcing white identity. "In the video age country and western has become the last oasis of white American values" (Ware and Back 1992:266). Country mainstreaming may imply the further mainstreaming of white identity.

Despite the strong correlation between country music and whiteness, several popular country music artists have been able to criticize and push the boundaries of the genre. Johnny Cash, who has recorded over a thousand country songs since 1955, has publicly defended the rights of convicts, Native Americans, illiterate people, and people of color. To show his identification with marginalized people, Cash almost always appeared wearing black (Danker 1992). In his song, "Man in Black," he says he "will wear black until the world is in better shape and he can wear colors" (Lawler 1996:140). Cash's popular "Six White Horses" describes his grief over the killings of Jesus, the Kennedy brothers, and Martin Luther King Jr. (DiMaggio, Peterson, and Esco 1972). Lawler (1996) points out that he "managed to appeal to the rugged individualism dear to the country music fan's heart, as well as maintain a sense of justice and compassion that led him to protest many conditions and situations in America" (p. 140).

Garth Brooks, one of the most popular modern country performers, has spoken explicitly about the environment, domestic violence, famine, civil rights, date rape, and LGBT issues. He has managed to redefine conservative country music ideology, without abandoning the country community. He once said,

> "I think the Republicans' big problem is that they believe family values are June and Walt and 2.3 children. To me it means laughing, being able to dream . . . if a set of parents are black and white, or two people of the same sex, or if one man or one woman acts as the parents, that the children grow up happy and healthy: that's what family values are" (Ellison 1995:259).

The statement sums up Brooks' challenge to traditional, white, patriarchal, and heterosexist country music values. He has managed to extend the boundaries of country music, without abandoning the genre all together.

Finally, k. d. lang, the first publicly lesbian country music star, poses the largest challenge to country music. Although she has not been

She finishes with a summary. Most instructors would probably prefer a fuller recap, reviewing the general points she made throughout.

widely accepted by conventional country fans, her presence and in-your-face image force country music to confront and question its conservative nature. She challenged country music ideas about white female performers in the genre. Lang has, in fact, acknowledged that country music is a white genre that alienated many people of color. Rather than being a puppet to the country music community, lang has redefined country music. For example, she once taped a PETA promotional spot saying, "meat stinks, and if you knew how meat was made, you'd probably lose your lunch," to the chagrin of country fans in cattle country. Although she directly challenged the conservative nature of country music, her confrontational approach has alienated the traditional country music audience (Lawler 1996:69-70).

Country music is white noise, literally. In this paper, I have outlined the social, political, and economic relationship between country music and white identity. Country music is music for and by white people. Massive societal upheaval and progress in the past century has been unable to penetrate country music, keeping the genre, its performers and its audience exclusively white. Country music is white noise, figuratively. Whiteness is omnipresent, but never explicit, in country music. It remains in the background, presenting itself as a race-free form, when it, in fact, reinforces white pride and existing racial hierarchies. As I stated earlier, I do not seek to vilify country music, nor do I advocate the complete annihilation of the genre. Rather, I encourage critical dialogue about country music's relationship to race, in hopes that further understanding will shape and open the future course of country music into a genre that truly represents the American people.

Mayank includes a Reference section in her paper as opposed to a Bibliography (see Chapter 3 for the difference). Following the guidelines in Chapter 3, she places the heading at the left-hand margin, types it in all capital letters, and triple-spaces between the heading and the first source listed. Consistent with the *ASA Style Guide* (2007), she starts the reference section on a new page and double-spaces the sources.

According to the *ASA Style Guide* (2007), with the exception of New York, both the city and the state of the publisher should be included.

Here Mayank includes the state but not the city of the source. Both the city and the state of the source should be included.

Both the volume number and the issue number should be included in the References for a journal article.

REFERENCES

Campbell, Gavin James. 1999. *Music and the Making of a Jim Crow Culture, 1900–1925*. Chapel Hill: University of North Carolina at Chapel Hill.

Ching, Barbara. 2001. *Wrong's What I Do Best: Hard Country Music and Contemporary Culture*. New York: Oxford University Press.

Danker, Frederick E. 1992. "The World According to Johnny Cash: Lyrical Themes in His Music." Pp. 131–154 in *You Wrote My Life: Lyrical Themes in Country Music,* edited by Melton A. McLaurin and Richard A. Peterson. Philadelphia: Gordon and Breach Science Publishers.

DiMaggio, Paul, Richard A. Peterson, and Jack Esco, Jr. 1972. "Country Music: Ballad of the Silent Majority." Pp. 38-55 in *The Sounds of Social Change: Studies in Popular Culture,* edited by R. Serge Denisoff and Richard A. Peterson. Chicago: Rand McNally & Co.

Dryer, Richard. 1997. "The Matter of Whiteness." Pp. 1–40 in *White*. New York: Routledge.

Ellison, Curtis W. 1995. *Country Music Culture: From Hard Times to Heaven*. Jackson: University Press of Mississippi.

Foley, Neil. 1997. *The White Scourge: Mexicans, Blacks, and Poor Whites in Texas Cotton Culture*. CA: University of California Press.

Green, Archie. 1965. "Hillbilly Music: Source and Symbol." *Journal of American Folklore* 78:204–28.

Gregory, James N. 1989. *American Exodus: The Dust Bowl Migration and Okie Culture in California*. New York: Oxford University Press.

Haney-Lopez, Ian. 1992. "White Race Consciousness." Pp. 155–195 in *White by Law: The Legal Construction of Race,* edited by Ian Haney Lopez. New York: New York University Press.

Horsman, Reginald. 1997. "Race and Manifest Destiny: The Origins of American Racial Anglo-Saxonism." Pp. 139–44 in *Critical White Studies: Looking Behind the Mirror,* edited by Richard Delgado and Jean Stefancie. Philadelphia: Temple University Press.

Lawler, Jennifer. 1996. *Songs of Life: The Meaning of Country Music*. Kansas: Pogo Press.

Lipsitz, George. 1998. *The Possessive Investment in Whiteness: How White People Profit From Identity Politics.* Philadelphia: Temple University Press.

Malone, Bill C. 1968. *Country Music U.S.A.* Austin: University of Texas Press.

Malone, Bill C. 2002. *Don't Get Above Your Raisin': Country Music and Southern Working Class.* Chicago: University of Illinois Press.

Malone, Bill C. 1998. "The Rural South Moves to the City: Country Music Since World War II." Pp. 95–121 in *The Rural South Since World War II,* edited by R. Douglas Hurt. Louisiana: Louisiana State University Press.

Malone, Bill C. 1993. *Singing Cowboys and Musical Mountaineers: Southern Culture and the Roots of Country Music.* Athens: University of Georgia Press.

[Note: To save space, only half of Mayank's references are reproduced here.]

The Textual Analysis (or Article Critique) Paper

You may be assigned a paper asking you to analyze a book or portion of a book—for example, Max Weber's *The Protestant Ethic and the Spirit of Capitalism* or Erving Goffman's *The Presentation of Self in Everyday Life*. We call this method "textual" analysis because the text itself, what the author wrote, provides your data. Your paper is *about* the text itself, not about the text's subject matter. For example, a textual analysis of Durkheim's *Suicide* might concern his theory of suicide or his use of statistical data to study suicide, not suicide itself. Your paper is an "analysis" because you take the author's work apart to examine the different components and then put them back together. This activity is called "explication"; a textual analysis explicates, or explains, what the author's main points are and how they are connected, and offers a critique of the author's argument. An analogy would be taking a car engine apart, explaining each part and how the parts work together, and evaluating whether the car is a good buy or a lemon.

Mastering the skill of explication will help you write better papers when a textual analysis is assigned. But, perhaps as important, this skill will help you evaluate more clearly all the books and articles you encounter in your academic career.

ARTICLE CRITIQUES

Students are often given assignments in which they are to critique a journal article or chapter rather than an entire book. The process of explicating or critiquing, which involves summarizing, analyzing, and evaluating, can be equally applied to articles (and chapters in edited books).

Critiquing is the same method your professor employs when she or he is asked to review an article submitted for publication. Before an article is published, high-quality journals send the article out for review by three specialists—or peers—in the field under study. This procedure is known as *peer review,* and hence journals that employ this system are designated *peer-reviewed journals* (see p. 79 in Chapter 4).

Moreover, article critiques are the building blocks of literature review sections of quantitative research papers (see Chapter 6) and of review articles. Review articles (such as those published in the *Annual Review of Sociology;* see p. 75 in Chapter 4) summarize, analyze, and evaluate whole bodies of literature on a topic rather than just a single article.

Thus, the valuable techniques described in this chapter can be applied not only to texts and individual journal articles but also to whole bodies of literature. Therefore, throughout this chapter, every time you come across the words "text" or "book," you could replace either with the word "article" and use the same techniques to write your article critique (or literature review).

ASKING QUESTIONS ABOUT THE TEXT

In textual analysis, the text is not only your data but also the source of your question. That is, your question will arise from the author's ideas and arguments presented in the text and from your analysis of them. Your question is a vehicle for conversing with the author about the thesis or argument of the work. This conversation should be conducted in an analytically critical manner, which means that to carry on your end you must raise questions about the logic of the argument, the type and credibility of the evidence, the soundness of the conclusion, and the fundamental assumptions on which the argument rests.

Your assignment may specify how you are to analyze a text, or the format may be left up to you. Here are three main areas generally addressed in a textual analysis:

1. SUMMARY

What is the author saying? This is the basic question in textual analysis. It involves considering the author's main point(s). In general, most people should agree on what the author is saying. Sometimes an instructor will assign a paper asking no more than this. He or she only wants students to demonstrate that they comprehend what the author is saying. But sometimes summary is not as easy as it seems. It requires seeing the forest and not just the trees, the entire book, not just the particular facts that are presented to support an argument. For example, Durkheim's *Suicide* is not just about the relationship between religious denominations and suicide; it is also about how social structure helps explain what is commonly considered the most private of individual acts, taking one's life.

To see the whole picture of a book, study carefully any preface, introduction, or conclusion and the first and last chapters of a book. Read through and think about the table of contents. What is the point of having the chapters organized the way they are? Why do the first chapters come first? Read through the section headings of the entire book. They usually give important clues about what the author thinks is important. They are like signposts along a highway that tell you the cities you are going through.

How does this author deal with one important sociological concept or issue in this text? Rather than analyzing all the ideas that the author presents, in this approach you focus in depth on one significant aspect of the text. If you are reading Talcott Parsons's book on the *Evolution of Societies*, for example, you might ask how Parsons views modern society. In that case, your questions would include: "How does Parsons define 'modern society'? Why, in light of the overall purpose of the book, does he discuss modern society? What evidence does he use to support his claims about it?"

2. ANALYSIS

Analysis involves going beyond what the author says. It means looking at relationships: relationships between evidence and conclusions, relationships between concepts in the text, and relationships between the concepts in the work being analyzed and other texts.

What devices does the author use to convince the reader that he or she is correct? One of the general skills students should learn in college is to analyze the devices that authors—all authors, not just sociologists or academic writers—use to convince a reader. All of these have their place in writing, but all can be misused. The key here is to learn to identify what an author is doing to persuade the reader to his or her conclusions.

Logical reasoning. The most common form of logical reasoning is the syllogism (an *if . . . then* statement). Here the author seeks to convince you that there is a logical connection between something you already believe and something he or she wants you to believe. For example, Durkheim essentially argues that if social groups have an effect on whether a person feels a moral wholeness and if moral wholeness influences whether a person might commit suicide, then there must be a relationship between social groups and suicide. Logical reasoning can also take the form of an analogy, in which something the author wants you to understand in a certain way is compared to something you are familiar with. For example, Durkheim argues that suicide is a form of deviance, just as crime is a form of deviance. Both stem from a sense of normlessness or "anomie." There are many other logical devices that authors use, but they all have in common that the authors' arguments *make sense.* They are *logical.*

Anecdote. Anecdotes are little stories used to illustrate a point. They are especially common in journalistic accounts. A journalistic account of crime would begin with a story about a particular criminal or crime victim, with the unstated assumption that this story is representative of all criminals or victims. A single statistic can be used anecdotally to add credence to a paper. Anecdotes can make a paper "come alive" and hold the reader's interest, but do not substitute for systematic evidence.

Appeal to authority. It is quite common to show that someone the reader respects agrees with the author's perspective. This can be either an "expert," whose knowledge of a subject qualifies him or her for respect, or an elite, whose social status or position makes the person believable.

Controlled study. This type of book is intended to answer a very specific and empirically verifiable question, such as "Are Catholics less likely to commit suicide than Protestants?" A study designed according to the rules of the scientific method is conducted for this purpose. Durkheim rests his case on a controlled study comparing suicide rates in Protestant and Catholic areas of Europe.

Rhetorical virtuosity. This includes a number of devices that can be employed to convince a reader by way of the writer's skill at using language. A well-turned phrase or metaphor may sound poetic due to its selection of words (for example, baby boom, sensuous sixties, animal rights, or law and order). Scientific jargon can give unscientific ideas the sound of authority. Big words or convoluted sentences can make the author sound intelligent and knowledgeable. Humor, satire, or irony can be used to make opposing views sound ridiculous.

What is important is that the student understand what the author is doing, to be able to analyze the devices being used.

3. EVALUATION

How well does the author answer his or her question and verify that answer? This is the realm of criticism (both positive and negative). It logically comes last. You can't really judge a text until you fully comprehend what the author is doing and how he or she does it. Evaluation is also the most subjective stage. While an instructor can grade how well you summarize or analyze a work, what you think of the work is your personal opinion. There may be disagreements about evaluation, but ultimately your opinions are your own. However, the line between analysis and evaluation is sometimes fuzzy, and an instructor may legitimately fault you for basing your evaluation on inaccurate summary or sloppy analysis. Instructors also have different tastes concerning how much evaluation they want. Some want students to express their opinions about a text, others just want summary and/or analysis. Evaluation involves asking the following questions:

Is the argument of the text clear? Is it clear what question the text is attempting to answer? Are the definitions precise and unambiguous? Are the concepts appropriate to the questions addressed? Are the conclusions explicitly presented or scattered throughout? This dimension of evaluation concerns the summary. If the summary is easy to do, the text rates high on this criterion.

Does the author make valid assumptions? Identifying and evaluating an author's assumptions are two of the intellectual skills often demanded in sociological theory classes. Authors necessarily make assumptions about the way the world works. For example, some theories assume that human beings act primarily on the basis of material self-interest, whereas others assume that people are motivated by the need for social approval. Some theories treat society as the aggregation of individuals, assuming that all social behavior should be reduced to individual behavior. Others assume that there are factors such as social class that can only be understood at the given level of society. Evaluating such assumptions means identifying the author's assumptions to see how plausible they are.

How well does the text use evidence? Is the evidence adequate to the conclusions? If the text is based on a specific study, how well was the study performed? If the evidence is less systematic, does it seem to be fairly drawn or carefully selected to favor the author's point of view? This is an area where many beginning students feel ill equipped because they have not been thoroughly trained in methods and may feel they don't know enough about a topic to gauge whether or not the evidence is selective. Some instructors, while admitting such limitations, encourage students to make a stab at this type of evaluation. Most students should have some sense of whether the evidence presented adequately supports the conclusion. One can ask, "Even if this evidence is true, does the author's conclusion necessarily follow?" You will find that the answer is often "no."

Are the conclusions and implications supported by other works? There are times when we assume that other works have validity and therefore we compare the text being studied to other works. This is especially common where certain works have achieved a sort of "orthodoxy," at least in the view of some sociologists. One might ask, for example, whether a work by a contemporary writer on deviance legitimately qualifies as a Durkheimian analysis.

Is the craftsmanship of the writing sound? Do the parts fit into a whole? Is the prose understandable? Do the ideas flow smoothly from one to another? Craftsmanship is basically the theme of this book. If you were grading the text according to the criteria we have set forth as good writing, how would that text stand up?

It is important to repeat that different instructors have different tastes concerning how much evaluation they want and along what criteria. Some want you to basically stick to the text itself. Others want the text evaluated relative to other works. Some emphasize an evaluation of the logic, others of the evidence, and still others of the assumptions. Make sure you understand the instructor's preferences.

COMPARE–CONTRAST ASSIGNMENTS

If you are asked to compare and/or contrast two authors' works (or two works by the same author), you must start by identifying the common topic under consideration and use that as the basis for your question. How do these two works deal with an issue that is central to each?

Any or all of these three aspects—summary, analysis, and evaluation—may be relevant to the particular work you are considering. Before you decide which questions will form the basis of your paper, you must read the text—and you must read it in a special way. We recommend that you buy your own copy of the book you will be using, if it is affordable. You will then be able to mark it up.

HOW TO READ THE TEXT

Before developing your question, get to know the text. As you read, keep in mind three general tasks. First, you must *identify the main points* that are explicitly presented as parts of the argument. Second, you must *identify the author's hidden assumptions*—that is, what she or he takes for granted about how the world works and does not question or bother to justify. These assumptions are like the principles of physics taken for granted in building an engine. Third, you must *evaluate* the text, asking, for example, in what ways the argument is not convincing. What are its problems? How could it be better? Evaluating the argument is like diagnosing which of a car's engine parts do not work and how they could work, or arguing that the whole thing should be junked and stating why.

In other words, as you read you must ask yourself and ask the text the same sorts of questions that you will address in your paper. Following is a more detailed description of the close reading required for textual analysis.

GETTING TO KNOW SOMETHING ABOUT THE TEXT

Here are some things you must find out in order to become acquainted with the text:

Who is the author? What is her or his background? This information is sometimes included in the introduction to the book. If there is no biographical information in the introduction, or if the information is insufficient to give you a picture of the author, there are resources you can use to find out the information.

The *Biography and Genealogy Master Index* contains a list of authors' names, followed by a list of references in which you will find biographical information. The reference book titles are abbreviated; consult the front of the book for the complete titles.

Information on well-known authors—for example, the founders of the discipline—might also be found in the *Encyclopaedia Britannica, Encyclopedia Americana,* or *International Encyclopedia of Social and Behavioral Sciences.*

When was the text written? What was the social climate of the period? To determine when the text was written, look at the copyright date in the front of the book. If you find more than one date, the first one indicates the date of the original printing or first edition. To determine the historical period in which the text was written, look first to your introduction. If this does not provide adequate information, you can use the preceding sources, paying particular attention to the historical information given in entries on the author or the countries where the author lived.

What is the polemical context? That is, where is the text located in the ongoing debate on the question? To whom is the author responding? Sometimes the text will reveal the polemical context by explicitly contrasting the author's argument with other perspectives. This information may be found either in the body of the text or in the preface or introduction. Sometimes it requires reading between the lines, paying attention to how the author refers to other works—for example, by drawing contrasts between her or his position and that of others. If the polemical context is not obvious, look for other books or journal articles about the author or the subject of the text. Often scholars write critiques or commentaries on others' work, especially if it is considered controversial or exemplary. This literature can be found in the library or in their electronic databases. (See Chapter 4 for guidelines about specific references.) Remember, the reference librarian can help you locate sources to help you get the information you need to write your paper.

READING TWICE

Read the text twice, for different purposes.

First, read for the big picture—get a feel for the text's organization and content. The author has major points that you are looking for. These major points, in turn, are supported by minor points. Pay special attention to the author's introduction, often called a preface, or to a foreword, written by an expert in the field.

After you have completed this preliminary reading, focus on the kind of question you will be addressing in your paper. If your instructor has specified a question, now is the time to consider it carefully. Be sure you understand what information to provide, how deeply to analyze the work, and how much of your own opinion to give. If the assignment is more general, look back over the categories of questions we listed earlier and decide which approach you will take: Will you analyze the text as a whole? Would you rather focus on a particular concept or aspect of the argument? Or should you compare this work to another one?

With your question in mind, read the text very closely the second time through; this reading forms the core of your "data collection." Your goal is to understand the interconnected points that constitute the author's argument and to record these important points. Notetaking during this second reading is an important step toward writing your paper. We will deal with it in detail later in the chapter.

What are you looking for in this detailed reading? Look for the author's argument—that is, the question the author is trying to answer and the evidence she or he uses to answer it. The following questions will assist you in identifying the text's argument; that is, the author's main points and the assumptions hidden beneath them:

- ✦ What is the author's question? For example, in *Suicide*, Durkheim asks, "What are the social factors that help explain suicide?"
- ✦ What is the author's answer—that is, what provides the core of the argument? What answers have other scholars given? Durkheim argues that the degree of social solidarity within groups that people belong to affects how likely they are to commit suicide. Protestants were more likely than Catholics to commit suicide (when Durkheim lived) because Protestantism provided less social solidarity than Catholicism. He was trying to demonstrate that psychological explanations that emphasized individual pathology were not sufficient.
- ✦ What evidence does the author offer to support this answer? Is the evidence logical or empirical or both? Does the evidence actually support the argument?
- ✦ How does the author get from point A to point B? How do the main points that you identified in your reading relate to one another?
- ✦ What are the assumptions? What does the author take for granted, points without which the argument could not be made? Some examples of fundamental assumptions are that people have free will, that our social order constitutes the normal state of affairs, and that free enterprise benefits everyone.

As you engage in this second reading, you may want to adjust your question. If you planned on analyzing the text as a whole, for example, you may now discover that for this particular paper that task is too broad. If you attempt to explicate a work that is too comprehensive, your analysis may touch on a little bit of everything but fail to cover anything in depth; the result will be a weak analysis. Conversely, you may discover that it is not possible to discuss one concept without analyzing the text as a whole or to explain this text without comparing or contrasting it with another work. If your focus is too narrow, your analysis won't make sense. In any case, remember as you read to adjust the breadth of your questioning to the particular materials you wish to analyze.

TAKING NOTES

As C. Wright Mills explains in his appendix, "On Intellectual Craftsmanship," to *The Sociological Imagination* ([1959] 2000), "You will have to acquire the habit of taking a large volume of notes from any worth-while book you read" (p. 199). Taking notes is a personal skill that varies somewhat from student to student. Specific techniques include any or all of the following: writing notes on separate note cards or sheets of paper, writing in the margins of your own copy of the text or on the back of photocopied pages, attaching Post-it notes to specific passages in the text, or writing notes in word-processed files opened up for that specific purpose.

Regardless of where they are physically recorded, carefully taken notes provide two benefits. As Mills explains, "the mere taking of a note from a book is often a prod to reflection. At the same time, of course, the taking of a note is a great aid in comprehending what you are reading" (p. 199). The first kind of note, what Mills calls "a prod to reflection," can take the form of annotations: definitions, cross-references, examples, questions, or other ideas that are triggered in your mind as you read. It is your part of the dialogue you are having with the author.

In the second kind of note, according to Mills, "you try to grasp the structure of the writer's argument" (p. 199). This second kind of note is more objective. It is a systematic restatement of all or part of the author's argument. This summarizing kind of note outlines the author's main points and the interrelationships between the points and the evidence on which they are based. In general, you should paraphrase the author's original words rather than quote them. You should quote only in a few special instances (see Chapter 3).

When you want to use the author's exact words, be sure to mark them as a quotation in your notes so that you will properly cite the source in your paper. You must also document paraphrases (see Chapter 3).

ORGANIZING YOUR PAPER

Once you have read the text carefully and made notes on the most revealing passages, the next step is to outline your analysis and plan how to present it. The essay format is more suitable than the journal format for textual analysis (see "Developing an Argument: Logic and Structure" in Chapter 1). Within the basic format there are a number of ways in which you can organize your paper. Here are three basic outline patterns you can use or modify:

I. *Organize the body of your paper into three main parts corresponding to the three main tasks involved in explication:*
    1. Summary: Your description of what the author is saying; the author's main points.
    2. Analysis: Your explanation of what is behind the author's argument; for example, the polemical context or debate being addressed, the author's hidden assumptions, the author's evidence, implications of the author's points.
    3. Evaluation: Your assessment of the strengths and weaknesses of the author's argument (How well do the main points fit together? How relevant is the evidence to the points being made? How convincing are the conclusions?).

II. *Organize the body of your paper into major points that assert what you believe is most important about the text:*
    1. In your introduction, identify the most important features and state your position. You might also want to state the positions of other scholars unless your assignment excludes the use of outside sources.
    2. In the second paragraph (or section, in a longer paper), summarize one main point you want the reader to know in order to accept your point of view and provide detailed evidence from the text to support this point.
    3. Do the same thing in the third and fourth paragraphs (or sections), presenting one more major point in each.
    4. In your conclusion, restate your claims and summarize your points supporting them.

III. *Organize your paper around comparing and contrasting:* There are two basic patterns you can follow to compare and contrast two works:

PATTERN I	PATTERN II
A (1st author)	1 (1st point)
1 (1st point)	A (1st author)
2 (2nd point)	B (2nd author)
3 (3rd point)	2 (2nd point)
B (2nd author)	A (1st author)
1 (1st point)	B (2nd author)
2 (2nd point)	3 (3rd point)
3 (3rd point)	A (1st author)
	B (2nd author)

WRITING YOUR TEXTUAL ANALYSIS

Generally, your goal is to answer in writing, in a logical and coherent way, the same questions you have been asking about the text as you read. A review of "Developing an Argument: Logic and Structure" (in Chapter 1) will help you in this task. A tip for developing a cohesive paper is to refer back to the questions you are answering as you write. They can serve as a guide in determining which information you need to make your point and which is extraneous. Keeping your key questions in mind as you write and revise will keep you from wandering. Remember to identify the author and text in your opening paragraph.

When writing a research paper, you must follow a special set of formal conventions for documentation. For textual analysis, however, it is usually sufficient to indicate only in the first reference the publication date of the text you are using. Thereafter you may document quotations with the author's name and appropriate page number. When referring to an idea or argument found more generally throughout the text, the author's name alone, included in one of your own sentences (for example, "Elias states . . ."), will suffice. See pages 53–55 for illustrations of these special citation formats. Consult your instructor for clarification and for her or his preference.

A SAMPLE STUDENT PAPER

Lysa Agundez's paper was written for a course in culture and personality. The text she chose to analyze is Norbert Elias's *The Civilizing Process*. It was an appropriate choice because Elias's goal is to show how individual psyches and actions take the same shape as the social structure in which they occur. We selected Lysa's paper not only because it illustrates a concise summary of a complex sociological work, but also because of its gritty and interesting subject.

Here Lysa attempts to show how Elias uses the sociological imagination to connect the most personal of experiences with large-scale social relations.

Lysa identified and designed her paper around two key issues in the text she analyzed. The format of her paper is, accordingly, a variation of the three-part essay format—in this case, a two-part format. Our comments on the pages facing the paper indicate how Lysa addressed the three questions we have recommended you consider in any textual analysis: What is the author saying (summary)? What devices does the author use to convince the reader that he or she is correct (analysis)? How well does the author answer his or her question and verify the answer (evaluation)?

Demonstrating a problem many students encounter, Lysa's summary is more complete than her analysis and evaluation. Follow both her well-written paper and our remarks to see the strengths of her work and how it could be made even better.

Because of the length of her paper, Lysa includes a title page (as suggested in Part 3); however, she should have included the date.

NORBERT ELIAS ON THE DEVELOPMENT OF CIVILIZATION
THROUGH REPRESSION OF INSTINCTS

Lysa Agundez
Sociology 134
Professor Heritage

"The nature of this essay" is a vague phrase, and its meaning is unclear. It would be more effective to say: "This essay will address the two most important aspects of Elias's work" or "I will address two important issues raised by Elias."

Note that Lysa plans to address only two issues. Nowhere is it carved in stone that the student *must* have three main points (unless, of course, the assignment specifically says so). Since Lysa has identified two truly key ideas, her paper will have enough substance.

The second paragraph begins Lysa's summary of the first point she intends to address. Her summary is longer and more complete than the analysis and evaluation sections that follow. Although this is a drawback to her paper, in the case of writing as complex as that of Elias, we give her credit just for being able to identify and describe his main points.

Lysa's paper should include a bibliography or reference page, including the publication information on both volumes. As you will see, this is a serious shortcoming of her paper.

While it is helpful to make it clear which ideas expressed are being attributed to Elias, it is a good idea to vary the form of attribution. The repetition of "Elias believes" in this paragraph could have been avoided by using "Elias argues," "Elias maintains," "Elias contends," or other phrases.

Lysa appropriately numbers the pages of her paper.

This paper will discuss the theories of Norbert Elias, who argues that the development of civilization involves a repression of instincts. The nature of this essay entails addressing two issues: (1) The stricter control of emotion and behavior developed following the Middle Ages; and (2) The relationship of shame and the structure of society. Then I will discuss Elias's distinctive contributions to investigation of the civilizing process.

Norbert Elias is a German sociologist, whose two-volume masterpiece is titled *The Civilizing Process.* The first volume, titled *The History of Manners,* is a complete presentation of basic attitude changes of European manners and morals. Examples include attitudes towards bodily functions, table manners, sexual behavior, and aggression. The second volume, titled *Power and Civility,* presents a thorough sociological analysis of the development of civilized behavior formed by the centralization of society.

The process of civilization, Elias believes, involved a progressively stricter control of emotion and habits of restraint which led to socially institutionalized frontiers of shame and emotional standards. Thus, the growth of civilization, Elias believes, involves the gradual intensification of instinctual repression over the centuries. In *The History of Manners,* Elias documents the gradual domestication of human affects and emotions from the Middle Ages to our days. His purpose is to show how the psychical make-up of modern men and women differs in significant ways from their ancestors. Compared to modern man, medieval people, Elias argues, were faced with few barriers to the acting out of affect, be that in the area of aggression, sex, at the dinner table, or in the bedroom.

To prove his point, Elias turns to various etiquette and manners books that have been steadily written and very widely read since the days of Erasmus of Rotterdam. Written mainly for members of European court society, these books exemplify right and wrong behavior. Systematically comparing their changing content over time, Elias takes them as guides to the changing life-styles and sense of propriety on the passing historical scene.

Many of the teachings of Erasmus's book of manners would be taken for granted by most children today. For example, medieval writers tell their readers in quest for refinements of manners that one should not gnaw a bone and then throw it back into the common dish, that diners should not

1

Lysa's use of these examples as evidence for her explication would be strengthened by citing their sources in Elias's text. In fact, with material as colorful as this, direct quotation would liven up the scholarly discussion and keep the reader's interest.

The quotation marks around "natural" are not necessary because the word is not being quoted or used ironically or in a special way.

Lysa does a good job of summarizing the advice offered in the etiquette books that serve as Elias's data. More direct quotations would provide the reader with a stronger sense of the materials he used to reach his conclusions.

It is acceptable to use language normally considered vulgar to describe a historical situation, especially if it is used in the text. Still, if it makes you uncomfortable, or you think it might offend your instructor, you can adopt a euphemism.

"Polite etiquette guides" is redundant, since etiquette by definition involves politeness. Never use two words when one will do!

wipe their nose on their hands or spit into the plate, nor poke in their mouth, nor scratch themselves while eating. These elementary rules were necessary for fifteenth-century feudal nobles, who, in fact, ate with their hands, threw bones to dogs gathered around the table, dipped their fingers in common dishes, and drank from a common goblet.

By the sixteenth century, however, the time of Erasmus, standards became gradually more demanding, and people more self-conscious of their public manners. As time went on, eating habits gradually became more refined. People began to use forks instead of searching with pieces of bread for chunks of meat in the common pot. They were taught that they should use their knives unobtrusively so as not to threaten their neighbors at the table.

Erasmus, in an effort to teach "civility" to the nobility and the aspiring bourgeoisie, did not limit his advice to table manners. With a lack of embarrassment that might seem gross to modern sensibilities, he attempted to teach his public the circumstances in which spitting, farting, urinating, or defecating in public might or might not be defensible.

Spitting, for instance, was a common "natural" bodily function in the Middle Ages. As a matter of fact, it was even considered a custom and was commonplace in the courts of feudal lords. The only major restriction imposed then was that "one should not spit on or over the table but under it" (I, p. 156). In the sixteenth century, people were provided with spittoons. And in our age, the "need" for spitting in public has been altogether abolished.

Farting in public also became prohibited over the civilizing process. In the Middle Ages, it was considered unhealthy to "hold back wind" (I, p. 130). It was better to be emitted with a noise than to be held back. Gradually, however, the feeling of embarrassment increased, and it was instructed to calm your body by farting only while covering the sounds with coughs, or, if one was in a holy place, to press your buttocks together. By the eighteenth century, farting, like spitting, was abolished.

People furthermore used to urinate and defecate in public, and polite etiquette guides simply taught their readers that one should avoid looking at people engaging in these activities. Even in the Palace of Versailles, people used to relieve themselves in corridors and on staircases. As a result, a

2

The contrast between the reader's stereotypical image of Versailles as a glamorous place and the graphic insight Lysa provides about the use of perfume stimulates a lot of reader interest.

In using "complementary movements," Lysa seems to be making a valiant effort to avoid repetitive use of "changes." Still, because "movement" implies a collective effort of some sort (particularly in sociology), it is somewhat confusing here.

In general, Lysa makes good use of the kinds of transitional words and phrases discussed in Chapter 2. In this case, "Moreover" indicates to the reader that what she reports in this paragraph is additional information relevant to what was discussed in the one preceding.

Did you catch "conceled" as a misspelling of "concealed"? Always proof your final draft for spelling errors, which detract from your presentation and make your ideas more difficult to follow. If you are using a word processor, a spelling check can be done electronically. See Part 3 for tips on correcting misspellings in your final draft.

Since "threshold of shame" is a special term that conveys one of Elias's key concepts, it would be good to define or explain it here, to be sure the reader knows what it means and how it is being used.

Note that, in contrast to the use of quotation marks around "natural" on page 135, their use with "primitive" and "civilized" are appropriate here, since Lysa is using the words to indicate certain analytical definitions of those terms.

This is where Lysa begins her summary of the second point she introduced in the opening paragraph. It is not covered as fully as the first one was.

huge consumption of perfume at the court was required to hide the offensive odors in the palace.

To Elias, these changes are not just curious: they indicate basic changes in the ways human beings perceive themselves and use their bodies in relation to those of others. People now began to mold themselves and others more self-consciously and deliberately than was the wont and use of the Middle Ages. Much of what we now consider "second nature" was the result of a century-long process of gradual domestication. As external restraint against personal emissions gave way to self-restraint, an "invisible wall" gradually grew up between one human body and another.

Elias also documents complementary movements involving sleeping habits and sexuality. Here, also, the public became distinguished from the private sphere. In medieval society it was quite normal for many people, even strangers, to spend the night in one room and even to share the same bed. Today, however, the bedroom has become privatized and separated from the rest of social life.

Moreover, in the Middle Ages it was customary for guests at a wedding to terminate the proceedings by undressing the bride and groom who were then obliged to consummate the marriage in the presence of the assembled company. By the late Middle Ages, the custom gradually changed to the extent that the couple was placed on the bed fully dressed. After this period, sexual life was conceled and dismissed behind the scenes altogether.

Elias argues that these examples of changes in sexual behavior, along with those illustrating changes in standards of self-restraint, mark the advance in the threshold of shame. Noting that restrictions of various kinds surround the elimination of natural functions in many societies, both "primitive" and "civilized," he concludes that the fears of natural elimination and the feeling of shame and repugnance in which it is expressed do not originate from a rational understanding of the origins of certain diseases, as one might think. Actually, our understanding of their dangers is attained only in the nineteenth century, at a very late stage in the civilizing process.

Elias argues that our feelings of distaste and shame are based on changes in the ways people live together in the structure of society. He

3

Because of this quotation's length, Lysa has appropriately indented and single-spaced the paragraph.

Here is a good example of why it is important to include full publication information for references: when we went to look for more information on this quotation (in this case, to check on correct punctuation), we could not find it on page 8 of our copy of the second volume. Perhaps it is because Lysa used a different edition than we have, but, since no publication information is provided, we cannot tell for sure.

When Lysa claims that Elias's thesis is "convincing," it sounds like she is ready to begin an evaluation of the text. However, she continues her summary without giving the reader any evidence of *why* she believes the thesis is convincing. See the following page for tips on how she might evaluate the text.

Again, Lysa has used quotation marks correctly here, since "courtoisie" is a foreign word. However, if you are using a word processor, you should italicize foreign words. (By the way, it might have been interesting if she had pointed out how it demonstrates the way the tips Erasmus provided became the basis for our idea of and word for "courtesy.")

But why does the phrase "invisible walls" also have quotation marks around it? If it is directly from Elias's work, there should be a citation for it.

By including the concept of "sociological imagination," Lysa is demonstrating her familiarity with basic sociological principles. However, she could apply the idea more fully here. "Sociological imagination" does not just mean using an imaginative approach to research. It involves relating individual experience to large-scale social structures and processes; Elias does this very well by connecting personal habits to the historical formation of a centralized political state.

discusses these changes in social structure at length in *Power and Civility,* in which he announces:

> . . . [T]he civilizing of conduct and the corresponding transformation of human consciousness and libidinal make-up cannot be understood without tracing the process of state formation, and within it the advancing centralization of society which first finds particularly visible expression in the absolute form of life. (II, p. 8)

Despite the cumbersome formulation, Elias's basic thesis is unexpectedly simple and convincing: as society became more centralized, individuals came into close contact and began to exercise greater self-constraint—"more affect control," in Elias's jargon.

For example, Elias believes feudal knights behaved like powerful and uninhibited children. These knights vigorously (and often violently) engaged in self-defense and self-gratification, clearly demonstrating minimal manners. "What was lacking," Elias observes of this impulsive personality, "was the invisible wall of affects which seems now to rise between one body and another, repelling and separating" (II, p. 256). The courtiers who congregated later in absolutist courts were far more careful types; relying now on central royal authority for physical protection, they vied (rarely violently) for influence and advancement. Consequently, the feudal knights increasingly had to regulate their behavior to secure protection and promotions.

Furthermore, crude feudal "courtoisie" was replaced by a more exacting code as courtiers strived to maintain their status, fending off the bourgeoisie below. The threshold of shame and embarrassment rose and rational forethought became a more important guide to conduct; bodily functions hidden, spontaneous impulses suppressed, and more elaborate proprieties established. Henceforth those "invisible walls" were everywhere, creating private selves who anxiously calculated their actions, thereby increasing self-control over passions and emotions.

Elias's ideas are similar to those of other authors, such as Sigmund Freud. So what makes for the distinctive contribution of this book? It is Elias's true leap of the sociological imagination when searching for data through which this process might be documented; his use of etiquette

4

To strengthen her paper, at this point Lysa could have begun an analysis of Elias's work, making clear the ways in which Elias goes about convincing the reader to accept his point of view. (He uses empirical data written during the time he's theorizing about.)

Lysa's evaluation of the text should follow her analysis. This is where she might tell the reader why she believes Elias's basic thesis is "convincing" (perhaps because the data are contemporaneous with social changes that are taking place in people's everyday lives). Alternatively, she might choose to criticize how Elias attempts to justify his argument. (She could, for example, question whether etiquette books, however "juicy" and graphic, are accurate representations of how people live: Would you consider "Dear Abby" books, one author's perspective on relations among those in a certain social class, reflective of *your* everyday life?)

Sometimes students neglect to include criticisms of work they are analyzing because they are afraid it will undermine the strengths pointed out in their papers. However, including Thomas's critique adds to Lysa's paper by showing she is aware of the intellectual discussion he has generated. Unfortunately, there is no citation for Thomas, so there is no way for the reader to judge his credibility or to further investigate his assessment of Elias.

Rather than expressing the author's personal feelings, the conclusion should bring the reader full circle by summarizing or drawing conclusions about the work being discussed or its significance.

manuals was very creative, and his research was very thorough. Even though his work was published forty years after it was written, it is not at all outdated. In fact, it is encompassing and stands complete today.

One might argue that Elias's focus is too narrow. Elias chose to focus only on the transformation of people from the Middle Ages to our times and has eschewed the occasion for a comparative treatment of the subject. As Keith Thomas (1978) has pointed out, Elias says next to nothing about the world of Graeco-Roman antiquity in which a similar process had surely taken place, even though the results of that process were largely lost during the Dark Ages. There is next to nothing in the book about other high civilizations, such as those of Asia, in which one can discern similar trends. But these are, after all, minor matters. One can hardly reproach an author who has given so much for not having written a world history of manners.

In conclusion, I was very happy that I got to work on such an interesting topic. I think one can learn from Elias's detailed method of research—looking in countless manners books and presenting the material the way things really happened and then giving a thorough sociological explanation of civilization.

5

The Quantitative Research Paper

In a quantitative paper, numerical data are collected to answer a sociological question. Because quantitative research depends on specific techniques of data collection and analysis, this chapter (unlike the previous three chapters) may be most useful to students who have taken or are taking an introductory research methods and an elementary statistics course.

Most quantitative papers are based on deductive reasoning—that is, the investigator, starting with a theory or with previous research, expects a certain answer to her or his research question. The investigator develops one or more hypotheses with the aim of predicting the results. However, some quantitative papers are based on inductive reasoning. The investigator, unsure of the answer but with some idea of what to look for, sets out to explore a particular topic. Here the purpose is description rather than prediction. No matter which approach is taken, the data collected can be represented numerically.

The sample quantitative research paper that appears at the end of this chapter illustrates both types of logic. The student writer, Shannon Prior, uses the deductive approach in examining: (1) the relationship between race/ethnicity and gender stereotyping, and (2) the relative frequency of the gender stereotype, *objectification*, vis-à-vis other forms. But she uses the inductive approach in examining which race/ethnic group will be stereotyped the most and in what way. Basing her expectation on previous research, Shannon anticipated that women from all race/ethnic groups would be portrayed stereotypically in magazine advertisements. She also estimated that the gender stereotype, *objectification*, would be the most common form for all three groups of women. However, her review of the literature did not suggest which racial/ethnic group would be gender-stereotyped most or which gender stereotype, other than *objectification*, would occur most frequently. Therefore, she was unable to make an educated guess as to the rate of occurrence of the six forms of gender stereotyping for each of the three groups of women.

Like most quantitative research papers, Shannon's is written in journal rather than essay format (see the section "Developing an Argument: Logic and Structure" in Chapter 1 for more information on these two formats) and is divided into four major sections, and within the Methods section, two to three minor subsections. Briefly, the issues that should be covered in each section and subsection of a quantitative research paper include:

1. **Review of the Literature.** After a review of the relevant theory and literature, what sociological question do you feel needs to be addressed? What, if any, expectations (hypotheses) do you have about the answer?
2. **Methods.**
   Sample. How did you select your sample?
   Measures. What measures did you use?
   Procedure. What method did you use in trying to answer your question?
3. **Results.** What patterns of numerical data did you find?
4. **Discussion.** Do the data support or refute your hypotheses? What do your data mean? How do they relate to theory and/or previous empirical research?

Although the length of the four major sections is about equal for published papers utilizing sophisticated methods and analyses, the introduction and discussion sections for student papers are generally slightly longer than the other two sections. However, the relative length of the sections will depend on the amount of detail required by your instructor for describing your methods and results. With the exception of the Review of the Literature, which requires no heading, you should identify the other major and minor sections with a heading. The major headings should be in all capital letters, left-justified, and bolded; the minor headings should be left-justified and italicized and have only the first letter capitalized. In addition to these major sections and subsections, other important components of your paper include the title, abstract, references, and appendix (which are discussed later in the chapter).

Since journal styles vary, ask your instructor which professional or scholarly journal format you should use. For example, the advice given in this chapter is based on the *American Sociological Association Style Guide* (2007) <http://www.asanet.org/>; however, many journals used by sociologists follow the procedures described in the *Publication Manual of the American Psychological Association* (2001) <http://www.apa.org/>. Both of these publications are available in the reference section of your library as well as available for purchase through the Web sites of each professional organization. It may be sufficient to simply follow the style used by the journal your instructor recommends. Before starting your paper, examine recent articles from the recommended journal. (If none is recommended, use the *American Sociological Review*, the top-tier journal published by the American Sociological Association). Download to a storage device, email, or photocopy one or two sample journal articles (as discussed in Chapter 4) to use as a model of format and tone. Your paper should not only look professional but sound professional as well. Scientific communication uses a formal prose style.

We have arranged the topics covered in this chapter according to the steps you should follow in writing your quantitative research paper. For example, although the title and the abstract go at the beginning of your paper, you should write them during the final stages so that they describe your entire study. Therefore, we cover these components toward the end of the chapter.

REVIEWING THE LITERATURE

Once you decide on a topic, use the reference sources listed in Chapter 4 (such as *CSA Sociological Abstracts* and *Google Scholar*) to search for similar empirical studies of the topic. Also gather books and articles on the theory you plan to use as a framework for your study. Read and take notes as you would for a textual analysis paper or an article critique (see Chapter 5). That is, the purpose of the literature review is not simply to discuss what has been done on your topic but to determine what has been done well. Rather than accept the existing research at face value, students writing a quantitative research paper are trying to develop a justification for doing additional research. To do this, a student needs to find a weakness in the logic and/or methods of previous studies. Alternatively, a student might look for gaps in what is known. After reviewing what has been done, it should become evident what has *not* been done or what has not been done *well*. By finding an area of research that has been understudied or one that has not been adequately studied, you will be able to justify new data collection. You will also be able to make a contribution to the literature. Thus, the purpose of the literature review is to provide a context for the formulation of your hypotheses.

In writing your review of the literature, provide enough background material to place the hypotheses in their proper setting. Begin your review with a summary of the theory (or theories) from which your question is derived, specifying its major tenets and focusing on one or two aspects (or major concepts) that you would like to test. Next, discuss each relevant study, summarizing in a few sentences the theoretical approach, major hypotheses, operational definitions (measures), and conclusions drawn in each one. It is often helpful to arrange the studies in chronological order. How do these studies fit together? Do they form a pattern or are they inconsistent? Do they fail to account for an important variable? What direction do they suggest for future research?

STATING THE PROBLEM AND CHOOSING A QUESTION

The statement of the problem reveals the gaps or contradictory findings that you found after reviewing the chosen theory and relevant literature. Its purpose is to point out theoretical inconsistencies in need of resolution, methodological problems apparent in the empirical literature, and/or the logical next step that research in this area should take. For example, you may want to concentrate on a different interpretation of a theory not adequately tested, set up a critical test of two rival theories, extend the theory to a new population or substantive area, use a new operational definition of a concept, correct the faulty methodology of a previous study, use a different design or method, or include more variables in order to look for possible interactions. For some class assignments a simple replication of a published study may be sufficient. Be sure to check with your instructor. However, unless your study is an exact replication of an earlier study, you must explain how your study differs from previous works, how your study will extend their findings, and what your study will contribute.

Following from the review of the literature, the statement of the problem should suggest questions that need to be answered (for example, "Is education always related to occupational attainment?"). These questions can be refined and developed into hypotheses (for example, "If ethnicity is held constant, an increase in education will be associated with an increase in occupational attainment"). Most quantitative papers examine more than one hypothesis.

STATING YOUR HYPOTHESES

A hypothesis in a quantitative paper is the counterpart of the thesis in a library research paper. Each is a formal statement expressing the relationship you expect to find between two or more of your variables. Your literature review and statement of the problem show the logic that led to the development of your hypotheses. They serve as a sort of preliminary evidence. If your reasoning is sound, the numerical data you collect will provide further support for each of your hypotheses.

Each hypothesis should be stated in such a way that it can be unambiguously confirmed or rejected by the results. Each should also be stated in such a way as to make clear the type (causal or correlational) and direction (positive or negative) of the expected relationships. That is, does any particular hypothesis postulate that one variable causes the other, or does it simply state that the two variables are correlated? If the relationship is believed to be correlational rather than causal, are the variables expected to be related positively (as X increases, Y increases) or negatively (as X increases, Y decreases)? Explain how the independent and dependent variables will be operationally defined, that is, the manner in which the variables will be measured. For example, occupational attainment may be operationally defined as whether the job involves the supervision of other workers. (In correlational studies where there is no assumption about the causal order of the variables, no distinction is made between the independent and dependent variables.) Be sure to specify your unit of analysis, for example, individuals, groups, institutions, or countries.

As we explained earlier, if your study is purely descriptive you will not have specific hypotheses. You may simply have questions that suggest themselves as interesting problems in need of further investigation. In this case, you should explain why you feel an exploration of these topics is important.

For some topics, a descriptive study is often an important first step toward the formulation of a good deductive study.

DEVELOPING A METHODS AND ANALYSIS PLAN

Once you have drafted the review of the literature and stated your hypotheses, you are ready to proceed with the development of a methods and analysis plan. Collecting and analyzing quantitative data can be time-consuming tasks. Unanticipated problems or events may interfere. Start early in the term and apportion enough time for these and other tasks. Conducting a sound investigation is crucial to writing a good quantitative research paper. Therefore, it is necessary to consider in advance all the decisions you must make in collecting your data. Drawing up a methods and analysis plan will greatly improve the quality of your paper and will make the writing process go more smoothly. Although it is beyond the scope of this book to discuss the multitude of methodological and statistical factors that need to be considered in conducting a good quantitative study, we do address those issues important to writing a good report of your study. These tips should be useful to both the novice and the more experienced student. However, if you are currently taking a research methods or statistics course, or have taken one or both in the past, you might want to consult your text(s) for further details.

You will be limited to certain methods depending on the hypothesis you are testing or the kind of research question you are trying to answer. For example, if you are interested in the mortality (death) rates of upper- versus lower-class men, you obviously would have to use archival sources rather than a survey. Your choice of method will also be influenced by your assignment and by time and cost constraints. However, the four most common methods are archival sources, structured observation, experiment, and survey.

Archival sources are records of preexisting data. Although some of these data are obtained from surveys—the census, for example—we include them as archival because the results are published in tables available in government documents and books. Most of these data consist of official records of "rates," such as birth, death, marriage, divorce, crime, suicide, and accident rates. For example, you may want to examine the change in divorce rates from 1977 to 2007, the crime rates in urban versus rural areas, or the suicide rates of males versus females. For statistics about the United States, two excellent government publications are the *Annual Statistical Abstract of the United States* (available online at <http://www.census.gov/prod/www/statistical-abstract.html>) and the *Historical Statistics of the United States: Colonial Times to 1970* (available online at <http://www2.census.gov/prod2/statcomp/documents/CT1970p1-01.pdf>), which are also available in most college and university libraries.

Structured observation can be conducted in a laboratory or in the "field" (real-world settings). Structured field observation, unlike ethnographic field research, is guided by set hypotheses or specific measurement objectives. Structured observation, whether it is done in a laboratory or in the field, can often involve simple counting, such as counting the occurrence of certain behaviors or counting the number of people in different situations. For instance, you may want to observe the frequency with which men as compared to women make supportive statements during group discussions, or count the number of students who attend political rallies on versus off campus.

There are many different *experimental* designs, but the basic model involves two groups—an experimental group and a control group. Both groups are treated exactly the same except for the independent variable(s), which is (are) manipulated. Although we usually think of experiments as conducted in a laboratory, experiments can also be conducted in everyday settings (called "field experiments"). For example, you may want to examine whether people in a shopping mall are more likely to come to the aid of a well-dressed victim or a shabbily dressed victim. You could manipulate the situation so that in half the cases your confederate (accomplice) comes to the mall wearing a suit and in the other half wearing dirty jeans and a torn T-shirt.

The *survey* method includes both questionnaires and interviews. The logic of the survey is to replicate the experimental method artificially, although without the same degree of control, by comparing two or more groups. The groups can be based on response scores (for example, those who score high or low on a particular attitude measure) or on demographic characteristics (for example, Catholics and Protestants, blacks and whites, young and old, or high and low socioeconomic status). If you are interested in the different responses of males and females to a series of questions, your independent variable would be gender of respondent. In a survey, unlike an experiment, the independent variable is not manipulated. Instead, the researcher focuses on response differences that result from the naturally existing differences in the respondents.

Whichever method you choose, be sure that your proposed research is in line with the guidelines set forth by the Institutional Review Board or Office for the Protection of Human Subjects on your campus (ask your instructor for details). You may need to get approval for your project from this committee before you collect your data.

Once you have decided on a method, draw up a plan for data collection and analysis to show your instructor. A methods and analysis plan ensures, *before you collect the data,* that your study will actually provide a test of your hypotheses. Further, it guarantees that you will be able to make sense of your data and analyze them successfully. Many students waste time and effort collecting large amounts of data only to discover later that the data do not provide a test of their hypotheses. Or, they find that they don't know how to go about analyzing the data. A methods and analysis plan can prevent these problems.

When you write your methods and analysis plan, address those issues relevant to your type of study:

1. What population will you sample? How will you select your sample? If you are conducting a field study, either a structured field observation or field experiment, what setting will you choose? Do you anticipate any problems in gaining access to the respondents or the field setting? How many observations will you need to make? With the exception of an archival study, no matter which type of method you decide to use to collect your data, you need to specify how many respondents (of each type) you will need to question or observe. Describe relevant characteristics of the sample, such as the number of respondents of each race/ethnicity, class, and gender.

If you are doing an archival study, documents, rather than people, constitute your sample. For example, in the sample student paper at the end of this chapter, the sample is magazine advertisements. Just as with human samples, you must describe the important characteristics of your archival sample. Shannon's sample included advertisements in women's magazines targeted to three different race/ethnic groups (African American, Hispanic, and white).

2. What measures will you use? That is, how will you operationalize your variables? (To operationalize your variables means to define the specific operations, methods, or procedures you will use to measure your variables.) If you are designing an interview or questionnaire, what question(s) will you ask to measure each concept? For example, if one of the concepts you are interested in is traditional gender role attitudes, you might operationally define this as an affirmative answer (either "strongly agree" or "agree") to the statement "It goes against nature to place women in positions of authority over men." On the other hand, liberal gender role attitudes would be operationally defined as a negative answer (either "strongly disagree" or "disagree") to the same statement.

How long will the questionnaire or survey take to answer? If you plan on conducting an interview or survey, will you use closed-ended questions (also known as "fixed-response") or open-ended questions? Closed-ended questions compare to open-ended questions as multiple-choice exams compare to short-answer essay exams. What will be the possible range of the response scale (for example, a five-point Likert Response Scale) for the closed-ended questions?

If you plan to do a structured observation, whether it is in a field or laboratory setting, what exactly will you look for? How long should each observation last? What things will you want to have on your observation checklist (the list of things that you intend to count or measure)? For example, if you want to observe differences in how near people of different cultures tend to stand to one another, you might want to have a checklist that includes several different races/ethnicities and distances.

If you plan to conduct an archival study, you will need to go to the library to find out the types of data that are available to you. Further, you will need to determine the form in which these data are presented. For example, if you are interested in comparing the birthrates of different religious groups, you will need to find out if the birthrates presented in the census tables are broken down by religious affiliation. Librarians can very often help you find what you need.

If you plan to conduct an interview or survey, you will need to develop a questionnaire. Even when conducting an experiment in the laboratory or in the field, you generally will want to interview respondents or have them complete a questionnaire at the conclusion of the experiment. Although it is beyond the scope of this book to discuss all the details of creating a sound instrument, there are general guidelines that you should consider in order to facilitate the writing of your report. Instructors often expect you to include a copy of your instrument in the appendix to your paper. It is best to include your instrument in your methods and analysis plan and to have it approved by your instructor before you collect your data.

In developing your measures, it is best to begin by looking at those developed by other researchers. Scales exist that have already been shown to be valid and reliable. Many of these scales are reproduced in the appendixes of books or journal articles; others appear in *Measures of Social Psychological Attitudes* by John Robinson and Philip Shaver of the Survey Research Center at the University of Michigan's Institute for Survey Research. If you use an existing scale, be sure to refer to the name of the scale and its originator in the body of your paper (for example, "Rosenberg's Self-Esteem Scale was administered to respondents") and to include the source of the scale in your list of references.

However, you might want to construct some original questions to use in conjunction with an existing scale or to modify existing questions to better suit the purpose of your study. In constructing your own questions, try to avoid the following pitfalls:

- Avoid using ambiguous terms or slang. Define the terms you use. For example, in the questionnaire on student dating, the term "date" is defined in question #7 (see Figure 6-1). Since dating patterns have changed over the years, there might have been some confusion as to what was meant by this term had this point not been clarified.
- Avoid "double-barreled" questions. Questions that contain "and" or "or" (such as "Do you feel that physical attractiveness or attitude similarity are important characteristics in a dating partner?") make it impossible to know whether the respondent views one or both characteristics as important.
- Avoid biased questions that lead the respondent to answer in a socially desirable way. For example, rather than asking, "Have you ever had a date?" You might ask the question, "Have you dated in the last year?" Respondents may be reluctant to say that they have never dated. However, they may feel comfortable saying they have not dated recently.

With regard to other aspects of your instrument, consider the following:

- If it is not necessary to know your respondent's name, do not ask for it. Anonymous questionnaires, that is, those that don't ask for a respondent's name, are more likely to yield honest answers.

Figure 6-1 EXAMPLE OF A QUESTIONNAIRE

Questionnaire # _____

Student Dating Questionnaire

The following questionnaire is anonymous. Your answers will be held in the strictest confidence.

Please circle your answers to the following questions.
1. What is your gender?
    a. male
    b. female

Using the five-point scale (where 1 = not at all important and 5 = extremely important), please rate how important each characteristic is *to you* in a dating partner.

		Not at All Important				Extremely Important
2.	Physical Attractiveness	1	2	3	4	5
3.	Personality	1	2	3	4	5
4.	Sense of Humor	1	2	3	4	5
5.	Potential Occupational Success	1	2	3	4	5
6.	Attitude Similarity	1	2	3	4	5

7. Have you dated in the last year (that is, gone out with someone of the opposite sex, or of the same sex, for purely social purposes with the possibility of developing a romantic involvement)?
    a. yes
    b. no

8. What is your sexual orientation?
    a. heterosexual
    b. homosexual
    c. bisexual
    d. prefer not to answer

Thank you for taking the time to complete this questionnaire. Your cooperation is greatly appreciated!

+ Provide adequate instructions about how to answer the questions. For example, the instructions ("rate how important each date characteristic is *to you*") let respondents know they are being asked for their own opinion, not the opinion they believe to be held by their peer group.
+ Number each question in the questionnaire. Space questions out on the page so that they are easy to read.
+ Be careful about the order in which questions are listed. Put easy questions first and difficult or sensitive questions last.
+ Show respect for your respondents. Thank them for their cooperation and retain the confidentiality of their responses, that is, do not reveal any information that could be used to identify them, including their names, if the questionnaire was not anonymous.

Alternatively, your assignment may allow you to use not only existing measures developed by other researchers, but their data as well. This is called secondary data analysis. Many large universities subscribe to the quantitative data library service provided by the Interuniversity Consortium for Political and Social Research (ICPSR). One of the most commonly used data sets provided by the ICPSR is the General Social Survey (GSS) collected by the National Opinion Research Center (NORC). Check with your instructor about this data library. If ICPSR serves your university, and if its use is acceptable for the purposes of your assignment, your task for the methods and analysis plan would involve the selection of an appropriate database, and, within that, the selection of specific questions to be used in your analysis.

3. How will you get the data into an analyzable form? For example, have you assigned an appropriate numerical equivalent (low = 1, high = 2) to each of the response categories of closed-ended questions? Have you developed a coding scheme for open-ended questions? For example, your coding scheme could involve counting the number of respondents who made some reference to social mobility in response to an open-ended question, or counting the number of times different types of respondents mentioned themes of alienation. Remember that in a quantitative paper, you must be able to represent all responses numerically.

If you are an advanced student planning on forming an attitude index or scale from a set of closed-ended questions, will the response scores of any of your questions need to be reversed? That is, before adding together the response scores of several questions to form a single scale, will the response scores of negatively worded questions be reversed so as to bring them in the same direction as positively worded questions? Will you leave the index as a continuous variable or will you divide it at the median so as to compare high and low scorers?

4. How will you analyze the data? Depending on your hypotheses and the level of statistical knowledge required for your assignment, there are different ways to do this. If you haven't taken a statistics course, the two simplest ways to analyze your data would be to calculate percentages or averages on each variable, independently of other variables. Independent percentages or averages are adequate for reporting the results of a descriptive study.

However, in testing hypotheses it is usually necessary to look at the relationship between two variables. The complexity of calculating percentages or averages increases when you examine the relationship between two variables, because the variables must be examined jointly. Some common methods of doing this include constructing a cross-tabulation table (see Table 1 in the sample quantitative paper), a table of means (see Figure 6-2), and a correlation matrix (not shown). In each type of table, one variable is designated as the row variable and the other as the column variable.

Although constructing a correlation matrix is most feasible for advanced students, beginning students may be able to calculate a cross-tabulation table or table of means (averages). For example, in Table 1 of the sample paper Shannon uses race/ethnicity as the column variable and type of gender stereotype as the row variable. In preparing the table, Shannon first sorted the magazine advertisements into three piles based on the race/ethnicity of the women (African American, Hispanic, and white). *Separately for each pile,* she counted the number of times each of the six gender stereotypes was found. She repeated this procedure for each pile, producing a set of frequencies to be used in calculating the percentages. Notice at the top of each column in Table 1 that Shannon specifies the number of advertisements analyzed for each of the three racial/ethnic groups: African American (N = 10), Hispanic (N = 10), and white (N = 10). This lets the reader know that the denominator used in calculating the percentages for each pile is 10. For example, Shannon found that out of the 10 magazine advertisements featuring African American women, 4 used the gender stereotype *objectification* (4/10 = 40%). At the bottom of each column, Shannon includes the total percentage so that the reader knows how to read the table (for example, 10% + 10% + 10% + 20% + 10% + 40% = 100%, indicating that the column variable is the independent variable).

In Figure 6-2, we present a table based on a calculation of means or averages instead of percentages to show the relationship between two variables (gender and desired date characteristics). We use date characteristic as the row variable and gender as the column variable. We designate in parentheses the number of male and female respondents. In preparing this table, we sorted the questionnaires into two piles: one for males and one for females. Then, *separately for each pile,* we added together the numerical scores given by every respondent for each date characteristic. We divided each sum by the number of students in the pile. For example, the responses of the 15 males in pile 1 for the date characteristic "physical attractiveness" summed to 69 (5 + 4 + 4 + 5 + 4 + 5 + 4 + 5 + 5 + 5 + 4 + 5 + 5 + 4 + 5 = 69). We divided 69 by the number of the respondents in the pile to obtain the average score for males (69 ÷ 15 = 4.6). We repeated this procedure for each date characteristic. We

Figure 6-2 SAMPLE TABLE OF MEANS

Table 1. Mean Level of Importance of Five Date Characteristics by Gender

	Males (N = 15)	Females (N = 15)
Physical Attractiveness	4.6	3.1
Personality	3.0	3.9
Sense of Humor	2.5	3.2
Potential Occupational Success	1.4	4.5
Attitude Similarity	2.2	2.4

then did all the same calculations for females. The table reports the mean level of importance of each date characteristic for males and females separately. The results show that males (mean = 4.6) place a greater importance on physical attractiveness than do females (mean = 3.1), while females (mean = 4.5) place greater importance on potential occupational success than do males (mean = 1.4).

Try to make a mock table for analyzing and presenting your results. That is, try to specify which variable you will use as your row variable and which variable as your column variable. Which variables will you use to sort respondents into piles? Determine whether the numbers in the cells will be percentages or averages.

If you are required to carry out more sophisticated statistical analyses of your data, determine the level of measurement of your variables (nominal, ordinal, interval, or ratio). This will allow you to decide which statistical tests can be appropriately calculated. Computer software packages that calculate social science statistics, such as SPSS and SAS, are available. Check with your instructor.

Don't proceed with your data collection or analysis until your instructor has approved your methods and analysis plan and answered your questions. Once you complete your data collection and analysis, you are ready to begin writing the other sections of your paper.

WRITING THE OTHER SECTIONS OF YOUR PAPER

THE METHODS SECTION

The methods section directly follows the review of the literature. It should contain three subparts: sample, measures, and procedure. Each subpart should be labeled with an italicized heading at the left margin; capitalize only the first letter. (See pages 167 and 169 of Shannon's paper for examples of these headings.) Begin the methods section by describing your sample.

Describing Your Sample

Specify the population studied. Discuss in detail how you selected your sample from this population. Did you randomly select respondents—that is, give every member of the population an equal chance of being included in the sample—or did you select whomever you could get? If respondents were randomly selected, describe the steps you took to ensure randomness (for example, tossing a coin or systematically selecting every fifth respondent). If you are a more advanced student, did you stratify your sample on any particular variable?

Describe all the relevant characteristics of your sample (for example, age, gender, race). If you had to eliminate any subjects because of incomplete data or for other reasons, state the number and the reason. Specify the final overall sample size and the size of each group.

Describing Your Measures

If you obtained your data from secondary sources, describe where the original data came from and how they were measured. If you did a structured observation, describe the behaviors, types of people, situations, and so on, that you observed.

If you used a questionnaire or interview, state whether you used closed-ended or open-ended questions, questions newly developed by you, or questions adapted from previous research. If you used existing scales or indexes, include information about their validity and reliability, if available. "Validity" refers to the extent to which the questions actually measure what they are supposed to measure. "Reliability" refers to the stability of measurements taken at different times.

In the body of the paper, quote the actual question(s) used to operationally define each variable. If several questions were used, as in the construction of an index or a scale, give a sample of the questions and include the others in a table or an appendix. For example: "Gender role attitudes were measured by agreement–disagreement with 20 statements, such as 'The woman's place is in the home' and 'I would vote for a woman presidential candidate' (see Appendix A)." If the questions were closed-ended, state the range of the response scale and describe the anchor points. For example, you might state that you used "a five-point Likert Response Scale ranging from (1) not at all to (5) extremely." If you averaged several questions together to form an index, state what the high and low scores on the index signify. For example: "A high score on the gender role index indicates liberal gender role attitudes; a low score indicates conservative attitudes." If the questions were open-ended, describe the coding scheme that you used to code the data.

Describing Your Procedure

Identify the method you used. Describe when (time of day, day of week, date), where (the geographic location, type of institution, building), and under what circumstances the study took place. This information is especially important if the study was conducted in a field setting.

If you conducted an experiment, be sure to also specify the design. Discuss the procedure by which the independent variable(s) was (were) manipulated and the instructions given to respondents in each group. Specify any additional precautions taken to control extraneous variables or to exclude bias from your sample. For example, did you randomly assign respondents to experimental conditions? (Random assignment to groups is different from random selection.) If you employed confederates (accomplices), describe who they were, what they did, and whether or not they were kept "blind" to (ignorant of) the hypotheses.

Whichever method you chose, summarize each step you took in collecting your data. A good rule of thumb is to describe your methods in enough detail that another researcher could replicate your study.

THE RESULTS SECTION

Discuss how you examined the relationship between your variables. Did you count the number of people who gave each type of response, or did you average the scores of several people? If you calculated percentages or took averages, state the number of people used as the denominator in your calculations.

If you have a large amount of data to report, consider displaying it in a table or figure. Put each table or figure on a separate page at the end of the paper, just after the list of references. Each table should be numbered consecutively. The word "Table" and the number should be bolded and end with a period and be followed by an indented descriptive title. The line consisting of the table number and descriptive title should be flush with the left margin, and it should be followed by a double rule, as shown in our Figure 6-3. A

Figure 6-3 SAMPLE TABLE OF PERCENTAGES

Table 1. Gender Role Attitudes by Gender of Respondent

	Gender of Respondent	
Gender Role Attitudes	Male (N = 100)	Female (N = 100)
Liberal	55%	85%
Traditional	45	15
TOTAL	100%	100%

good title allows the reader to tell what is in the table without having to refer to the text. For figures, the number and descriptive title should also be flush with the left margin and bold, but they should be positioned below the graph or diagram, as shown in Figure 6-4. Figures should also be numbered consecutively. In the body of the paper, refer to each table or figure by number; then explain it. Remember that the numbers presented in the table never speak for themselves.

Another way to present your results is to use graphs or charts. You can use one of the many computer graphics programs that are available. The best known of these programs for the advanced student are SPSS (formerly known as the Statistical Package for the Social Sciences) and the SAS (Statistical Analysis System), which can also be used to perform statistical analyses. Programs such as Microsoft's Excel can be most useful for the less advanced student. Often visual aids can dramatically illustrate the relationships between variables. Whether you should use a bar chart, a line graph, or a causal model will depend on the type of data that you have and the analyses you perform. Ask your instructor for suggestions on the best way to present your results.

If your assignment required statistical analyses, state the statistical tests performed; their critical values, degrees of freedom, and significance levels; and the direction of the results. For example: "The relationship between gender role attitudes and gender of respondent is reported in Table 1. The results of a chi-square test indicate that a significantly greater proportion of females (85%) than males (55%) hold liberal gender role attitudes ($x^2 = 24.24$, d.f. $= 100$, $p < .01$)." In the discussion section, you will take this explanation a step further.

THE DISCUSSION SECTION

In the discussion section you should tie your results back in to your hypotheses. Did the data support any of your hypotheses? Remember that the statistical significance of your findings does not indicate the theoretical, substantive, or practical significance of your findings. The latter is a judgment you must make in the discussion section. What does a relationship between X and Y mean in the larger theoretical context? How do your findings com-

Figure 6-4 SAMPLE FIGURE

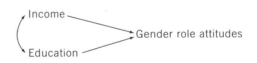

Figure 1.   Measurement Model of Gender Role Attitudes

pare with previous research? That is, are your findings consistent or inconsistent with those found by other researchers? What has the study contributed to the existing body of literature on this topic? What are the practical implications of your findings, if any? What ethical issues were raised?

What is the internal and external validity of your study? That is, to what extent does your study provide an adequate test of your hypotheses? To what other populations can your findings be generalized? Discuss any methodological or design flaws, particularly if your hypotheses are not supported. Make suggestions for improving future research. If the study is methodologically sound, how can you account for your unexpected findings? Do the data support an alternative theory?

What conclusions can you draw? What direction should further research on this topic take?

THE TITLE

Now that you've completed the main sections of your paper, you will be able to come up with a good descriptive title. It should be short (rarely over 12 words) and include the theoretical perspective taken and/or the major variables examined (both independent and dependent, where appropriate). (See Part 3 for guidelines on formatting a title page.)

THE ABSTRACT

The abstract, usually about 100 to 200 words in length, is a very brief summary of your paper. It describes the problem, methods, sample, results, and conclusions of your study and should contain only ideas or information already discussed in the body of the paper. The abstract goes on a separate (labeled) page right after the title page. For a heading, type ABSTRACT (in capital letters) and left-justify it. Triple-space between the heading and the body of the abstract. Indent the first line. (See page 163 of the sample paper for an example of an abstract.) Although almost always included in a journal article, an abstract may not be required by your instructor.

THE LIST OF REFERENCES

If no specific journal style is required, follow the guidelines given in Chapter 3 for formatting your list of references. Include in your list only those sources you actually cite in the body of your paper. The list of references should appear on a separate page at the end of your paper (see page 179 for an example).

THE APPENDIX

The appendixes (also called appendices) are optional. Some instructors may want you to include your questionnaire, observation checklist, instructions to respondents, raw data, statistical calculations, or other items in an appendix. Each appendix should be numbered or lettered (see Part 3) and given a descriptive title. The appendixes, when included, go after the list of references.

SUGGESTED READINGS

Babbie, Earl R. 2007. *The Practice of Social Research.* 11th ed. Belmont, CA: Thomson-Wadsworth Publishing Co.

Babbie, Earl R. 2008. *The Basics of Social Research.* 4th ed. Belmont, CA: Thomson-Wadsworth Publishing Co.

Babbie, Earl R., Fred Halley, and Jeanne S. Zaino. 2007. *Adventures in Social Research.* 6th ed. Thousand Oaks, CA: Sage Publications, Inc.

A SAMPLE STUDENT PAPER

The following sample quantitative research paper, a study of gender stereotyping in magazine advertisements, was written by Shannon Prior for an undergraduate course in writing for sociology. Shannon's study reveals that women are portrayed stereotypically in the advertisements of women's magazines, regardless of their race or ethnicity.

Shannon's assignment required her to review the literature on a topic, design a study, and construct measures; however, she only had to simulate rather than collect the data. (She included this simulated "raw data" in Appendix B [not shown], so that her instructor could verify that she tabulated the results correctly). Because Shannon wrote this paper for a class in writing rather than in research methods, the purpose of the assignment was to demonstrate critical thinking about a sociological topic all the way from the formulation of a research question and/or hypothesis to the analysis, interpretation, and discussion of findings. Thus, there was less emphasis on the mechanics of collecting data than on the logic behind the entire research and writing process. If your assignment entails the collection of data, it would be prudent to share your methods and analysis plan with your instructor beforehand, to ensure you're on the right track.

Shannon reviewed the relevant literature on stereotyping in magazine advertisements and developed her main hypotheses to address questions raised by this review. Shannon went beyond other studies by looking at gender stereotypes of African American and Hispanic women, in addition to white women, in magazine advertisements. Thus, this work is located within an ongoing discussion but also contains something original, both of which are important considerations in designing sociological research.

The paper follows a journal article format and is based on simulated quantitative results from an archival study. Notice that it contains the major and minor sections discussed in this chapter: title page, abstract, review of the literature, methods (including subsections on the sample, measures, and procedure), results, and discussion. Shannon also provides a table that presents important results in an easily read format. Her list of references appears toward the end of the paper, but it should have been placed just before her table and appendixes. Our comments on the facing pages detail other important features of the paper as well as ways in which it could be improved.

Because of the length of her paper, Shannon includes a title page (as suggested in Part 3). Shannon correctly begins numbering the pages of her paper *after* the title page.

Shannon produces a descriptive title that appropriately identifies the dependent variable (stereotypes) and the independent variable (race/ethnicity), and hints at the method (examining magazines). (Note that this reference to magazine advertisements implies that she uses archival data to examine the relationship between the independent and dependent variables). However, this title is ambiguous. It does not identify the kinds of stereotypes investigated, whether these stereotypes are racial/ethnic stereotypes, class stereotypes, or gender stereotypes. Since Shannon's paper is on gender stereotypes, this topic of gender stereotypes should be specified in the title.

**STEREOTYPES OF AFRICAN AMERICAN, HISPANIC, AND WHITE WOMEN
IN MAGAZINE ADVERTISEMENTS**

Shannon Prior
Sociology 301
Dr. Giarrusso
December 18, 2006

OUR COMMENTS

Shannon includes an abstract or brief summary of her paper. In less than 200 words she describes the purpose of the paper, the methods, and the results. Because Shannon follows the *ASA Style Guide* (2007), she left-justifies, bolds, and capitalizes all the letters of the heading. However, she begins the fourth sentence with a number; instead, she should write it out, "One hundred and twenty advertisements. . . " Also, she could strengthen her abstract with the addition of a concluding sentence, such as "Two explanations that could account for the present findings are 'the beauty myth' and old fashioned economics."

ABSTRACT

Research by Lindner (2004) indicates that women have been consistently stereotyped in magazine advertisements since the 1950s. However, her research does not address how women of different races are stereotyped. A content analysis of African American, Hispanic, and White women's magazine advertisements is conducted to compare the stereotypes of each group. 120 advertisements are analyzed using the coding categories *relative size, function ranking, licensed withdrawal, body display, location,* and *objectification.* The results show that all groups of women are stereotyped. Advertisements of white women are slightly more likely than advertisements of other women to contain *licensed withdrawal* and *body display. Objectification* occurs most frequently in all groups.

Appropriately, Shannon begins the review of the literature section on a separate page without a heading. At the outset of the paper, she provides a statement of the problem: advertisers often use stereotypes to sell products. This paragraph creates a context for the rest of the paper, explaining why it is important to study the use of stereotyping by advertisers. However, at this point it is still unclear whether Shannon will be focusing on gender stereotypes or racial/ethnic stereotypes.

Shannon provides a concise description of a relevant empirical journal article that includes key information about the: (1) independent variable (race/ethnicity), (2) dependent variable (types of roles in which minorities were cast), (3) method (archival), (4) sample (four types of magazines—business, women's, general interest, and technical), and (5) results. Importantly, she ends the paragraph with a critique of the article, setting the stage for her study to make a contribution to the literature. However, her description of the study would be stronger if she indicated the gender of the individuals studied in the advertisements—it is unclear whether the study by Taylor, Lee, and Stern is based on males and/or females. Also, this is the first time Shannon suggests she is interested in studying gender role stereotypes rather than racial/ethnic stereotypes. The paper should have prepared the reader beforehand to expect this emphasis. Moreover, the reader still doesn't know at this point whether Shannon studied the stereotyping of one or both genders.

Again, Shannon provides a concise description of an empirical journal article. Without using the actual terms, she specifies the independent variable (time), dependent variable (gender role stereotypes), method (archival), sample (mainstream magazines), and results (stereotypes remain stable over time). Once more, her critique of the study (the findings cannot be generalized to minority women) shows critical thinking skills. Further, she is careful to give the operational definitions of the gender role stereotypes that are studied (for example, objectification is "when the woman's sole purpose is to be looked at"). However, because Shannon uses the ASA publication style, she should not include Lindner's first name in her citation.

The power of advertising is clear. The fact that companies annually expend over $200 billion on advertising is a testament to its power and prevalence in our society (Kilbourne 1999). Advertising not only sells products, it also sells images (Baker 2005). Too often these images are stereotypes of women and minorities. These portrayals, good or bad, influence our perceptions of the people in our society. For these reasons, the study of minorities and women in advertising is the focus of this research.

Taylor, Lee, and Stern (1995) explore the portrayal of minorities in magazines by conducting a content analysis of four types of magazines (business, women's, general interest, and technical). The researchers analyze the types of roles (major, minor, background, etc.) minorities are cast in and the types of products they are selling. The authors conclude that some stereotypes still persist. African Americans are over-represented in minor or background roles. Asian Americans are consistently represented as tech-savvy workaholics while Hispanic Americans are either non-existent or somewhere in the background. Although the study includes women's magazines in their content analysis, they do not provide a specific analysis of gender role stereotypes.

To gain a better understanding of gender portrayals in advertising, I consulted Katharina Lindner's (2004) longitudinal study of women in *Time* and *Vogue* magazine advertisements. The study utilizes Goffman's frame analysis and coding scheme, which is designed to detect subtle messages in advertising. Lindner finds that 78% of the advertisements portray women stereotypically. The study finds decreases over time in certain categories of stereotypes. For instance, the *feminine touch* category in which the woman depicted is touching her hair, face, or clothing in an unnatural manner or stroking an object declines throughout the years. However, Lindner was surprised to find that the other types of stereotypes measured remain relatively stable over time. Overall, *objectification,* when the woman's sole purpose is to be looked at, occurs most frequently. Although this study provides insight into gender portrayals, it only includes publications directed toward a mainstream, predominantly White audience. Therefore, the results do not apply to minority women.

1

Shannon provides another succinct description of an empirical journal article, clarifying how the dependent variable in this article differs from the other articles she reviews. It appears that the Baker article is not as relevant to her topic as the previous article by Lindner; however, there may not have been another article that more closely related to her topic. Notably, Shannon shows the limitations of the article in addressing her research question, thereby adding to her argument for the need to study gender stereotypes among women from different race/ethnic groups. Because Shannon uses the ASA publication style, she should not have included Baker's first name or middle initial in her citation.

This reference to the source being cited is correct according to *ASA Style Guide.*

This paragraph ties all the studies reviewed together leading to the conclusion that a study of gender stereotypes among African American, Hispanic, and white women in corresponding women's magazines will make a contribution to the literature. A common error is capitalizing the word "white." According to the *ASA Style Guide,* the words "black" or "white" should not be capitalized; however, it is appropriate to capitalize the words "African American," "Asian," and "Hispanic" because these names represent groups with a common geographic location or language.

The final paragraph in the review of the literature section is where most researchers propose their hypotheses. Appropriately, Shannon offers two hypotheses, each about the frequency with which she expects various gender stereotypes will be found; she is able to provide "educated guesses" about the likelihood of these findings because there is adequate literature on this aspect of her research in the literature. These hypotheses constitute the deductive component of her research. Conversely, the inductive component of her research deals with "which race/ethnic group will be stereotyped most frequently" and "what ways." Because there is not enough literature on these topics for her to render hypotheses, she poses these as research questions.

Shannon divides her paper into four major sections. She indicates the beginning of the second section with the heading, METHODS, all in capitals, bolded, and left-justified. She then goes on to divide this major section into several subsections: sample, measures, and procedure.

In contrast to Lindner's study, Christina N. Baker (2005) studies the portrayal of African American and White women's sexuality in advertising. She conducted a content analysis of African American and White-oriented men's and women's magazines to compare the portrayals of African American and White women's sexuality. Included in her study is an analysis of the role of women and the authority of the women in relation to the men. In women's magazines, Baker finds that African American women are more likely to be portrayed as independent compared to White women. White women are more likely to be portrayed as "partners" or have their faces hidden, signifying subordination. However, the results are not generalizable because Baker only includes advertisements that display women in a sexual manner.

It is clear from the previous research that White and minority women are stereotyped in magazine advertisements. These stereotypes are not simply images, they are powerful messages that "depict for us not necessarily how we actually behave as men and women but how we think men and women behave" (Gornick 1979:7). Therefore, I wish to further explore the types and frequencies of gender stereotypes in magazine advertisements. I contribute to the literature by examining and comparing the stereotypes of African American, Hispanic, and White women in African American, Hispanic, and White oriented women's magazines.

Based on the literature reviewed, I hypothesize that all groups of women will be stereotyped. Based specifically on Lindner's (2004) study, I hypothesize that *objectification* will occur most frequently out of all the stereotype categories. Due to the lack of research on the topic, I explore rather than hypothesize which racial group will be stereotyped most frequently and in what ways.

METHODS

Sample

A content analysis is conducted to examine and compare the portrayals of African American, Hispanic, and White women in magazine advertisements. Since minority women are underrepresented in mainstream magazine advertising, I analyze African American and Hispanic-oriented

2

The word "amount" is used incorrectly here because "women" is a count noun. The correct term is "number."

Although for most research studies, the sample refers to people, in an archival study, the sample refers to existing documents. Importantly, Shannon specifies how she selected her sample (magazines): she purposefully chose magazines that would provide her with a close-to-equal representation of women from each race/ethnic group. Moreover, she shows her critical thinking skills by selecting the January and June issues to control for possible seasonal biases in the advertisements.

Again showing her critical thinking skills, Shannon integrates the coding schemes of different researchers in examining her hypotheses and answering her research questions. She also provides an operational definition of each type of stereotype to be investigated in an appendix at the end of her paper. While many students believe they will impress their instructor by developing new measures, it is best to use existing measures unless your instructor tells you otherwise. Better to use "tried and true" measures, especially if they are based on classic studies like those of Goffman, than risk using inadequate or inappropriate measures. Because Shannon includes more than one appendix, she assigns a letter to each one (as suggested in Part 3), designating the first one as Appendix A.

Shannon provides further specification about how the advertisements are selected and coded. To her credit, she trained two coders to examine the data and made sure that there was high interrater reliability before having the coders analyze the rest of the advertisements. The fourth sentence of the paragraph begins incorrectly with a number. Shannon could have eliminated this error by putting a semi-colon at the end of the previous sentence and joining them to make one sentence or by writing out the number in words: "Twenty-five percent."

Shannon uses the major heading, RESULTS, to delineate another major section. She refers the reader to Table 1 for the results and then goes on to explain the content of the table. Although Shannon uses the word "significant," she does not mean the term "statistically significant," which means that the differences found could not be attributable to chance. To avoid any possible ambiguity here, Shannon should have substituted the word "noteworthy" or "noticeable" when she was revising her final draft.

magazines in addition to a mainstream or White-oriented magazines. I do so in the hope of obtaining a close to equal amount of Black, Hispanic, and White women. I chose *Redbook* for White women, *Latina* for Hispanic women and *Essence* for Black women. All of the magazines contain similar topic matter including sections on beauty, fashion, sex, and health. The sample of advertisements is taken from the January and June issues published in 2005. I chose a winter and summer month to control for any bias that one season might create. For example, summer months would most likely contain more advertisements with *body display*.

Measures

Goffman's (1997) coding scheme categories *relative size, function ranking,* and *licensed withdrawal* are used to analyze the advertisements. In addition, Umiker-Sebeok's (1996) category *location,* Lindner's (2004) category *objectification,* and Kang's (1997) category *body display* are used. See Appendix A for the full list of the categories including their operational definitions.

Procedure

Only full-page advertisements containing at least one woman with or without one or more men were coded. At least one woman in the advertisement had to appear to be Black, Hispanic, or White. Other minority women were excluded from this study due to the lack of a comparable magazine that targets them. Two coders were trained to use the coding scheme and were not informed of the exact purpose of the study. 25% of the sample was analyzed by each coder. The results were compared and inconsistencies were resolved. Each coder then analyzed half of the sample.

RESULTS

Table 1 displays the percentage of each gender stereotype by race/ethnicity. I found that African American, Hispanic, and White women are all consistently stereotyped. There were significant differences in the frequencies of stereotypes based on race with the exception of the

3

Shannon explains how she derived the percentages presented in the table. She also provides the raw data from which she constructed the percentages in an appendix at the end of the paper (not shown); she distinguishes between the two appendixes by assigning the second appendix a different letter ("Appendix B").

Here Shannon provides further description about how she obtained the percentages presented in the last column of Table 1, and she talks about how the gender stereotypes differ in their frequency. Shannon could have avoided beginning the fourth sentence with a number (13.3%) by combining it with the previous sentence. In that case, she would need to be very careful to avoid a common grammar error of run-on or comma splice sentence. A correct version would be *"Location* occurred in 13.3% of the advertisements, while 13.3% of the advertisements contained the stereotype *licensed withdrawal."*

Students need to be careful about the use of the word "significant" in quantitative papers. Although Shannon does not use the word "statistically significant," the reader may not be sure whether she understands the difference. A better way to note the differences in occurrence among the types of gender stereotypes when statistical tests were not calculated would be to say that "large differences" were found.

Shannon should avoid beginning the sentence with a number (0%).

Shannon uses the major heading, DISCUSSION, to divide her paper into the last major section.

To avoid the confusion of the reference to "we," Shannon should have omitted it here by revising the statement to "Whether acknowledged or not, advertising. . . ."

Be careful about using the pronoun "this" ("This was consistent with Lindner's . . .") when it is not clear what it refers to: Hypothesis? Category? Women? Note as effective examples that Shannon writes "these reasons" and "This hypothesis" in sentences before the ambiguous "This" here.

categories *location* and *objectification.* I also found particular categories of stereotypes to be more prevalent than others among all women tested.

To obtain percentages of the stereotypes for each group of women, I took the total number of times the stereotype occurred within that race and divided it by the total number of women in that group. To calculate the average percentage of stereotype categories, I added up the percentages of each category and divided it by three. See Appendix B for the raw data.

I averaged the percentages for the three race groups to determine which categories occurred most frequently overall. The categories *relative size* and *function ranking* occurred the least among all of the categories at 6.7%. *Location* occurred in 10% of the advertisements. 13.3% of the advertisements contained the stereotype *licensed withdrawal. Body display* occurred in 23.3% of the sample. *Objectification* was the most frequent stereotype, occurring in 40% of the advertisements.

There were significant differences among the women in the categories *relative size, function ranking, licensed withdrawal,* and *body display.*

0% of the advertisements of White women contained *relative size* or *function ranking.* In contrast, 10% of advertisements depicting African American women and 10% depicting Hispanic women contained *relative size* and *function ranking.* Advertisements depicting White women contained more instances of *licensed withdrawal* (20%) and *body display* (30%) compared to African American (10% and 20%, respectively) and Hispanic (10% and 20%, respectively) women.

DISCUSSION

Whether we acknowledge it or not, advertising permeates almost every aspect of our lives. The images in advertisements define and solidify gender roles (Baker 2005). For these reasons I studied the stereotypes of African American, Hispanic, and White women in magazine advertisements. I hypothesized that each group of women would be stereotyped. This hypothesis was supported by my findings. African American, Hispanic, and White women were stereotyped in almost every category tested. This was consistent with Lindner's (2004) study, which found that 78% of the advertisements examined in *Time* and *Vogue* contained stereotypes of

4

As with most sociologists, Shannon begins the discussion section by reiterating the reason for her study and reminding the reader of the hypotheses she set out to examine. She goes on to conclude that the data supported her first hypothesis. Moreover, she ties her first finding back to the literature she reviewed at the beginning of her paper by indicating whether or not her results were consistent with those of other researchers. She is careful to state that the study by Taylor et al. was not similar enough to make a meaningful comparison.

Shannon follows the same strategy in discussing the results for her second hypothesis. Because she already cited all the authors of the Taylor article, she now refers to this article using the "et al." convention.

These two paragraphs are very strong because they provide an interpretation of the results. The purpose of the discussion section is to give meaning to the numbers that were presented in the results section, rather than simply repeat the findings that were reported. Shannon explains how her findings support the idea of a beauty myth.

women. This finding was also supported by Baker's (2005) study which found that African American and White women were stereotyped in White and African American men's and women's magazine advertisements. Although Taylor et al. (1995) found minorities to be stereotyped in magazine advertisements, they did not specifically examine stereotypes of women. Therefore, our findings could not be confirmed or denied by their study.

My second hypothesis, that *objectification* would be the most prevalent stereotype, was supported by my data. *Objectification* occurred in 40% of the advertisements analyzed, more than any other category. This finding was consistent with Lindner's (2004) study, which also found *objectification* to be the most common stereotype in *Time* and *Vogue* magazine advertisements. Since Baker (2005) and Taylor et al. (1995) did not use *objectification* in their content analysis, their studies could not substantiate or deny my second hypothesis.

The prevalence of *objectification* can be interpreted as a reaction against the economic and social freedoms enjoyed by the modern woman. In Naomi Wolf's (1991) book, *The Beauty Myth,* she argues that the beauty myth, the unattainable image of women perpetuated by the mass media, is a tool of patriarchy. As women have become stronger materially they have been weakened psychologically by the beauty myth (Wolf 1991). This unrealistic ideal of beauty keeps women mentally and physically preoccupied with their bodies (Wolf 1991). This theory was supported by the frequent occurrence of *objectification* in advertisements. *Objectification,* which occurs when a woman is depicted for the sole purpose of being looked at, fully acquaints women with the ideal they must strive to attain.

Wolf's theory was also supported by the low occurrence of *function ranking* and *relative size. Function ranking* occurs when the man in the advertisement plays a dominant role as a boss or instructor. *Relative size* occurs when the man in the advertisement is larger or takes up more space than the woman. Both of these stereotypes display more traditional gender roles in which the woman is subordinate to the man. Since the women's movement, these gender roles are considered to be outdated and unacceptable to today's woman. Hence the emergence of the modern beauty myth and the prevalence of more subtle forms of stereotypes like *objectification.* However, the requirement of a man and woman to be

5

This is another strong paragraph because Shannon postulates yet another possible explanation of her findings. The two explanations are mutually exclusive, that is, only one of them can be correct. Also, telling the reader about Lasn's credentials as founder of *Adbusters* effectively supports the credibility of the borrowed explanation cited here.

A comma is necessary after "profitable" in order to clarify the meaning of this sentence. Without the comma, a reader might think "profitable" referred to "advertisers."

Here Shannon explains the implications of her findings and gives some concrete ways to counter the pernicious effect of gender stereotyping in advertising.

Shannon proposes several interesting ways to extend her work in future research. Any one of these ideas would produce an interesting quantitative research paper.

depicted together could also account for the low occurrence of *function ranking* and *relative size.*

The high occurrence of *objectification* can also be explained by economics. Kalle Lasn, the founder of *Adbusters* magazine, argues that advertising starts a vicious cycle. It bolsters our insecurities by bombarding us with unattainable images of beauty and then it "offers us a variety of ways to buy our way back to security" (Lasn 1999:17). For Lasn, the beauty myth does not discriminate based on gender. He argues that because it is more profitable advertisers launch their psychological assault on both men and women.

Although my study was not perfect, the results suggest that women should be aware of the images they are absorbing. Women can resist the psychological assault of the beauty myth by being conscious of the subtle messages conveyed in advertisements. We must also teach our children to be media literate and aware of damaging stereotypes perpetrated by the media. In addition, we can take action by writing letters to advertisers and magazine editors expressing our disapproval of the stereotypes conveyed in their advertisements and magazines.

For the future, it would be interesting to focus on the racial stereotypes present in women's magazines. It would also be interesting to study the stereotypes of men in men's magazines. If stereotypes like *objectification* are also high, it would mean the beauty myth is less about gender and more about money. I would also like to study stereotypes in teen magazines. It would also be interesting to expose teens to popular advertisements and then test their perceptions of themselves and the opposite sex.

According to the *ASA Style Guide,* Shannon puts the table on a separate page at the end of her paper; however, she should have put it after the References. By giving the table a descriptive title, the reader can understand what's in the table without having to read the text. Shannon includes the sample size of each race/ethnic group and gives the total percent for each column; this indicates that race/ethnicity is the independent variable and that the type of gender stereotype is the dependent variable.

In line with the *ASA Style Guide,* Shannon should have put the appendix on a separate page after the References. However, at least she provides the appendix with a descriptive title.

Table 1. Type of Gender Stereotype by Race/Ethnicity of Women in Magazine Advertisements

| Type of Gender Stereotype | Race/Ethnicity | | | |
	African American (N = 10)	Hispanic (N =10)	White (N =10)	Average of Three Groups
Relative Size	10%	10%	0%	6.7%
Function Rank	10%	10%	0%	6.7%
Licensed Withdrawal	10%	10%	20%	13.3%
Body Display	20%	20%	30%	23.3%
Location	10%	10%	10%	10%
Objectification	40%	40%	40%	40%
Total	100%	100%	100%	

APPENDIX A

Operational Definitions of Coding Categories

1. *Relative Size.* In advertisements with both men and women present, the man is larger than the woman and more space in the ad is used by him.

2. *Function Ranking.* When both men and women are depicted, the man plays a dominant part as a superior or instructor.

3. *Licensed Withdrawal.* The woman is mentally not present. Her gaze is off in the distance or she is smiling or laughing, covering her face or mouth.

4. *Body Display.* The woman depicted is wearing revealing clothing or no clothing at all.

5. *Location.* The woman is depicted in a domestic or unidentifiable environment. Examples would be a kitchen, bedroom, bathroom, or a setting that does not lend itself to any purposeful activities.

6. *Objectification.* Occurs when being looked at is the major purpose of the woman depicted.

Shannon uses the term "references" rather than "bibliography" because she includes only those articles and books that she actually cites (see Chapter 3). A bibliography is rarely, if ever, appropriate for a quantitative journal article, unless indicated by your instructor. Shannon follows the *ASA Style Guide* in formatting the bibliographic information for the articles and books she cites.

Consistent with the *ASA Style Guide*, Shannon includes both the volume number and the issue number of the journal articles in her References.

Following the *ASA Style Guide*, with the exception of New York, Shannon includes both the city and state for all book references.

REFERENCES

Baker, Christina N. 2005. "Images of Women's Sexuality in Advertisements: A Content Analysis of Black- and White-Oriented Women's and Men's Magazines." *Sex Roles* 52(1-2):13–27.

Goffman, E. 1979. *Gender Advertisements.* Cambridge, MA: Harvard University Press.

Gornick, V. 1979. "Introduction." Pp. vii-ix in *Gender Advertisements* by E. Goffman. Cambridge, MA: Harvard University Press.

Kang, M.E. 1997. "The Portrayal of Women's Images in Magazine Advertisements: Goffman's Gender Analysis Revisited." *Sex Roles* 37(11-12):979–97.

Kilbourne, Jean. 1999. *Can't Buy My Love: How Advertising Changes the Way We Think and Feel.* New York: Touchstone.

Lasn, Kalle. 1999. *Culture Jam: How to Reverse America's Suicidal Consumer Binge-And Why We Must.* New York: Harper Collins Publishers.

Lindner, Katharina. 2004. "Images of Women in General Interest and Fashion Magazine Advertisements from 1955 to 2002." *Sex Roles* 51(7-8):409–21.

Taylor, Charles R., Yu Yung Lee, and Barbara B. Stern. 1995. "Portrayals of African, Hispanic, and Asian Americans in Magazine Advertising." *American Behavioral Scientist* 38(4):608–21.

Umiker-Sebeok, J. 1996. "Power and Construction of Gendered Spaces." *International Review of Sociology* 6(3):389–404.

Wolf, Naomi. [1991] 2003. "The Beauty Myth." Pp.515–524 in *Signs of Life in the USA: Readings on Popular Culture for Writers,* edited by Sonia Maasik and Jack Solomon. Boston, MA: Bedford/St.Martin's Press.

c h a p t e r
S E V E N

The Ethnographic Field Research Paper

In an *ethnographic field research* project, your data come from observing or interacting with people in everyday social settings, which are known as "the field." The data are gathered when a researcher visits the setting (allowing him or her to conduct *observational* research), takes part in the setting's activities (called *participant observation*), and sometimes *interviews* participants in the setting.

Ethnographic research is one type of qualitative method used by sociologists, as well as by their colleagues in fields such as anthropology, education, social work, journalism, nursing, and management. Other qualitative methods include narrative analysis, comparative historical methods, ethnomethodology, and conversational analysis.[1] These are likely to be assigned with very specific instructions from your instructor.

What makes a research method "qualitative" is a subject of considerable lively debate among sociologists. Some suggest that qualitative methods are defined by what they are *not:* they do not involve counting or measuring the social phenomenon of interest. Others argue that qualitative methods take a distinctive approach to exploring the social world, setting out to represent as accurately as possible the process of social life *from the point of view of the participants* (or "members") in the setting (or "field") being investigated. Since a scientific hypothesis is an explanation of social processes proposed by someone *outside* the research setting, the qualitative researcher who adopts an ethnographic approach generally does not engage in the testing of hypotheses. (The kind of fieldwork in which sociologists *do* use fieldwork to test hypotheses about what happens in social settings or why it happens—which we refer to as "structured field observation" or as a "field experiment"—is discussed in Chapter 6.) The following list of goals and methods defines the specific type of qualitative research—ethnographic field research—that we describe in this chapter.

[1]For more information on the range and nature of research methods considered "qualitative," see Denzin, Norman K. and Yvonna S. Lincoln. 2005. *The Sage Handbook of Qualitative Research*. 3rd ed. Thousand Oaks, CA: Sage Publications; or Merriam, Sharon B. 2002. *Qualitative Research in Practice: Examples for Discussion and Analysis*. San Francisco, CA: Jossey-Bass.

GOALS AND METHODS OF ETHNOGRAPHIC FIELD RESEARCH

The ethnographic researcher usually conducts research by closely observing what people are doing, by talking with them informally, and often by participating in activities with them. If interviews are conducted, the ethnographer uses open-ended questions that encourage respondents to answer in their own ways and with their own words. The choice of methods used in ethnographic research depends on the characteristics of the setting and its inhabitants and on the personal style of the researcher.

Unlike most deductive researchers, then, the ethnographic field researcher does not use a predesigned research instrument, such as a written questionnaire. And unlike the structured fieldwork and field experiments described in Chapter 6, ethnographic field research rarely involves quantitative measurement. While predesigned and quantitative methods are useful for measuring some aspects of the social world, they do not convey the intricate and subtle transactions that the ethnographer seeks to understand.

Reports based on ethnographic field research—called *ethnographies*—often produce new theoretical insights, but they are most distinctive for their vivid descriptions of actual social scenes and transactions. In other words, even after collecting data, the ethnographer typically does not attempt to propose a hypothesis about *why* something happens in the social world. Instead, ethnographic research attempts to uncover *what* happens in a social setting, *how* social relationships are conducted, and *what* those events and relationships mean to those involved. Assignments involving these methods may require you to connect these descriptions to specific concepts covered in the class.

In doing ethnographic research, your sociological imagination is exercised by the opportunity to see society's institutions, such as the police, the judicial system, and the health care system, as they are enacted by specific individuals in everyday settings. Because it takes sociology out of the classroom and into the "real world," and because it allows you to view the world through the eyes of people often very different from yourself, an ethnographic field research project can be especially challenging and exciting.

ASKING AN APPROPRIATE QUESTION

Often the goal of your research project—whether to explore unfamiliar settings or to see a familiar environment through a sociological lens—will be specified by your instructor, who may ask you to do one of the following:

1. Look at social interaction in your everyday life—among family members, friends, fellow students, or coworkers, for example—in new ways. The goals are to describe patterns and processes that often pass unnoticed in your daily interactions and to use your sociological imagination to relate these

personal patterns and processes to specific course concepts. This kind of project might ask you, for instance, to talk to fellow students about their relationships with friends; to observe how those in your dorm, apartment, or family deal with odd behavior; or to watch how individuals attempt to present a certain impression of themselves to others.

2. Visit a setting selected by your instructor, in which social activities of special concern in your course occur, and investigate how those present carry out routine activities and make decisions. Examples of this kind of assignment are going on a police ride-along, observing small-group interactions, or interviewing a mental health professional.

In some classes, however, you may have to develop your own question to address through ethnographic research, or you may simply be assigned to visit a setting of your choice and describe what it is like. If so, remember that, unlike much other sociological research, the goal of ethnographic field research is not to determine what causes some social event or relationship. Therefore, avoid devising a research question that asks *why* something happens in your research setting. Instead, concentrate on asking *what* (for example, "What does a police officer do during his or her time on the job?") or *how* (such as, "How do those sharing an elevator ride deal with one another in the limited space available?"). In the sample student paper at the end of this chapter, the author addresses this question: *"How* do students act in academic settings?"

REVIEWING THE LITERATURE

In a deductive research process, a review of relevant research done on the same topic is used to develop a hypothesis for testing through data collection. However, because the kind of fieldwork we are describing here does not involve hypothesis testing, instructors assigning ethnographic research projects often do not require that you use a summary of relevant research literature for that purpose. Nevertheless, your instructor, in order to encourage you to become familiar with work already done on the question you are investigating, may prefer that you conduct an overview of relevant research on your subject. Or you may find a literature review useful in getting a feel for ethnographic research, perhaps as you choose a setting or a question for your research or understand the issues of concern to those you will be observing in the field. In this case, use the guidelines for library research in Chapter 4 to get an overview of the sociological literature relevant to your project.

COLLECTING YOUR DATA

UNDERSTAND THE ASSIGNMENT

It's important that you understand the instructions you've been given for completing the assignment. Where are you supposed to go? What are you to look for? Is there a specific question you should address?

The most common mistake that students make in conducting an ethnographic research project is to focus so intently on describing a setting that they neglect to discuss it from a sociological perspective. Be sure you are clear on whether the assignment requires you to provide a detailed account of interaction in the observed setting, to demonstrate your ability to apply course concepts to what you see, or both. Ask the instructor for any necessary clarification.

PLAN AHEAD

1. Begin early in the quarter or semester. Field data cannot always be collected predictably or on short notice. Furthermore, you may have to return to your field setting several times to get the additional information or understanding that you need.

2. Make arrangements to interview and/or observe. While the prospect of getting permission may make you nervous at first, you will find that most people are receptive to showing or telling you about their lives. You can assure them that, if they prefer, their identities will not be known to anyone besides you and your instructor. Be sure to follow the procedures established by your college's Office for the Protection of Research Subjects or Institutional Review Board, which might require you to submit your research plan for approval or to obtain written permission from those you observe or interview. Consult your instructor for details.

When scheduling your observation or interview, allow plenty of time. Unanticipated events may occur, your subject may begin to talk at length about some particularly interesting topic, or you may think of additional questions on the spot. Also, you will need to allow time to record, transcribe, or elaborate on notes immediately after the contact.

3. Plan how you will record your data (a summary of recording options follows later in this chapter). In interview situations, it is best to electronically record or to make notes during the interview. Likewise, notes made while observing are more reliable than those made after you've left your field setting. The data collection methods you choose will depend on the situation,

your personal style, and the ethical constraints of the situation. But, whatever approach you take, be prepared ahead of time with adequate supplies, such as blank recording tape, batteries, paper, and pencils, as appropriate.

LOOK AND LISTEN

Although you may know a lot about the setting and the interactions you observe, it is crucial that you leave behind your previous assumptions and even your knowledge about them in order to learn something new. Adopt the attitude of a naive newcomer (as though you are a visitor from another planet!) so that you can begin to look in a new way at events and experiences you used to take for granted. In other words, don't try to figure out beforehand what conclusions you should come to or how you will use the information you are collecting. Just be as attentive to detail as you can in order to get as much valuable information as possible.

When observing, don't presume you know which events or interactions matter most. Keep your eyes and ears open to everything that is going on around you. Notice your surroundings, all the people who are present, the time taken by events, and so on. Attempt, above all, to look at the setting or situation through the eyes of the participants.

When interviewing, consider your place within the interview situation. How might the person you are interviewing see you or think about the questions you are asking? How might he or she relate to someone of your age, race/ethnicity, gender, and/or educational level? Your sensitivity to these social dynamics will be helpful in managing the interaction successfully. In terms of the interviewing process, follow these guidelines:

1. Don't talk more than you have to. Listen carefully to the respondent's comments.

2. Ask open-ended questions. Avoid leading questions that define the respondent's answer, and avoid questions that point to "yes" or "no" answers.

3. Rather than asking why something happened, concentrate on asking what transpired and how it occurred. "Why" questions often put people on the defensive, making them feel forced to justify their actions or lifestyle. Also, respondents' answers to "how" questions are usually more specific about real events, providing you with the concrete examples you need to describe in detail what goes on in the setting.

4. Don't overwhelm your interviewee with multiple questions. If you are a new interviewer, you may be uncomfortable with silence, but don't rush in with comments, requests for clarification, or further questions if the respondent pauses. Allow the respondent time to think and to complete his or her responses fully.

5. Encourage the respondent to be fairly specific about the details of events or experiences: Exactly who was involved? What happened? When did it take place? Remember, however, that probing should be gentle (for example, "Could you tell me more about that?"), not an interrogation.

6. Relax, allow your natural curiosity about your subject to direct you, and *listen*.

RECORD YOUR DATA

Since the final paper you produce will be only as good as your recorded data, it is crucial that you record observations or interview responses accurately, in detail, as soon as possible after the event. Otherwise, you will inevitably forget or distort what was said or done.

In observational research, take notes on what you see or hear as it happens. If that is impossible or bothers those you are observing, then write notes on what you observed as soon as possible afterward. You may even want to take periodic note-taking breaks away from the setting during your observation to jot down a few words or phrases that will trigger your memory later. A camera, or even your cell phone, makes it possible to easily create a video record of the setting; however, your obligation as a researcher to respect the privacy of all subjects would require you to get the written agreement of everyone involved in order to use their video images. Check with your instructor on any questions regarding these ethical issues.

If you are interviewing, it is best to electronically record the conversation (with the interviewee's permission). The most effective way to record is to use an audiotape recorder with a microphone. In a pinch, though, it is also possible to record it as a voice message by using a cell phone to call yourself. Don't be shy about asking permission to tape or take notes during the interview. People are often agreeable once they understand your interest in accurately representing what they say.

If subjects seem reluctant to let you tape, don't force the issue. Just listen to their responses and reconstruct the interview in writing as soon as you can afterward. Don't editorialize in your reporting of what was said. Likewise, don't edit your interview to make responses seem more sensible or because something seems "inconsequential." If you edit or editorialize, you may leave out something significant. Report all the respondent's comments, keeping them in their original order. And be sure to include all your questions, as well as the answers to them.

If you do tape-record an interview, it will be helpful to transcribe it into written form. There are special dictation machines that make transcription easier. Or, at the least, you should listen carefully to the interview and take notes on both your questions and the responses.

In all cases, make your notes specific. Describe in detail what you observed, did, and/or heard. Like a good reporter or a novelist, give the specifics of who, what, when, and where. Include concrete details about the physical setting, what went on, and your reactions: How did you feel about the people with whom you were involved? Remember that in ethnographic field research, you are the research instrument; it is through your own thoughts and feelings, your interactions, and your relations that you learn about the people and settings you are studying. For that reason, your personal reactions are especially important.

You may be required to submit the originals, or a typed version, of your field notes as an appendix to your paper (see page 218 of Part 3). Or you might choose to include your notes in an appendix, in order to give your instructor a better appreciation of what happened in your setting or interview (and of how hard you worked to gather your data!). Even if you will not be submitting your notes, keep them legible and organized. Be sure, for example, to date every entry. The quality of your paper relies on the quality of your field notes and interview notes or transcript; the more clear data you have available, the stronger your paper will be.

EXAMPLE OF OBSERVATIONAL FIELD NOTES

The following sample observational field notes will give you an idea of their general format and content. The example is excerpted from the notes written up by Gloria Fong, an undergraduate student in a class on the sociology of student and campus culture at a large university. The assignment asked participants to investigate aspects of student life. The field notes were in preparation for Gloria's paper, which is presented later in this chapter. Her observations focused on the non-academic activities in which students engage while in lecture and seminar classes.

Gloria is careful to identify where and when her observations took place.

Unlike your paper, which should be double-spaced, it is usually acceptable to single-space your field notes. Be sure to leave wide margins for making notes, as described later in the chapter.

It's perfectly normal to be nervous about beginning observations, even in a familiar environment. Generally, though, people being observed are friendly and willing to talk about their experiences.

Gloria describes the setting. Elsewhere in her field notes she includes descriptions of all students in the seminar room. The set-up turns out to be significant: by noting the seating arrangement, she eventually realizes that students sitting a certain distance from the instructor are more likely to engage in non-academic activities.

Remember that your notes are not a formal treatise. Describe gestures, sounds, even smells, through whatever means necessary, to bring the setting or interactions alive. This will help you to remember and to analyze what happened. It will also bring the field notes alive for your instructor.

Be careful not to make assumptions. It's obvious that the two students look up at the instructor. But we don't know why: Is it to keep from getting caught, out of interest in what the instructor is saying, or some other reason?

Wherever possible, make a note of direct quotations right away. Otherwise, paraphrase as accurately as possible.

As with the seminar setting, Gloria carefully describes the academic setting in which her observations took place. We really get a sense of the large size of the room and the distance between students and between students and instructor.

EXCERPTS FROM GLORIA'S FIELD NOTES

SEMINAR FIELD NOTES, May 11, 1–3 p.m.

    I entered the seminar room through the one and only door. I was nervous about observing, even though I usually attend this class anyway. In the middle of the small room is a large rectangular table with sixteen chairs around it, seven on each long side of the table and two individual chairs at each end of the table. The room is cramped, to say the least. There are fifteen students and one professor. The students sit around the table, and the professor sits at the head of the table, the seat facing opposite the door. A wall of windows is behind the professor, and the other three walls are blackboards.

    Two females are each sitting seven seats away from the professor, directly across the table from each other, one on the left and one on the right side of the table. The female on the right side of the table (female A) is a Hispanic female, wearing a white t-shirt and black pants. She has black hair pulled back with a black elastic into a ponytail. The female on the left side of the table (female B) is a Caucasian female, wearing a tan sweatshirt and blue jeans. She has long, dark brown hair, and it hangs loosely around her face.

    During the seminar meeting, these two females pass back and forth female A's copy of a newspaper clipping and female B's open notebook. I can see that the two students are doing the campus newspaper's daily crossword puzzle together, even though they are across the table from each other. They signal to each other when they need help, and take turns filling in the blanks of the crossword puzzle. They both look up at the professor periodically to see where he is in the room so they do not get caught. Neither of them seems to notice that they are being very obvious with their passing the crossword puzzle and notebooks back and forth across the table. When I asked them about it later, female A said, "We're not trying to disrespect the professor, but we just get bored and it's a challenge to try to finish the puzzle. We help each other out."

LECTURE FIELD NOTES, 5/13, 2-3:30 p.m.

    I walked into the large lecture hall through the left set of doors. There are three main sections of seats, a left, right, and middle section. The right

1

It is important to separate out what is obvious (the exact words or movements or gestures that anyone in the same setting would be able to see or hear)
and what is assumed (what we conclude based on those observations). Gloria
is careful to document the exact things she observed that led her to conclude
that the student was intermittently sleeping and that he was nonetheless attempting to take notes.

and left sections each consist of fourteen rows of seats with three seats across each row. The middle section consists of thirteen rows of seats with eight seats across each row. There are no windows in the room, and the ceilings are much higher than in the seminar room. The professor stands at the front corner of the lecture hall, behind a lectern. Behind the professor is a large movie screen with a picture of lecture notes projected upon it. The class is not full at all, and only the first five rows and the last two rows of the room have students in the seats.

One student I observed was an Asian male in a black t-shirt and black pants, wearing a red baseball cap backwards, sitting alone in the last row of the lecture hall. The student is hunched over his desk, with his elbows on the desk, his arms supporting his head, and his eyes are closed. His notebook is open on the desk, supporting his arms and head, and he has a black pen uncapped in his right hand. He opens his eyes wide and shakes his head from side to side. He looks to the front of the room when his eyes are open and then looks down at his notebook and begins to write. He writes in his notebook for ten minutes and then rests his head on his arms and closes his eyes again. Five minutes pass and his whole body hunches over the desk. He drops his pen on the floor and does not pick it up. His body moves up and down in rhythm with his breathing. My assumption is that this male student is attempting to take notes, but falls asleep in lecture instead. He is trying to pay attention, but just keeps falling asleep in between his frantic note taking sessions.

EXAMPLE OF INTERVIEW NOTES

Following is a brief excerpt from the interview notes that Gloria Fong (GF) took while researching her paper on college student and campus culture (see pp. 199–213). Although she could have asked for permission to make an electronic recording of the interview, this is an example of the type of notes jotted down during or immediately after speaking with one of the students (S1) she had observed.

> GF: What do you think of attending class?
>
> S1: It's okay. Sometimes kind of boring.
>
> GF: How do you deal with it?
>
> S1: I try really hard to take notes but then I just space out. But I don't want to skip lecture because then I might miss something that is on the final. I stop by and get a newspaper every time I come to this class. I rip out the crossword and put it in my notebook before I walk in. I just can't take notes the whole time so I need something else to do to pass the time.

The interview excerpt illustrates how Gloria's attempt to speak directly to a participant in the process she observed paid off. Being able to convey the voices of actual actors in a social scene makes her paper much richer and more graphic.

Gloria's' inquiries are phrased as "what" and "how" questions, which typically elicit more useful information from interview subjects than "why" questions do. If she had asked, "Why don't you pay attention in class?" the student might have felt too defensive to share her thoughts about classroom behaviors. Also, her questions are open-ended rather than phrased, so they cannot be answered with a "yes" or "no." She might have gotten more specific responses, though, if she had been able to focus her questions. For example, "What do you think of attending class?" is a broad inquiry, to which the reply was very general. She might have learned even more if she had asked specifically what the subject thought of a particular aspect of attending a college class, such as "What do you do during class besides listening and taking notes on what the instructor says?"

ORGANIZING YOUR DATA

The observations and answers you collect in your fieldwork are the data on which your paper will be based. In this step of your research process, you use the material you have collected to analyze the setting and/or to answer the question that your instructor assigned or that you formulated. In order to do that, you will need to identify, sort, and order and re-order segments of your notes, either electronically or on hard copy. This is an exciting process; as you work with your notes, you will notice that the setting you have learned about in a personal way reveals interesting information about the nature of social life.

ANSWERING AN ASSIGNED QUESTION

If your instructor asked a specific question in your paper assignment, now is the time to consider how what you saw, heard, and experienced addresses that question. Here are some guidelines:*

1. Go through your notes and make a mark by every comment, observation, or response that seems relevant to the question being asked. Some researchers prefer to do this kind of review in the margins of a printout; others do it on screen (as described in Warren and Karner 2005). Either way, don't be too discriminating at this point. Better to include too much at this stage than too little. Use a relevant word (or "code") in the margin to highlight what is important about that section of the data.

2. Extract these relevant pieces of data so that you can review them together and put them in categories. You can do this by copying them by hand onto separate note cards; by photocopying your original notes and cutting and pasting the relevant excerpts onto the cards; or by electronically blocking and copying the identified sections into a separate file. Whatever approach you take, you should be able to see the bits of data side by side, much as you would for materials in a library research paper (see Chapter 4).

3. Now consider what the information on each card or segment says in response to the question asked in the assignment. What does it tell you about the setting you observed and/or the people you interviewed?

4. Look for patterns among your data excerpts. Move them around (on cards or electronically) to illustrate to yourself how the information fits together. For instance, you might stack together cards or put together blocks of data to which you assigned the same code because they contain examples of the same kind of behavior. Or you might arrange data sections to reflect stages in a process.

Course materials and the paper assignment itself may be useful in helping you notice the patterns in your data. Recall concepts covered in the class that are relevant to your project. Review carefully just what the assignment directs you to look at. Then consider how your data illustrate those concepts or teach you something about the social relations you observed.

Gloria Fong, the student author of the sample ethnographic paper that appears at the end of this chapter, was asked by her instructor to observe and write about some aspect of college student life. Several class readings,

---

* These guidelines assume you will be doing this sorting on hard copy. If you have the time and resources, the coding and sorting process can also be done electronically, with a program such as The Ethnograph <http://www.qualisresearch.com/>.

including the classic work by Horowitz (1987) that she cites, focused on how college students do and don't feel engaged in their studies. In organizing her data, she might have listed the different roles that Horowitz noticed that students take, then stacked in separate piles (or moved to separate electronic files) the excerpts from her data that illustrated them. Or, looking for stages, she could have arranged her description of students in the "back of the class" as they selected their seats, began their non-academic activities, and moved from one activity to another.

ANSWERING A BROADER QUESTION

Perhaps you were simply assigned (or chose as your project) to participate in and describe a social setting. It will still be useful to sort out excerpts from your notes as described in the preceding section, but you will probably have more freedom to establish the categories in which you will organize your observations.

Begin by carefully rereading your field notes to refresh your memory about the events. Then start to look for patterns in your notes. As in the case of an assigned question, you might use course concepts to organize this search. Better yet, you might try to find the categories and terms used by people you observed, asking yourself how *they* understand and describe their activities.

For example, if you were taking a course in deviant behavior, your text would probably spend considerable space defining "deviance" in terms of breaking social norms. But in ethnographic research, you would find that the people you observe don't talk about "deviance" or "norms." Thus, rather than looking in your notes for examples of what your text would define as "deviance," it would be more enlightening to pinpoint what specific behaviors your subjects perceive as odd or disruptive and to note the ways in which they categorize and describe those who exhibit disliked behavior (such as referring to them as "weird" or as "different from us"). Similarly, a course in stratification may present sophisticated ways of measuring socioeconomic status; but, since the most interesting and valuable findings from your ethnographic field research concern the ways in which the people you observe perceive their own position in relation to society, you might look through your notes for all the ways they compare themselves to other groups.

Some of the most common themes ethnographers look for include the ways members characterize their group; the ways they distinguish between insiders and outsiders; the special language they develop to describe their shared activities and values; their patterns of interaction; the ways they teach new members the ropes; the ways they identify and respond to behavior they don't like; and the ways in which members experience their setting through the course of an event, a workday, or any other unit of experience. You may find some or all of these reflected in your notes, and you may find interesting themes not listed here. You may choose to focus on one area or on several related themes.

As you begin to identify themes that run through your field notes, you can proceed to sort the excerpts, either electronically or on hard copy, as described in the preceding section.

WRITING YOUR PAPER

Because ethnographic field research does not involve hypothesis testing, the essay format discussed in Chapter 1 is more appropriate than the journal format for this type of paper. Simply modify the essay format slightly: in place of the three (or more) "claims" or "points" relevant to a paper that proposes and supports a thesis, substitute the themes or concepts that you identified in your field notes. These will serve as the body of your paper. Remember that you are responsible for demonstrating, through effective use of your data, why your description of the setting is believable. Be sure to describe your research methods—where you went, how long you stayed, with whom you spoke, and so on—and to include as evidence the most illustrative excerpts from your field notes.

If the question you are addressing was assigned, you can use one of two approaches to present a written report on your observations:

One approach is to describe what happened or what was said, chronologically, and comment on how course concepts apply to the things you describe, as you report them in the order in which they occurred. This strategy requires you to be especially careful to avoid spending too much time on describing "what happened next."

Another approach is to organize your paper around concepts, defining and indicating the importance of each and using your data to illustrate them. In this case, you can follow the essay format, taking for each of your main points a selected concept or group of concepts.

Unless your assignment specifically requires one approach, either can be successful. If you are uncertain about which approach to take or which may be preferred, discuss your plans with your instructor. In either case, return to course concepts and themes frequently. Ask yourself how the events or comments you are describing reflect or illustrate sociological ideas. This will help you avoid the common mistakes of focusing too much on description or making overly psychological interpretations of those whom you observe or interview.

If your assignment doesn't specify a particular question for you to answer or a specific setting for you to analyze according to course concepts, then you can simply organize the themes you discovered in your notes in the essay format. You might choose three points to make about one of the themes that you found most interesting or revealing. Or, you might develop your paper around three different themes.

Whichever format you use, it is important for your paper to incorporate the reactions you experienced in your research and recorded in your notes.

Inevitably, those engaged in ethnographic field research encounter people, events, and experiences that fascinate, surprise, confuse, or even upset them. It is a challenge to make effective use of such reactions without getting side-tracked into self-analysis. A good way to make your personal reactions relevant is to ask yourself what they illuminate about the setting. Describe in your paper how your own feelings and thoughts helped you better understand the people you studied and their interactions.

When writing your paper, you may quote your field notes directly. When you do, punctuate and cite them as you would any other source. Or, you may choose to summarize an incident or a response in an anecdotal way to illustrate a point. As long as they are relevant to your assignment, use your collected data in as many ways as you can; they make up the empirical basis for your discussion.

SUGGESTED READINGS

Denzin, Norman K. and Yvonna S. Lincoln. 2005. *Handbook of Qualitative Research.* 3rd ed. Thousand Oaks, CA: Sage Publications.

Emerson, Robert M., Rachel I. Fretz, and Linda L. Shaw. 1995. *Writing Fieldnotes.* Chicago, IL: University of Chicago Press.

Merriam, Sharon B. 2002. *Qualitative Research in Practice: Examples for Discussion and Analysis.* San Francisco, CA: Jossey-Bass.

Warren, Carol A.B. and Tracy X. Karner. 2005. *Discovering Qualitative Methods: Field Research, Interviews, and Analysis.* Los Angeles, CA: Roxbury Publishing Company.

A SAMPLE STUDENT PAPER

The following sample ethnographic field research paper was written by Gloria Fong for a class on the sociology of student and campus culture. She describes in her paper how she came to focus her research on the non-academic activities in which students engage in classroom settings. She observed students' activities both in a large lecture hall and in a small seminar room, noting where the students sat and what they did besides listening to the lecture.

Gloria used her original data to answer three research questions. Her findings are illustrated by specific observations, which she summarized in her field notes. Sometimes her field notes and interview notes are quoted directly, and sometimes they are incorporated into the text of her paper.

Gloria's paper demonstrates that she is a capable and diligent student. Her creative brainstorming resulted in an attempt to fill a hole in the research literature on higher education. Although research has been done on students' academic activities and on their out-of-class activities, little is known about their non-academic activities in the classroom settings that Gloria explored. She is a good example of a student whose basically good writing could be made even better by applying a closer eye to such details as grammar and punctuation.

Because of the length of Gloria's paper, she has included a title page (as recommended in Part 3).

NON-ACADEMIC ACTIVITIES IN ACADEMIC SETTINGS

Gloria Fong
Sociology 197-A: Sociology of
    Student and Campus Culture
Professor Richlin-Klonsky
June 2004

Gloria's first paragraph introduces her research question: In what non-academic activities do students engage in a college classroom? Then she shows how it fits into existing research literature in higher education, such as the studies on student involvement by Astin and by Horowitz, and indicates its significance. Despite the length of time it's been since these studies were published, Gloria's use of them is acceptable because they are considered classics and because they were key readings for the class. You should be sure to look for recent relevant research whenever possible.

Gloria's writing would be more straightforward if she would use fewer descriptors, such as adverbs like "really," "actually," and "certainly."

Gloria includes a description of how her research question was selected, because she feels that the roundabout way it occurred to her says something about the question she's studying. It also illustrates how the research question may emerge from personal experience.

Gloria's informal narrative style (telling about her walk home and how the question came to her "in a flash") was acceptable for this assignment, which was meant to lead to a preliminary research report. It might not be appropriate for more formal research papers.

INTRODUCTION

Researchers in higher education have been interested in the ways that students either are or aren't involved in their college experience (Astin 1993; Horowitz 1987). There seems to be quite a lot of research about the academic activities of students in the classroom and about the non-academic activities of students outside of the classroom. But there is not much about the non-academic activities of students in academic settings. No one seems to have really researched in depth what students actually do in class, even though it is certainly a part of student and campus culture. Such data could certainly help improve the quality of the college experience, particularly by helping faculty understand how things look from the students' point of view.

RESEARCH DESIGN AND METHODS

I originally was interested in studying fashion on campus, but because there were already so many students in the class studying that, I was assigned to study something about academics. I spent a while trying to figure out what aspect of academics I wanted to look at most. Then in class the professor suggested that somebody look at where students sit in classrooms. Then another student in the class suggested that I look at how students do the daily crossword puzzle all the time during classes. As I was walking home after class, I started thinking back to all of the lectures and seminars I have been in during my four years in college. And I realized that the back of the class is usually more interesting than the front of the room because of the non-academic activities that take place in the back of the room. And so it came to me in a flash that I should just combine the two topics suggested to me in class and explore where people sit in classrooms and what people do depending on where they sit in class. The amount of time that it took me to string the suggested topics together to make my own topic shows how strongly people tend to separate the two realities of academics and non-academics.

I became an ethnographer to investigate, (1) whether there is a front-of-the room culture and a back-of-the-room culture, (2) whether students from one racial or economic background are more likely than others to sit in

1

Although making only one visit to each kind of academic setting (lecture and seminar) does not produce enough data to draw any conclusions about them, it was sufficient for this preliminary study.

Gloria included her interview notes and field notes as an appendix to her paper (as suggested in Part 3), which will allow her instructor and any other readers to review the detailed data she collected. (However, due to space limitations, Appendix A is not included at the end of her paper.)

In this introduction to this section, Gloria clearly identifies her major findings and organizes them around her research questions. This will serve as a road map for someone reading her findings.

Be careful to use the correct form of pronouns. The object of a preposition ("to") should be "whom" rather than "who."

It is not unusual that in the course of qualitative research, new insights lead to additional questions.

Gloria quotes her field notes directly to illustrate the distribution of students in the classroom.

the front or the back of the classroom; (3) whether there is a difference between what students do in the back of the room in large lectures and what students do who sit in the back of the room in small seminars. I made various observations and inscriptions during one three-hour seminar I attended and one two-hour lecture I attended. I sat in the back of the classrooms and took notes on what students were doing and I also asked a few of the students I had observed some quick questions after each class was over. I recorded small notes to myself while in the classes I chose to attend. I then took the inscriptions I made in the classroom back home and turned them into formal field notes, which I later reviewed for themes and patterns (see Appendix A).

FINDINGS

In reviewing my field notes, I found answers to my three questions. First, there are definitely separate areas in the front and back of the lecture hall which can be seen either from where people are sitting or from who is talking to who. Second, social factors such as race, ethnicity, gender, and class standing did not seem to affect who sat in the back of a class versus who sat in the front of a class. Third, non-academic activities take place in both overall settings (lecture hall or seminar room).

Even though it wasn't part of my original questions, I also learned something about why students bother going to class when they are doing so many other things besides listening to the lecture. This was a question that came to my mind while I was doing my research.

Is there a back of the room culture?

The "front" and "back" areas in the lecture hall were easy to see because they were physically separated.

> There are three main sections of seats, a left, right, and middle section. The right and left sections each consist of fourteen rows of seats with three seats across each row. The middle section consists of thirteen rows of seats with eight seats across each row. . . .The class is not full at all, and only the first five rows and the last two rows of the room have students in the seats.

2

Watch out for accurate capitalization. All proper names ("Game Boys" and "Palm Pilots") need to be capitalized.

Gloria's notes do a good job of setting the scene for the reader. We can easily visualize the setting she was observing.

The middle of the room was basically a no-man's land. When it comes to interactions, it seemed that only those who sat in the front of the class spoke with and/or interacted with the students in the front of the class. And furthermore, only those who sat in the back of the class spoke with and/or interacted with the students in the back. The non-academic activities that I observed in the back of the class were: sleeping, eating, talking, doing the crossword puzzle from the school newspaper, doodling, and listening to music. And with the exception of listening to music, all of the non-academic activities were low-tech. I did not observe anyone text messaging on their cell phones, playing with gameboys or other portable video game devices, playing with their palm pilots, talking on their cell phones, or any other types of high-tech, non-academic activities in the back of the room.

In the seminar room, there was no space for the "front" and "back" to be physically separated.

> In the middle of the room is a large rectangular table with sixteen chairs around it, seven on each long side of the table and two individual chairs at each end of the table. The room is cramped, to say the least. There are fifteen students and one professor. The students sit around the table, and the professor sits at the head of the table.

Before I observed the classes, I thought for sure that there would be less of a "back of the room" culture in a seminar room because of its size. I was surprised to find so many people doing the same types of non-academic activities in both academic settings. The back of the room in the seminar was just as active with non-academic activities as the back of the lecture hall. It is interesting to note that even though there were only 15 people in the seminar, there was still definitely a "back of the class" area. All the people sitting four seats or closer to the professor sat quietly and wrote down notes on their notebooks. They did not look at other people in the class and only looked up at the professor or the board when he was writing things down. All the people sitting five seats or more away from the professor felt that they were far enough away from him to be able to do other things besides take notes. This was the "back of the class" area for the seminar room.

3

Sociologists are always interested in the role of social factors in the type of experience under study. This conclusion was made possible by Gloria's detailed field notes, which included descriptions of social characteristics of the students she observed, and by her interviews, in which she asked students about their class standings (first year, sophomore, and so on).

This kind of unexpected finding is not unusual for qualitative research and makes it especially interesting.

Are students of certain social characteristics more likely to be in the back of the room?

There is no one type of person who sits in the back of the room and engages in non-academic activities. All races, ethnicities, genders, and class standings are represented in the back of the room. Students' social characteristics did not appear to play a role in how involved they are in the academic part of what goes on in the classrooms.

Do non-academic activities take place in both lecture halls and seminar rooms?

Before I observed the classes, I thought for sure that there would be less of a "back of the room" culture in a seminar room because of its size. I was surprised to find so many people doing the same types of non-academic activities in both academic settings. The back of the room in the seminar was just as active with non-academic activities as the back of the lecture hall.

> Two females are each sitting seven seats away from the professor, directly across the table from each other, one on the left and one on the right side of the table. During the seminar meeting, these two females pass back and forth female A's copy of a newspaper clipping and female B's open notebook. I can see that the two students are doing the campus newspaper's daily crossword puzzle together, even though they are across the table from each other. They signal to each other when they need help, and take turns filling in blanks of the crossword puzzle. They both look up at the professor periodically to see where he is in the room so they do not get caught. Neither of them seems to notice that they are being very obvious with their passing the crossword puzzle and notebooks back and forth across the table.

But because the professor was very close to them, students in the seminar setting did check on where he was looking and what he was doing far more often than the people in large lecture halls checked.

Why do students engage in non-academic activities while in class?

This wasn't one of my original research questions, but after observing students engaged in non-academic activities during class, I became curious about why they bothered to attend class at all. Two of my interview subjects

Gloria tries to highlight the different types of students in Horowitz's typology. However, capitalizing an entire word is the written equivalent of yelling.

Gloria neglects to point out one difference between her observations and Horowitz's analysis, which suggests that "outsiders" and "college men and women" were of different racial and ethnic groups and different social classes.

indicated that they wanted to be sure that they don't miss something that may be on a test. As one student put it:

> I try really hard to take notes but then I just space out. But I don't want to skip lecture because then I might miss something that is on the final.

There also seems to be a strong norm among students that one has to go to class to feel like, and appear as, a "good student." Being a "good student" means you attend all of your classes. One of the students I interviewed said, "I feel like I have to come to lecture, so I come."

DISCUSSION AND IMPLICATIONS

In my study, there were distinct groups in the front and in the back of the classroom. This is like the "OUTSIDERS" and the "COLLEGE MEN AND WOMEN" that Horowitz (1987) described in higher education. She describes college men and women as those students for whom "classes and books exist [only] as a price one has to pay for college life. . . .but no real college man or woman ever expects to live in the classroom" (1987:12). The outsiders are "studious, polite, and respectful of authority. . . .hardworking students [who] sought the approval of their teachers, not of their peers" (1987:14).

The findings are relevant to campus policy and programming because they could lead to some changes in campus policy and programming that are aimed at decreasing the amount of non-academic activities in the back of classrooms directly. However, while there are obviously a lot of non-academic activities occurring in lectures and seminars, I do not feel that there is really any reason to try and stop them, and really no way to stop them, because there is already an established culture of students sitting in the back of the room sleeping, eating, reading, etc. I feel that no matter what rules and regulations are put in place to stop them, there will always be students in the back of the class doing other things besides taking notes. This is because there will always be students who are just showing up to class to appear as a "good student," but not to take notes.

5

Instead, I would suggest that classes not be scheduled earlier than 11:00 a.m. to cut down on the amount of sleeping in class. Classes should also not be longer than two hours so students do not get bored and fidgety. Classes should not be scheduled around mealtimes so that people will not have to eat in class or fall asleep in class from being too tired from not eating. Also, I think online classes, video classes, or other types of distance learning should be considered for large lectures.

My findings could also be used to help foster a better understanding between students and faculty and therefore better relationships between the two, which would facilitate students' academic and personal development.

Appropriately, Gloria started her References on a separate page.

Gloria should have included her interview and/or field notes in her list of references. Since the format was not specified in the assignment, she should have discussed the required information and preferred format with her instructor. Here is one possibility:

Fong, Gloria. May 11, 2004. Field notes, observations of seminar room, California.

REFERENCES

Astin, Alexander. 1993. "Effects of Involvement." Pp. 365-395 in *What Matters in College? Four Critical Years Revisited,* edited by A. Astin. San Francisco, CA: Jossey-Bass.

Horowitz, Helen Lefkowitz. 1987. "Introduction: The Worlds that Undergraduates Make." Pp. 3-22 in *Campus Life: Undergraduate Cultures from the End of the Eighteenth Century to the Present.* New York: Alfred A. Knopf.

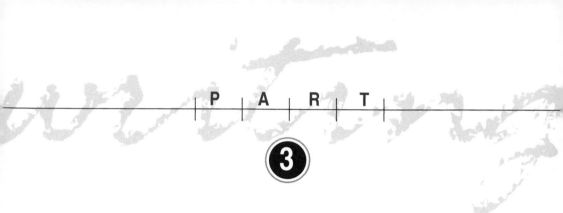

Finishing Up

> It has long been an axiom of mine that the little things are infinitely the most important.

> SHERLOCK HOLMES IN ARTHUR CONAN DOYLE'S
> "Adventure of the Copper Beeches"

POLISHING

First impressions count. What your paper *looks* like is important. Its appearance will create expectations in the instructor who picks it up to read and grade. A professional-looking paper promises quality. So take the necessary trouble at the very end of the process of writing your paper to proofread and polish it before you hand it in. Now the most difficult stages are behind you. In fact, some writers who do anything "to avoid writing that first word" actually *enjoy* polishing their final draft.

Think of polishing as a way of showing hospitality, and your reader as a special guest whom you would not dream of putting to work. In some cases, your paper will be among dozens that your probably overworked instructor or reader must evaluate. Imagine your own irritation if, after reading students' papers for hours, you picked up one that was printed with a spent cartridge that should have been replaced long ago; or, conversely, imagine your sigh of relief and gratitude when the next paper in the stack is easy to read. Although a nicely presented paper that lacks substance will not likely fool even the weariest instructor, studies reveal that a professional-looking paper implies a smart and serious student and often contributes to a better grade. Taking the time to "package" a carefully written paper also shows respect for your instructor's workload—a respect that he or she may well be inclined to return.

At this stage you are on the last lap, but do not underestimate the importance of a strong finish. Therefore, allow ample time for a careful—not rushed—polishing of your paper. Doing so can often turn "poor" into "satisfactory," or "good" into "excellent."

EDITING

Edit your draft to find and correct inadvertent errors in spelling and punctuation, repeated words and phrases, and omitted words. After you print out what you hope will be your last draft, get away from it—for several days if possible, or for a good night's sleep at least. Efficiency in spotting weaknesses increases dramatically with distance from the paper, and flaws that escape your bleary eyes at 2 A.M. often leap off the page when you are rested.

The way to spot such mechanical problems is to proofread. To proofread efficiently, you must *see*, not just *look at*, your draft. The way to *see* errors is to examine a hard copy of your paper (not just a computer screen) to engage hand, brain, and eye coordination. Take a pen or pencil and then point to each word as you read it silently, or, better, out loud, to yourself. Only through this hand movement will you make yourself actually see what you have written; otherwise you will be consulting your short-term memory and will literally not see your draft. Once you have proofread your paper, have someone else proofread it, too.

A computer tip. Most word-processing programs have spellcheckers. Use your spellchecker to detect and correct misspellings. There is no excuse for spelling mistakes in a word-processed paper. But do not depend on your spellchecker alone to edit your paper.

Especially be on the alert for these two common problems in word-processed papers that spellcheckers cannot detect: (1) repeated passages in the paper that you moved from one location to another but did not delete from the first location and (2) incorrect sentence structure caused through revising on the computer. As an example of this second problem, consider this sentence in a revised draft: "This paper will to show how Robert Parks's model of racial and ethnic group contact explains Latino discontent about the recent UCLA student body elections." The author of this mangled sentence originally wrote "The purpose of this paper is to show how . . ." and then changed it to "This paper will show how." But when she edited her draft she did not completely delete the original phrase.

A number of computer programs go beyond spellchecking in order to check grammar and style. Although not foolproof, they can be useful aids.

Corrections. Despite your best efforts, however, you may need to make some last-minute corrections. Even though there should be no handwritten corrections on a word-processed paper, it is better to correct any mistakes by hand than pass in an uncorrected paper. Here are several of the most common corrections, which can be made in ink by using conventional proofreader's marks.

To insert, put a caret ($_\wedge$) just below the line at the place where you want to insert and then write in the word or phrase directly above the caret.

Example

This is what you do if you have left$_\wedge$a word or phrase.

To delete, put a single line through the word or phrase.

Example

the ~~good~~ word

If you neglected to indent a paragraph, put the paragraph sign (¶) right before it.

FORMATTING

Begin by setting up the following automatic features on your computer. Use the tabs, not the space bar, for measurement (for example, one inch, not eight spaces) so that the format remains constant when you print out your text, even if you change fonts, pitch, or typeface.

+ Margins (one to one-and-a-half inches on all sides)
+ Double-spacing (quotations longer than five lines should be single-spaced and indented one inch from the left margin)
+ Paragraph indentions (one-half to one inch)
+ Left margin justification. Do not justify the right margin; a ragged right margin is friendlier and the spacing between the letters often looks better.
+ A header with your last name and the page number only

Word processing turns writers into designers. The creative possibilities of printing out a final draft, once the completed draft has been saved in the computer's memory, can be very satisfying. Here is an opportunity to experiment with typeface, pitch, font, italics, boldface, boxes, borders, underlining, and so forth. Unfortunately, the result is sometimes a mess and distracts the reader from your ideas. To avoid this problem, keep these design principles in mind:

+ Make the shape follow sense. What you do to the printed words should emphasize their meaning. For example, 12-point Helvetica Narrow is

excellent for tables and other types of writing that require lots of information in a very small space. Zapf Chancery is a display face that gives headings a decorative look. New Century Schoolbook looks traditionally academic.
+ Use restraint. If you emphasize everything, nothing stands out.
+ Use your page preview function or scroll through the document to identify and repair "widows," which are single lines separated from the rest of their paragraph by a page break, or other breaks such as captions separated from figures.
+ Stick with 12-point fonts. Smaller ones are hard to read.
+ Use your italics function to indicate titles of publications.
+ Use the bold command for emphasis, not italics, underlining, or capitalization.
+ Simplicity is best. Just because you can create elaborate headers and footers, for instance, doesn't mean that the reader needs all that information.

If you use a title page, center your title horizontally and place it halfway down the page. In the lower right-hand corner, put your name, the course number (for example, Sociology 101), the name of your instructor, and the date. Number pages beginning with the first page of the text, not with the title page. Sometimes instructors do not require a title page for short papers (approximately five or fewer pages). If you're not using a title page, provide the same information (your name, the course number, the instructor's name, and the date) in the upper right-hand corner of page 1; triple-space and center the title; and triple-space again before you begin the first paragraph.

A quick review of Chapter 3 will remind you of the proper form for citing sources in the text of your paper and for the list of references that follows the text.

Depending on the type of paper you've written, some instructors may want you to include your raw data, statistical calculations, questionnaires, observation checklists, instructions to respondents, ethnographic field notes, or other items. As appropriate, you should make each of these items an appendix to your paper. (The *American Heritage Dictionary* defines "appendix" as "supplementary material.") The appendix belongs after the References or Bibliography on a separate, titled page. If your paper requires more than one appendix, number or letter each one (Appendix 1, Appendix 2; or Appendix A, Appendix B, and so on). Number the pages of the appendix(es) as if they were additional text pages—if, for example, the last page of the text is numbered 5, the first page of the appendix would be 6.

You may single-space or double-space an appendix depending on the nature of the material and how it can most easily be read. The spacing need not be the same for all appendixes. However, the heading is ordinarily centered and triple-spaced—that is, you triple-space between "Appendix" and the title and triple-space again between the title and the body of the appendix.

As with any work created on a computer, save your document often and back it up on a portable media device (such as a CD or flash drive) or to a hard disk, or e-mail it to yourself as an attachment. For insurance against hardware problems, make an extra copy on another portable media device.

A FINAL CHECKLIST FOR SUBMITTING YOUR PAPER

1. Can you quickly identify your thesis (your central argument) or, if you're writing a quantitative research paper, your hypothesis (or statement of the expected relationship between two variables)?

2. Does your thesis, or the logic behind your hypothesis, remain evident and central throughout the paper?

3. Do you support your thesis, or hypothesis, with adequate evidence? One trick for checking the quantity and quality of your evidence is to put a mark in the margin of a rough draft wherever you see evidence for your thesis, or hypothesis, pausing at each point to review its soundness. Instructors sometimes use this method when evaluating the reasonableness of an argument.

4. Is there a clear, logical relationship among all the paragraphs? If one is irrelevant to your thesis or hypothesis—no matter how dazzling—delete it; if one wanders from the topic, bring it back into line. Stick to the subject.

5. Repeat 4 (above), substituting "sentences" for "paragraphs."

6. Does the writing flow back and forth between generalizations and specifics that support and clarify those generalizations?

7. Are there transitions between paragraphs? Sometimes transitions seem to create themselves naturally during the writing process. Other times you have to create them, very deliberately, at the polishing stage. But make them look natural, not slapped on. The smoothest transitions, perhaps, come in the first sentence of each paragraph, deftly referring back from where you came and forward to where you are going. Your reader will be grateful for transitions because the ride through the paper will be smooth, not bumpy.

8. Now pay attention to transitions between sentences.

9. Do all your words mean what you think they mean? For those occasional moments of doubt, we recommend your owning a good hardcover dictionary (*The American Heritage College Dictionary* is one good choice) as well as a portable paperback if you sometimes write and study in the library. Or if you're working on a computer with Internet access, you can access Web sites such as <www.dictionary.com>. As we mentioned in Chapter 2 (page 39), be especially careful when using terms that have become part of everyday

language and yet retain special sociological definitions (the examples we gave were "stereotype," "status," and "self-fulfilling prophecy"). If you're uncertain about the sociological definitions of your key terms, you might find them quickly in sociology textbooks by using the index and/or glossary. Several dictionaries of sociological terms are also available.

When dealing with words that do not have special sociological meanings, a thesaurus can help you both to locate the most precise word that expresses what you want to say and to find synonyms for varying your word choice. The popular paperback *Roget A to Z: The Classic Thesaurus in Dictionary Form* is simple to use because words are alphabetized just as they are in a dictionary. Or if you're working on a computer with Internet access, you can access Web sites such as <www.thesaurus.reference.com>. However, before you use a synonym from a thesaurus in your paper, check its meaning in a dictionary. Mark Twain said that "the difference between the almost right word and the right word is really a large matter—'tis the difference between the lightning-bug and the lightning." Believe it or not, the search for "just the right word" can be fun.

10. Have you looked carefully for errors in style (sentence structure, punctuation, spelling, citations)? As we mentioned in Chapter 2, reference books that present style guidelines are available online (see page 42) as well as in bookstores and libraries.

11. What about contractions (for example, "it's," "don't," "you're")? If you do not know your instructor's preference, avoid using contractions.

12. Have you stated your conclusion clearly and forcefully?

13. Have you avoided sexist language (for example, using the masculine pronoun "he" exclusively)?

THINKING BIG

If you or your instructor is particularly pleased with the quality of the paper you produced, you might consider submitting it for presentation at a national or regional meeting of a professional sociological association or for publication in a scholarly journal. Paper presentations and publications that demonstrate good communication skills will increase your chance of getting into graduate school and will enhance your résumé.

The main professional organization in sociology is the American Sociological Association (ASA). The ASA holds an annual national meeting for the presentation of both theoretical and empirical research. Usually, several sessions are devoted to undergraduate and graduate student papers. The international sociology honor society, Alpha Kappa Delta (AKD), also holds both regional and national meetings at which students have the opportunity to present their work. Ask your instructor or undergraduate counselor for more information about these and other professional associations.

If you wish to submit your paper for publication in a scholarly journal, refer to the list in Chapter 4. Always look inside the cover of the latest issue of the journal for the name and address of the current editor and the guidelines for submission. Ask your instructor how to draft a cover letter to accompany your paper submission.

References

American Psychological Association. 2001. *Publication Manual of the American Psychological Association.* 5th ed. Washington, DC: American Psychological Association.

American Sociological Association. 2007. *American Sociological Association Style Guide.* 3rd ed. Washington, DC: American Sociological Association.

Becker, Howard. 1986. *Writing for Social Scientists: How to Start and Finish Your Thesis, Book or Article.* Chicago, IL: University of Chicago Press.

Bryant, Clifton D. and Dennis L. Peck. 2007. *21st Century Sociology: A Reference Handbook.* Thousand Oaks, CA: Sage Publications.

Durkheim, Emile. [1897] 1951. *Suicide.* Translated by J. A. Spaulding and G. Simpson. Glencoe, IL: Free Press.

Gibaldi, Joseph. 1998. *MLA Style Manual and Guide to Scholarly Publishing.* 2nd ed. New York: Modern Language Association of America.

Goffman, Erving. 1959. *The Presentation of Self in Everyday Life.* Garden City, NY: Doubleday.

Hochschild, Arlie Russell. 1990. *The Second Shift.* New York: Avon Books.

Mills, C. Wright. [1959] 2000. *The Sociological Imagination.* New York: Oxford University Press.

Parsons, Talcott. 1977. *The Evolution of Societies.* Englewood Cliffs, NJ: Prentice-Hall.

Robinson, John P. and Philip R. Shaver. 1978. *Measures of Social Psychological Attitudes.* Ann Arbor, MI: Survey Research Center, Institute for Social Research.

Turabian, Kate L. 2007. *A Manual for Writers of Term Papers, Theses, and Dissertations.* 7th ed. Chicago, IL: University of Chicago Press.

The University of Chicago Press. 2003. *The Chicago Manual of Style.* 15th ed. Chicago, IL: University of Chicago Press.

Weber, Max. 2002. *The Protestant Ethic and the Spirit of Capitalism.* Translated by Stephen Kalberg. 3rd ed. Los Angeles, CA: Roxbury Publishing Co.

Index